'JUST TELL THEM
I SURVIVED!'

ROBIN BURNS

'JUST TELL THEM
I SURVIVED!'

Women in Antarctica

ALLEN&UNWIN

This project has been assisted by the Commonwealth Government through the Australia Council, its arts funding and advisory body.

The poem 'The Music Makers' on page 176 is reprinted courtesy of Caroline Caddy. It was first published in Antarctica, *Fremantle Arts Centre Press, South Fremantle, 1996.*

First published in 2001

Allen & Unwin
83 Alexander Street
Crows Nest NSW 2065
Australia
Phone: (61 2) 8425 0100
Fax: (61 2) 9906 2218
Email: info@allenandunwin.com
Web: www.allenandunwin.com

National Library of Australia
Cataloguing-in-Publication entry:

Burns, Robin.
 Just tell them I survived: women in Antarctica.

 ISBN 1 86508 382 8.

 1. Women—Antarctica. 2. Women—Employment—Antarctica.
 3. Women explorers—Antarctica. 4. Women scientists—
 Antarctica. I. Title.

305.409989

Set in 11/14 pt Baskerville by Midland Typesetters, Maryborough, Victoria
Printed by Griffin Press, South Australia

10 9 8 7 6 5 4 3 2 1

This book is dedicated to my mother, Laura Burns,
*   who sadly did not live to see its completion;*
to Anja Kate Bremmers,
*   who arrived just before it was completed;*
and to those who hear the challenge of wild places,
*   who respond to their call,*
*   and who work to preserve them for humanity.*

Foreword

The story of Antarctica is overwhelmingly *his*tory, and this book attempts to redress the balance by adding chapters from the stories of many women who have lived and worked on the continent and sub-Antarctic islands, most of them with ANARE (Australian National Antarctic Research Expeditions). Indeed, parts of my own Antarctic story are recorded here, derived from the sixteen months I spent down South in 1990–92, as station leader at Mawson in 1991 and as field leader of the 1991–92 summer Prince Charles Mountain Expedition. Like many Antarcticans of both genders, my original inspiration for seeking to experience the physical and personal challenge of the extreme environment of the last continent came from the great stories of the heroic age of Antarctic exploration, especially the saga of Shackleton's expeditions and the qualities of leadership and comradeship they displayed.

The actors in the saga of the heroic age were exclusively male, and this was the norm until the 1950s. The first women went South with ANARE in 1959, and over 400 have followed them since. As this book describes, women as well as men now share the awesome beauty of a midwinter aurora, the perils of glacier travel, the discomforts of a blizzard-bound tent, the exhilaration of boundless icescapes, the joy in companionship of special friends on a 'jolly', the trust and interdependence generated by a longer field expedition, the satisfaction of a successful resupply operation, the depression and loneliness of isolation from friends and family, the wonder of the wildlife—in fact, the whole kaleidoscope of experiences which create for almost everyone who has been there the most *intensely lived* period of their lives.

But this experience has come at a price and this book also records the battles against indifference, discrimination and harassment—the familiar occupational and psychological obstacles to women entering a traditionally male domain—as well as those against the unique physical obstacles of the Antarctic and sub-Antarctic environment.

For my own part, the vividness, the heightened sense of being, has taken me back to Antarctica almost every summer as a guide on tourist ships to many parts of the continent, and finally back to ANARE for another season as station leader, this time on sub-Antarctic Macquarie Island in 2000.

What struck me on returning to ANARE after nearly ten years is how much had changed, both for myself personally and as a woman. Rereading my Mawson diaries, I appreciate my greater self-assurance and reduced anxiety about how to do my job, born of more experience and maturity—which in turn makes me more relaxed, and helps me do it better. But I also find my job is easier, because of the change in culture. There is far greater acceptance of me as a woman station leader—even though there have still only been seven in over 50 years of ANARE—and there are far more women amongst the expeditioners: 25 per cent of both the summer and winter groups. The men are far less 'blokey', exclusive or antagonistic, but what draws my greatest admiration and respect is the competence and confidence of the women.

Many are young scientists, some on their first Antarctic season, but their ability to learn the ropes, their dedication to their projects and their infectious enthusiasm for their work set a standard for the whole station. Their professional credibility draws willing responses to requests for help from other expeditioners, both men and women, which they in turn reciprocate. The critical mass of between ten and fifteen women on station creates a joyous sisterhood that defines the social ambience of the community and embraces all members equally. The spirit of the station manifested such energy, conviviality and caring that the end of summer brought real sadness with the departure of so many dear friends. However, the same spirit prevailed into the winter, again with the large proportion of women on station playing a defining role.

To me, Macquarie Island 2000 represents the future of ANARE and of women as full participants, and I believe this goal is shared by many of the new generation of managers as well as expeditioners. This book describes the struggles that many women have faced in striving towards that goal. For the early pioneers, times were difficult although their expectations were often modest. Harder perhaps was the period of the 1970s–90s when women were seeking and achieving access and success in increasing numbers in so many fields of 'normal' life, yet Antarctica seemed caught in a time warp contingent on its 'special' status. But now the icy barriers are falling in ANARE. The focus of Australia's Antarctic program has shifted from station-building to science, which is the field in which most women work in Antarctica. This will give them both greater opportunities and greater status. It will also tend to reduce the power of the dominant male 'trades' culture, while opening more of those jobs to women as well.

The beginning of these trends is apparent in the stories told here. So this book gives us the opportunity to honour those women who first breached the geographical and social boundaries of the last continent, to acclaim those who struggled with both inner and outer weather to consolidate their foothold in hostile climes, and to celebrate with those now claiming with competence and confidence their right to share equally in the unique experience of living and working in Antarctica.

Louise Crossley
Macquarie Island
Midwinter Day 2000

Contents

Preface and acknowledgments

I began this book with the conviction that it was time to record the ways in which women contribute to our knowledge of Antarctica, and to the life on Antarctic stations, field sites and expeditions. I wanted to find out how women came to go South; about their longings, persistence in the face of opposition, expectations and experiences; and to celebrate the diversity of occupations, projects and achievements there. In a way, it was intended as a vicarious experience, since I did not believe when I began that a social scientist in her fifties would be able to join a national expedition. However, as I met women who had been to Antarctica, they suggested that I should try, and helped and encouraged me at every stage, so that in the austral summer of 1995–96 I spent three months at Casey station on an Antarctic Science Advisory Committee (ASAC) project.

It has been difficult to find adequate ways to capture and present the rich diversity of women's experiences of Antarctica, and their perspectives on gender issues, station life, the future of expeditions and the Antarctic itself. My apologies for any omissions, and for the brevity of most of the quotations from interviews: with 130 interviews in total, it has been a huge task to sort and select! I undertook not to present the interview material as biography; some women have requested anonymity, so I have used pseudonyms for them, as well as in dealing with sensitive material. I have tried hard to avoid material that would cause distress or embarrassment.

Inevitably, my beliefs and perceptions—as an older woman and a feminist concerned about women's suppression and oppression anywhere—have played a role in the presentation of the material. As an author, I invite you—the reader—to a dialogue, and ask you to bring your imagination, perspectives, experiences and dreams as you listen to the stories recorded here.

I was able to travel for interviews, have notes transcribed and employ research assistants thanks to an Australian Research Council (ARC) small grant, and one from the Australian Antarctic Foundation. ASAC and ANARE enabled me to go to Antarctica, though I worked there on a separate project. Assistance from all these bodies is gratefully acknowledged. Amanda Watson, Kathleen Orr and Annie Rushton were research assistants at different stages. Amanda helped with initial library searches, Kathleen with analysing the interviews and with tracking down references, while Annie did the archival work in Hobart, including searching the Antarctic Division's press cuttings, and conducted some interviews. I have enjoyed working with all three, and thank them heartily for painstaking, often tedious work and for their interest and insights. Both Bonnie Simons and Elisabeth Gallagher did a wonderful job typing up the interviews and making sense of my field notes, and also showed interest in the content.

Many people have been significant in enabling me to complete this work. My husband, Roger Douglas, not only managed our household and three feline companions during my research absences, but has listened attentively to my accounts, discussed issues with me, and nourished my enthusiasm. Friends have also encouraged and supported me, especially during the dark days when breast cancer interrupted the project, and then during my absence in Antarctica, even when they wondered why on earth I could want to go there! They are many, but I would like to mention Una Allen, Carol Anderson, Irene Baker, Bev Blaskett, John McLeod, Libby Morrison, Eve Oakley, Allan Peisley, Judy Rassaby, Priscilla Robinson, Margaret Sheehan, Sally Went and Jane Westman. The late Noni Holmes did understand my fascination with the challenge of Antarctica, and I cannot forget her generosity and warmth, nor my final phone call from Antarctica with the late Chasely Kratzmann.

My former colleagues at La Trobe University, Lyn Yates, Keith Simkin, Lois Foster-Fry, Mirna Cicioni and Tom Weber believed in the project and gave me generous encouragement. Many of my students have been genuinely interested, and I would like to name Dot Angell, Kate Brook, Samantha Hodgkins, Pam Martin, Kim McLeod and Milena Mirabelli. I am also grateful for advice and support from overseas colleagues Inga Elgqvist-Salzmann (Sweden) and Esther Rothblum (US).

Michael Henderson and Ray Snyder of St Vincent's Hospital, Melbourne, not only treated me for cancer in 1994, but believed in my dream and let me think it would be possible to realise it. Mary Rose Stewart has also helped me to meet the challenges. The writing period coincided with the final agonising illness in Sydney of my mother. I cannot find adequate words to thank Brian Burns and Mary Jamieson, my cousins, and Baiba Berzins, Heather Cox, Mee Mee Lee, Barbara Leigh, Beryl Pegler, Rosemary Snodgrass and Ruth Toop for the ways in which they 'were there' for me. In Melbourne, in the final days before my mother died, there was Dawn Ellis, a very special person.

It is difficult to single out people within the community of Antarcticans, for I am in danger of naming one and not another. However, Louise Crossley has been significant in believing in the project, in bringing it to life, and for her advice and friendship. She introduced me to a number of Antarctic players who were especially helpful in getting a project approved for me to conduct in Antarctica. Elizabeth Chipman has been generous with encouragement and with assistance with locating women. Tim and Ros Bowden kindly shared their taped radio interviews, and have shown helpful interest in the project. I will never forget my astonishment when Jo Jacka offered to let me work with his group at Law Dome, and am enormously grateful for his support, trust and friendship. My thanks to the 'Domies' (Alan Elcheikh, Russell Brand, Mark Richardson, Suenor Woon and Ross Anderson), to Ruth Lawless and Robin Thomson with whom I worked on Shirley

Island, and their supervisor, Knowles Kerry, as well as to the station-based people at Casey in the 1995–96 summer, especially Murray Parkinson and Damien Thomas, who have become good Antarctic mates. At the Division in Kingston, Martin Riddle (Human Impacts Program Leader) and Des Lugg (Head, Polar Medicine) have been especially helpful and encouraging. I would also like to thank Rob Easther, Tom Maggs, Mary Mulligan, Peter Sullivan and Warren Papworth of the Division, who have each made a contribution to the completion of this research.

The women whom I have interviewed have been unstintingly generous with their time, patience and material. I have shared hospitality in many of their homes, and their interest in the project has sustained me through the long process. I hope this book does some justice to the confidence you placed in me. The extent of my gratitude is difficult to convey. In particular, I would like to thank Morag Anderson, Liv Arnesen, Susan Barr, Helen Beggs, Isobel Bennett, Hope Black, Caroline Caddy, Robyn Carter, Ros Codling, Gillian Deakin, Liza Fallon, Melanie Fitzpatrick, Phillipa Foster, Beth Gott, Robyn Graham, Pene Greet, Mandy Holmes, Janet Hughes, Elizabeth Hynes, Susan Ingham, Jeannette Johanson, Midj Jones, Anne Kerle, Ulla Knox-Little, Gina Price, Pauline Reilly, Clare Robertson, Annie Rushton, Joan Russell, Patricia Selkirk, Kerrie Swadling, Robin Thomson, Maria Turnbull, Anitra Wendin and Lynn Williams for the special ways in which they have contributed to my task.

Pene Greet has been an unfailing source of support and practical assistance, and I have enjoyed our lively and wide-ranging discussions. She, Louise Crossley and my long-standing friend Elizabeth Swanton generously read drafts of the book, providing invaluable feedback. At Allen & Unwin, Rebecca Kaiser has been enthusiastic and helpful. Ultimately, of course, the responsibility rests with me for errors of interpretation, judgment, omission and commission. It has been a long journey, and an enjoyable one. I hope that readers will share our Antarctic dreams.

Robin Burns

'I want to go too!'

'Yes, I'll talk to you about my time in Antarctica, because I don't think a lot has been written about women who do unusual things.'

'The Antarctic brings these wonderfully diverse people together.'

'I'm just a little brick in the whole process of going down. There's nothing to it now, it's not pioneering or exploring.'

'Women are not "seen" and their contribution, especially creative, (policy, writing, management) is not valued as highly as similar men's.'

'Going to Antarctica was my big dream, since I was a little kid!'

'There's less overt sexism or harassment than 10 years ago but it's still there.'

'I really can't describe the good feeling of being in the Antarctic environment!'

'There's a long way to go till there are more women there, but there's no reason why we shouldn't be there.'

The quotes multiply, and entice. That women have been to Antarctica—numbers of women—and that there is a story to tell was my main motivation for writing about their experiences. And while, to some expeditioners, women have been given too much

1

prominence recently, the extent of their participation is barely known outside very limited circles. As I talked about this project, people speculated about the size of the task: Twelve? No? Twenty, perhaps? No? Not a hundred, surely? *Four hundred!* 'Why don't we ever hear about them?' they asked.

Yes, this is the approximate number of women who have been with the Australian expeditions. Of these, over 80 have spent the winter there (several on each of the four stations), while growing numbers have wintered twice or more. Some summer scientists and one support person have been four or more times. Others have been on marine science voyages, when they may barely sight land during six or more weeks away, working in the shipboard laboratories, sampling in icy conditions and mountainous seas, with no possibility for a weekend away from their research.

Still nowhere near half the population, but a solid minority on several stations over the now-lengthy summers, women are present in all Antarctic activities. And how they view their participation is diverse: some don't want to be seen in any way as different to their male companions; others are insistent that their different experiences be told; while yet others are simply voices wanting to be heard.

A STORY WITHIN THE STORY

If my first motivation for writing this book was to celebrate women's participation in Antarctic work, the second motivation was personal. The Antarctic, and other remote environments, have attracted me since school days. In December 1965, a close friend sailed off in the *Nella Dan* to spend fifteen months at Mawson as a cosmic ray physicist. I ground my teeth in envy as I farewelled him, and declared that I wanted to be the first woman to go to Antarctica, to study the effects on the men of my presence there! I did not know then that some female scientists had been to the sub-Antarctic, or that the first Australian woman had stepped ashore on the continent in the 1960–61 season.[1]

2

For three decades, other travels and tasks pushed Antarctica aside. Then, to celebrate my fiftieth birthday, I joined an Australian and New Zealand Scientific Exploring Society (ANZSES) women's expedition to the Great Victoria Desert, led by Louise Crossley. Several of the women revealed a longing to go to Antarctica; Louise had recently been station leader at Mawson. She invited me to an international conference on women in Antarctica, and that confirmed my plan to write a book about women in Antarctica, little dreaming that I too would go there.

Investigation of women's work in Antarctica led me to Jo Jacka, then head of the Australian glaciology program. To my utter disbelief, he matter of factly said that if my project was officially accepted, and if his research group approved of me, then I could work with them at the remote inland deep core drilling site at Law Dome! My first application was unsuccessful: the committee was doubtful about having a 'watcher' there. 'Try again,' they said. 'We also want to see if you are serious about your research.' The project evolved into a study of scientists working in remote areas, but just before the next application round I was diagnosed with breast cancer. The prospect of Antarctica sustained me through that. To help me deal with the nausea of chemotherapy, I even used an image of a rolling ship on the wild Southern Ocean, the distant icebergs promising the pack ice, calmer water ahead, and my goal. I took day leave from hospital to complete my new application, which was successful.

And so I, too, have been a summer expeditioner, experiencing the whole Antarctic process from medical and psychological assessment, through field training, to the ship journey South, to life on a modern station and at two field locations. I have used authorial privilege to place my story in this account woven from many stories, encouraged by other women to include my tale.

The other great privilege of having worked in Antarctica, as a social scientist on a research project supported by the Antarctic Science Advisory Committee (ASAC), is that my present task has been given a legitimacy that it could not have achieved had I merely looked through other women's eyes. I have only been for one summer, to one station, but I *have* voyaged South. I know what it can be like in the Southern Ocean, I've thrilled as the first iceberg appeared, and have sampled the community life and interactions, the station duties, the fun of learning new skills, the wildlife, the vivid skies and the scents and sounds.

GATHERING THE STORIES

My aim in this book has been to discover and depict the variety of women's work and women's experiences in Antarctica and the sub-Antarctic islands, predominantly as seen through the eyes of women with the official Australian program. There are some common themes, and also great diversity, in perspectives as well as experiences. I made a commitment to those who agreed to talk to me that I would respect and try to present that diversity. I have interviewed 130 women since June 1994.[2] Some of them have been with other national expeditions and with private ones. Their perspectives are included, as the Antarctic is international, managed under the Antarctic Treaty System.[3]

The international dimension is reflected in the composition of national expeditions, and in the present sample of expeditioners: I have met women from France, the United Kingdom, the United States and South Africa who have been to Antarctica with the Australian National Antarctic Research Expeditions (ANARE), and others who have spent seasons with the British Antarctic Survey (BAS), the US national program, the New Zealand program, and on Argentinian, Chilean, French, German, Italian and Norwegian stations, as well as private ex-peditions. The non-ANARE women expanded my understanding of women's Antarctic experiences, and of the ways in which Antarctic expeditions work.

There is no definitive list of all ANARE expeditioners, nor access to their names and addresses, so I had no idea how many women I was looking for. At the 1993 conference I met eight who agreed to be interviewed. I then asked each of them to suggest others who might be prepared to talk to me. This method of using existing networks is called—very appropriately for such a study—the 'snowball' recruitment technique, and has proved invaluable. Its major limitation is that those people not visible within networks may have systematically different experiences and perspectives to those who are more visible. I therefore used other strategies to locate women to interview and to gain an overview of the nature and extent of women's participation.

Two valuable lists have been published, one by Elizabeth Chipman (women from all nations who visited Antarctica up to 1984) and one compiled by the ANARE Club for the jubilee history of all wintering expeditioners.[4] I pieced together an overview, estimating that around 400 women have been South with ANARE. This includes Antarctic Division staff on familiarisation visits and supervisory visits, as well as voyage management trainees. It also includes 'round trippers' who go and return on the same voyage, a category covering special guests including politicians and media representatives, those on humanities programs such as artists, writers, photographers, and a philosopher, as well as representatives of the Treaty system and conservation interests. For a period, two school children were selected annually from a national competition to go with a chaperone, and in the first decades, Queen's scouts were also sent to Macquarie Island— boys allowed to go before women, as one interviewee commented. For a time, too, there was an annual ballot for partners of expeditioners to go.

Two groups of women who have been to the Antarctic are especially transient because of their occupation and have been hard to trace: Bureau of Meteorology staff and members of the Armed Forces, from which a number of the female radio operators and technicians have been recruited. In general, those who go to the Antarctic tend to be restless and seek new places and experiences.

The women included here are not a representative sample in the statistical sense. However, I have set out to give both temporal and occupational breadth to their stories, going back as far as I could to locate early female expeditioners, as well as some of the recent ones. The best time in the academic calendar for interviewing unfortunately coincided with the summer Antarctic season, which restricted my opportunities from 1996 onwards. As far as possible, at least five women have been included from the main occupational groups: station leader, doctor, scientist, Meteorological Bureau staff, radio and communications operator, chef and tradesperson. The greatest number were interviewed in Hobart, but I also tried to talk to women in as many other places as possible.[5] The biggest gap is for women who went to Antarctica during the 1970s and early 1980s. They proved extremely elusive. The loss of their perspectives is acknowledged: they went when it was still quite unusual for women to do so, and were more likely to be the only woman in their group. They are also from a period when more women were entering the workforce, small numbers were beginning to enter gender atypical occupations, especially in technical fields, and with second wave feminism still fresh, many were re-balancing career and motherhood priorities.

Contacting women has been an intriguing process. 'I think I know of someone . . .' usually led—eventually—to a contact being made. Sometimes the links were tenuous. A school newspaper reported that someone had gone to Antarctica, and a student in a class I took once for a colleague found the address for me. Others were traced from old newspaper clippings in my Antarctic file. My 'uncle-in-law's wife's niece' is another Antarctic woman, as is the daughter of 'a friend of an old school friend of my father-in-law'! It has been a detective job that has in itself been satisfying, and that owes much to the cooperation and assistance of many people.

Each woman was interviewed and ten themes were used to guide these interviews. The themes were suggested by early discussions with female expeditioners, issues raised at the conference and in the scant literature on the subject. The interviews were open-ended and confidential, and all the women had the choice of what to disclose as well as the right to withdraw at any stage. Interviews took up to five hours, sometimes over several sessions. I frequently only needed to ask about the decision to go to the Antarctic to elicit an hour or more of almost uninterrupted recollection. And, as a hesitant visitor to others' lives, I was delighted to hear that the interviews served as a debriefing for many, providing an enjoyable opportunity to talk to an interested listener. Written accounts of the interviews were returned for correction and additional comments. Three women withdrew at that point. Some edited their transcripts heavily, while others gave additional, sometimes detailed notes, told about subsequent visits South, and even invited a further interview.

In the small group of Antarctic women, to which I was admitted as an expeditioner myself, friendships have developed. I have heard different sides of an incident or memories of a season. Not one woman asked about the substance of other interviews, and all have respected the sometimes difficult position I found myself in as party to different versions of an event. Personally, ethically and methodologically, I have tried to approach each interview open-mindedly, and have received no feedback suggesting I have broken confidences.

For the pioneers, 35 years had elapsed between their first experience in Antarctica and when I spoke with them. Memory can play tricks, highlighting or smoothing out events and feeling-tones, blurring details, altering—mostly unconsciously—the individual's role or reactions, the importance of events, and even the place of some of the key figures. However, there was still a vividness about their recollections, which was outstanding with Isobel Bennett, 83 at the time of the interview and one of the first four women to go South. Her exquisite photographs, publications and diary were all laid out when I arrived at her home, and she spoke about the experience as I imagine she would have at the time.

Interviews conducted shortly after return from the Antarctic might record the raw, immediate reactions, but I know from my own experience and the words of others that most want time to process the experiences, both positive and negative. On first return they are not willing to talk to anyone, including in some instances close associates. This book, therefore, contains stories of women's lives filtered through many lenses. Not a single account of 'women in Antarctica', but rather many variations, will emerge. An interview, too, is but a moment in a person's life, reflecting an ongoing story.

The processing of experience is also ongoing, as transcript comments indicate: 'It was a bit of a shock seeing what I thought then. I've moved on since!' Through regular contact with some of the women, I have noted changing perspectives. Mostly the pain has lessened, though sometimes the healing process is prolonged and help has been hard to find. Several exclaimed: 'Gosh, didn't I dramatise then!' or: 'I feel rather differently about it now.' The cliché holds that 'time heals', and for some the telling has been part of the process.

The 1993 conference on women in the Antarctic owes much to the dedication of Robyn Graham, the organiser.[6] The conference was a watershed for a number of participants, for it was the first time that female expeditioners had gathered to talk about this important part of their lives. To hear their experiences and reactions named provided a sense of enormous relief at not being alone. For some, that triggered the ability to deal with the issues. For others, hearing strong feminist perspectives on male–female relationships, and the situation of women in Antarctica discussed within a formal anti-discrimination and anti-sexual harassment framework, was offensive, and seemed unwarranted, unrepresentative and unfair to their fellow, male expeditioners. I try to report these different perspectives throughout the book. In so doing, I have found that some feminist views on the significance of difference are reinforced and many other issues regarding perceptions, values and understandings are raised.

TELLING AND RETELLING THE STORIES

To say that interviews were conducted 'at a time and in a place of the interviewee's choosing' is a bland statement of how my discussions with the women took place. Undertaking this project has been a journey in itself. I experienced a stormy Sunday night in the Hobart Bureau of Meteorology, discussing the Antarctic in between regular forecasts and inquiries about an oncoming storm. One day I shared the life of an island-based ranger. Interviews have been suspended to comfort babies, to rescue my tape recorder from a jealous toddler, to admire a pet mouse, and to collect youngsters from school. Partners and grandparents have hovered and helped. I disappointed one 10-year-old by not squealing in horror at her live blue-tongued lizard necklace! I've sat in laboratories, in small corners in offices, in cafes and in parks, as well as in many homes from Hobart to Darwin as well as in the United Kingdom and at Tromsø in Norway's Arctic. I've listened to tales of missing chemicals, unsympathetic supervisors and cranky chefs surrounded by the noise of phones and the bustle of life. I've enjoyed home-cooked pasta and couscous, and have shared home-grown vegetables, chocolate cake and ginger muffins. I even met Muffy the cat, a pampered Hobart pet retrieved from Macquarie Island!

The volume of material I gathered is enormous, rich and diverse. It has, however, been hard to stop collecting because every woman interviewed has provided some new angle, some new insight, or told me of some situation about which I had not heard. And, as Louise's foreword points out, rapid changes are occurring, so that this is a story that has no end. However, the last interview was conducted in February 2000, with a woman who was in Antarctica during the previous summer. The volume of material and the nature of the interviews also means that this is not a collection of traditional biographies: it is a celebration of the many, and of the extent to which women have participated in Antarctic work.

Some women are named, with their permission; however, to personalise and protect, in some instances pseudonyms have been used, while others requested full anonymity. If this sometimes frustrates readers, think of the damage that can be done by stories, remarks, hints—especially if taken out of context and changed in the telling.

Women continue to work in Antarctica. My work is to present the textures, the richness and the range that is the fabric of their Antarctic experience. (Demographic details are found in Appendices 1 and 2.)

This book locates women, side by side with men, as people who travel South to work, who undergo an expeditioner experience. In order to do this, I have talked to many men too, but the foreground here is women's stories.

———

As I sit writing, I can see the *Aurora Australis* unloading at the Hobart docks, reminding me of the moment when, in late November 1995, our voyage leader quietly announced to the crowd below: 'Would all those who would like to come to Antarctica please come on board.' 'I'm *really* going there—at last!' reverberated in my mind, and I thought back to the time I farewelled my friend 30 years earlier.

The Antarctic ships bring back strong memories and tears, both fond and sad. You can try to describe the experience, in words, on film, in a work of art, but all agree that it eludes such endeavour. We women have taken our place with others, privileged beyond words, heading into the Southern Ocean and all that lies beyond.

ONE

'Finally we were on our way!'
Women become Antarctic
expeditioners

Frontiers are defined, approached and inhabited by men. The
women who may accompany them to the place between the
known and the unknown are often nameless. The role traditionally assigned to women, even in frontier situations, was through
the part they played in the men's domain as daughters, lovers,
helpmates, mistresses, wives and mothers—all terms defined by
relationships to men.[1]

The women who ventured South in the early days were no
exception—mostly nameless 'wife of ...', or only hinted at as a
near-invisible presence, for they were not whalers, ships' crew
or explorers. Elizabeth Chipman's comprehensive account of
women in Antarctica begins with the story of Louise Séguin, the
first woman recorded to have travelled South, in 1773–74.[2]
There are other accounts of early women travellers. Marnie
Bassett wrote of Rose de Freycinet, the young wife of a ship's
captain who stowed away on a round-world voyage in 1817–20
that called at several sub-Antarctic islands.[3] On 20 February
1935, Danish-born Caroline Mikkelsen, wife of the captain of
the Norwegian whaler *Thorshavn*, became the first woman
recorded to step ashore on the Antarctic continent, near the
present Davis station.[4] The story of twentieth century female
Antarctic scientific pioneers is found in Barbara Land's account,
while Esther Rothblum and colleagues gathered a range of

women's Antarctic stories from the second half of the twentieth century.[5]

A trickle of other personal stories is emerging, both from autobiographical writings and from research by others (see Appendix 3). There is an accumulation of accounts of women's ventures beyond our concept of normal, everyday, achievable life. As their numbers swell, questions remain concerning the way to write about such women. We delight in reading of their particular experiences and views, yet history is often written as a general narrative, where individual and group differences are absorbed into the dominant story. Thus, women have been accorded little place in historical accounts, including those of Antarctica.

Women *are* newcomers on the Antarctic stage in roles similar to those of men. Their arrival parallels the broader social and cultural changes as women enter an ever-increasing range of occupations and activities. However, this change was slower to happen in Antarctica because the occupations and skills required there have been strongly in male preserves.

This account seeks to interweave many women's views of life in Antarctica. It is inspired both by my strong belief that women's voices should be heard, and that there is a story about being a woman in Antarctica. Antarctica is also a special place that has been directly experienced by few people, and for that reason has an attraction of its own. It is a microcosm, but one that is coloured and enlarged by the place. The human community in Antarctica, and its treatment of fellow members, can enlighten the larger human condition. This book results, therefore, from a desire to commemorate women's enjoyment of and achievements in Antarctica and the sub-Antarctica, and to acknowledge some of the costs.

THE BARRIER OF THE ICE

The three early 'eras' in Antarctica—whaling and sealing, discovery and exploration—were initiated and conducted by men, occasionally with one or two accompanying women. The tales of those eras have become part of the history of the West reaching out to the wider world. They form, in scaled-down versions, the legitimating stories for the men and a number of women, who go South today. Fifty years after permanent bases were built and regular, scientific expeditions began women remain a minority in Antarctica. But minorities have stories, too.

To spend a winter in Antarctica is the 'real' Antarctic experience. Extensive summer programs are relatively new (enabled by better shipping, long-range helicopters and, for some countries, air services)[6] and now stretch for up to six months on the continent, and eight months on Macquarie Island. However, it is the handful—mostly between sixteen and 22 people—who keep the stations running when the shipping season ends who are considered the 'true Antarcticans'.[7] There is both a mystique about wintering, and a harsh reality: it is just about totally isolated and there is virtually no possibility for repatriation should a life-threatening or acute personal emergency occur. For nearly six weeks the sun does not appear above the horizon, temperatures hover below minus 20°C, and blizzards rage. Before satellite communication was established, telex and radio telephone (radphone)—the only means to contact the outside world—were often unreliable and used sparingly. And while the continental stations now have comfortable living conditions, accommodation is quite old and spartan on Macquarie Island. During summer, and on Macquarie Island in winter, too, those working in the field are housed primitively, with conditions sometimes resembling those that existed in the days of exploration.

In winter, with the blanketing, numbing, perspective-defying snow piling deep or ever-moving with the blizzard, the summer fractal landscape disappears, replaced by an encapsulating nothingness. Stephen Pyne's dramatic depiction of Antarctica epitomises what the wintering expeditioners encounter:

> Its extraordinary isolation was not merely geophysical but
> metaphysical . . . The Ice stripped civilization (and exploration) to

its most elemental forms. Exploration often became a matter of simple survival ... Paradoxically, what began as a richly imagined continent not unlike others became, when finally explored, a white spot on the globe.[8]

We are used to an ever-changing landscape, and those who experience winter in Antarctica learn to recognise and appreciate the subtle changes in ice, snow and light. However, it is far more monotonous than most visual environments we know, and this tends to turn people inwards. It is perhaps this reduction in outer cues, and the isolation from new stimulation and contact, that marks the difference between the experience of wintering and summering. This sensory deprivation, added to the material hardships, the quality of the isolation rather than just its presence, mark the boundary between the two sets of experiences of Antarctica. It is something that those who have wintered on the continent instinctively know, though it is hard to communicate to others. Louise Crossley remembers 'driving a Hägglunds[9] out to the ship on the first, ice edge voyage after the winter, and there was WATER beyond the ice. It was as if I was about to fall off the edge of the known universe'.

Women have only wintered on the continent since 1981,[10] whereas men have done so since 1954. They constitute 3 per cent of all winterers on Australian stations, or 7.5 per cent of all winterers since a woman first wintered on Macquarie Island. This reflects the occupational range of winterers: most women who go to Antarctica are scientists, and scientists are the minority on stations over winter, Macquarie Island in 1999 and 2000 being a recent exception. Correspondingly, in the summer science season, female numbers are higher, now reaching 25 per cent on some stations in some seasons, notwithstanding the additional maintenance crews at the bases at that time, too. However, women are occupying a greater variety of positions, and in 1997 the first female wintering tradesperson, a carpenter, went South.

While some hardships have changed, the challenges remain. And there is an element of personal odyssey about each person's

14

journey South. Gina Price suggests that 'the internal journey is as important as the external, going to extremes geographically challenges you to go deeper within'. For some there are merely a few inconveniences involved in working in a harsher clime; for others it is a preferred lifestyle, entering: 'a utopia [where] ... there's no push, there's no McDonald's up the road. Because there is no money, there's no consumer items; consumerism is not an issue, you take what you need, you use it but there's not that kind of element of competition, who's got what, is eliminated largely. And that's what I really like about it.' (Phillipa Foster) Indeed, the greatest competition may be verbal, about the exploits of 'my year'.[11]

Expectations, job, companions, weather that season, station dynamics, even events back home, combine to define the individual experience. Recent research suggests the interpersonal and group aspects of life in Antarctica can be the most stressful.[12] For some, once the ship docks in Australia, the task ends, while for others it is just beginning, since the data they bring back have to be analysed, interpreted, presented. It is a mosaic. Therefore, the portrait of the total human experience of Antarctica is immense, contains different pieces and can be viewed in varied ways.

BREAKING THE ICE: WOMEN ENTER THE ANTARCTIC ARENA

This book focuses on women who have gone on voyages and expeditions as colleagues and fellow workers. However, there was a transitional time, between the accompanying women on the whaling ships of previous centuries and the formal deployment of women, when wives of some senior men were given specific roles. Thus Edith Ronne and Jennie Darlington, on the 1947–48 Ronne Antarctic Research Expedition, were the first wintering women, and Edith was nominated a 'recorder'. In the 1952–53 summer Edna Petersen acted as stand-in during the filming of background shots for the movie *Hell Below Zero*.[13]

The first woman selected to work in the sub-Antarctic was the New Zealander G.L. Hammond, who was a theatre sister on Campbell Island during the summer of 1945–46. In 1955–56, Marie V. Klenova worked as a marine geologist on the Russian ship *Ob* at Mirny, and from then on the Russian ships had stewardesses. The following season, two more female Russian scientists went South: hydrobiologist V.S. Korotkevich and geomorphologist L.M. Nikolaeva. The most publicised women, however, were the two PanAm 'hostesses' Patricia Hepinstall and Ruth Kelly. They were employed on a commercial flight from Christchurch, New Zealand, to McMurdo station in October 1957.

Australia's national Antarctic operation was next to include women when Isobel Bennett, Mary Gillham, Susan Ingham and Hope MacPherson left for Macquarie Island in late 1959. Susan, a graduate scientific secretary with the Antarctic Division, is credited with successfully confronting the director with a request to go on the changeover voyage and, in order to fill a four-berth cabin, the other three were invited to accompany her. Then came the French geophysicist Jeanne Baguette and engineer Ge' Pillet on the Iles Kerguelen in 1961–62, and in 1962–63 Christiane Gillet went as the engineer for the construction of the French Dumont D'Urville station, spending many summers there. Also during 1962–63, the first four female American biologists joined the marine science voyages of the USNS *Eltanin*.

The increase in scientific activity in Antarctica in conjunction with the International Geophysical Year (IGY) in 1957–58 perhaps paved the way for more women to be among the Antarctic scientists. Women took part in voyages to Macquarie Island continuously between 1959 and 1968, and have done so every year since 1974. France, the former Soviet Union and the United States continued to include women in their expeditions. The first two female Chilean scientists went for the 1963–64 summer, followed by Argentinian women scientists in 1968–69, while in 1969 New Zealand was the first nation to appoint a woman to a permanent scientific position for Antarctic work. And women were among the crew of the *Dan*s, ships taking expeditioners South in the two decades following 1967. Scientists Mary Odile Cahoon and Mary Alice McWhinnie were the first American women to winter in Antarctica as team members, at McMurdo in 1974, and in 1979 Michele Raney, a doctor, was the first wintering woman at the US South Pole station.

Doctors were also the first female winterers at Australian stations, with English Zoë Gardner on Macquarie Island in 1976, and Louise Holliday at Davis in 1981. In 1976–77 the British scientist Janet Thomson gained a place on an American research vessel travelling South. In the 1983–84 season she became the first British woman to go with the British Antarctic Survey (BAS).[14] BAS engaged the first two women to winter for 1993–94, and in 1990 there was an all-female wintering team at the West German station. More recently, South Africa has admitted women as winterers. With the addition of new national Antarctic actors the situation of wintering women is changing rapidly.

There is little ethnic diversity among the national expeditions, something that is particularly noticeable with Australian groups since Australia is a country with a highly diverse population. This may highlight the cultural embeddedness of meanings of Antarctica, though selection bias cannot be excluded. It has not yet become a place for Indigenous Australians, only two having been there, artists Lin Onus and Miriam-Rose Ungunmerr who both went on a round trip in 1994.[15] And, given the nature of the stations and the work there, the occupational range is restricted. The age of expeditioners ranges between 20 and 60, with the early thirties the most common. While partners engaged in relevant work can and do go South, there is an ongoing issue in Antarctic service about the enforced lengthy separation of families. The mothers of pre-teen children are highly unlikely to winter, and wintering poses other difficulties for expeditioners and their families. Even with modern communications between Antarctica and Australia, twelve to fifteen months is a long time for couples to be separated. New relationships can form that are difficult to explain, and each may find it hard to understand the experiences of the other; for example, the intensity of life in Antarctica, or the new-found independence of the partner left at home. It is also hard to keep up with children's development, though use of the internet now enables closer contact and the exchange of photos. Even a six- to eight-week round trip can be problematic for a parent.

Women have been employed by the shipping operators carrying the expeditions South. Inger Knudsen was the radio operator on the *Thala Dan* from 1967, and Ulla Knox-Little (née Sommers) was on the *Nella Dan* and later the *Icebird*. Australian Peta Bragge became the first female ordinary seaman on the German *Icebird* in the mid-1980s, and Barbara Massing, from Germany, was its first female chief mate in 1990.

Tourism has increased women's opportunities to sample Antarctica, though a tourist visit, which is expensive, is very different from a working one. Tourists ships have also provided another avenue for women to go South, as guides, reporters and leaders. The first to do so was the New Zealand journalist Dorothy Braxton, who went as a guest on the *Magga Dan* in the summer of 1967–68. Her quest to go South echoes many of those recounted in this book: a childhood longing, repeated attempts to join official national expeditions, and then finally a breakthrough.

Private expeditions have provided another opportunity for women. They link the two major phases of Antarctic work, exploration and science, and range from the purely adventurous to the scientific. There is an ambience surrounding them that suggests they, rather than the official expeditions, carry the exploratory tradition today. Perhaps they are a contemporary answer to the routinisation of national Antarctic activity. Interestingly, given the 'explorer' tradition, women have readily found a place on these expeditions since the 1970s. On voyages today, roles are less clearly defined in domestic, assistant and principal actor terms, and women share the rigours of small boats on huge seas, at least one of which has sunk in pack ice.

Norwegian glaciologist Monica Kristensen led three men in a 1986–87 attempt to retrace Amundsen's dog-drawn polar trek of

1911–12. They were the first to climb the Axel Heiberg glacier since Amundsen, and undertook an impressive scientific program, but had to turn back at 86°S. Monica eventually reached the Pole as program coordinator of multi-nation expeditions in 1991–92 and 1993–94. Fellow countrywoman Liv Arnesen skied solo and unsupported to the Pole in 1994, the second person to do so, reaching it in an amazing 50 days. The first attempt by women to mount an all-female expedition in 1968 failed for lack of sponsorship. However, women finally succeeded in funding all-female expeditions in the 1990s, with four American women reaching the South Pole in 67 days in 1993, followed by Liv Arnesen's 1994 solo journey, then a group of British women in 1999–2000. Liv Arnesen and Ann Bancroft, one of the American four, are skiing across the entire continent, taking a new route, in 2000–01.

Other female Antarctic adventurers include Brigitte Muir, who climbed Mt Vincent Massif in 1994,[16] and Margaret Werner who participated in the 1987–88 Bicentennial Expedition to Mt Minto, though she did not climb the peak. Women have been members of each expedition for Project Blizzard. This project has been involved with the conservation of Douglas Mawson's historic hut at Cape Denison. The first voyage, in 1985, was also linked to a multi-nation expedition, 'In the Footsteps of Scott', that set out to re-trace Robert Scott's attempt to be first to the South Pole. He reached the Pole in January 1912 to find the Norwegian Roald Amundsen had beaten him, and Scott and all his party died on the way back to the coast. Women were included in the support crew for the re-enactment, and were present when the ship sank a year later, crushed by the ice.

They have also participated in Greenpeace expeditions, in all roles including leader. And, as couple venturers, Sally Poncet and her husband Jerome first wintered in Antarctica in 1978, on a personal and scientific mission, leading the way for subsequent wintering twosomes. In fact, there seems no role, except several of the more obscure trades, in Antarctica today that has not been undertaken by a woman.

GETTING A FOOT IN THE DOOR

Many of the women I interviewed echoed stories of yearning, and persistent attempts at inclusion in official Antarctic activities. Monika Puskeppeleit's image of women knocking at the castle gates of the Polar King is apt. It is interesting to trace the opposition that controlled access of women to this last earthly frontier. It focused on women's inferior physical and psychological strength, the primitive living conditions and the possible deleterious psychological effects on men of having women in their midst.

There are still barriers to women's participation in Antarctic activities. Their representation in the relevant occupations is in similar proportions to their representation in Australia, with the result that there are few skilled female tradespeople but a significant number of female scientists and doctors. And family responsibilities, especially caring for the very young and the elderly, still largely devolve on to women. Equal employment opportunity (EEO) principles and practices are redressing discrimination in selection procedures. Even though word can spread among potential applicants about perceived negative aspects of Antarctic service, there is very strong competition for places in some fields, such as science, especially when other employment opportunities are low. All these factors affect female numbers on Antarctic expeditions. And, as with most Antarctic positions, women are still a minority in professional grades in the Australian Antarctic Division headquarters.

After allowing women on summer voyages, there were still three major hurdles to be overcome: being allowed to stay overnight on station, being allowed to visit the continent, and being eligible for winter appointments. Overcoming the first hurdle was largely up to the station leader who determined if women would be allowed to overnight when they came on brief changeover round trips. In the summer of 1975–76, Elizabeth Chipman, Shelagh Robinson and Jutta Hösel visited Macquarie Island together with Zoë Gardner, who was to winter there. Elizabeth recalls that the three persuaded the Macquarie station leader to let them stay overnight in a field hut. This was 'really breaking ground to stay overnight for those times—[only] a few female biologists had', including the first four women. International Women's Year (1975) provided the political environment to topple the second and third hurdles. It allowed Elizabeth, Shelagh, Jutta and Zoë to go ashore at Casey on their way to Macquarie Island. But it was another five years before women could stay on the continent. Louise Holliday was the first wintering woman, and scientist Patricia Selkirk stayed several months at Casey the following summer (1981–82).

Initially, most summer visits were brief. The logistics of the ANARE operation in the 1960s and 1970s did not allow extensive summer projects, except for special surveys such as those undertaken by the Prince Charles Mountains (1969–70) and Heard Island (1971–72) expeditions. Logistics have always played a dominant role in determining the size and composition of ANARE groups, and bigger ships, long-range helicopters and more summer voyages from the early 1980s have enabled the conduct of more, and longer, science projects. This in turn has brought more women to Antarctica.

RESISTING THE FEMALE 'FATAL IMPACT'

An early proponent of women's participation in Antarctic voyages was Mr Turner, Master Warden at the Hobart Marine Board. Addressing Sir Douglas and Lady Mawson in 1930, on the eve of the departure of the Antarctic research ship *Discovery*, he commented: 'One thing disappoints me a little—that no women are accompanying the expedition. In these enlightened times, women have invaded all professions and all businesses, with credit to themselves, and to the advantage of the professions and businesses. It is said that no woman could survive the rigours of life in the Antarctic but, as Mrs T. Murdoch reminds me, Miss Nina Demney, 28 years of age, a graduate of the

Leningrad Geographical Institute, is now second in command of the Soviet Arctic Expedition ...' The *Mercury* reports that 'Sir Douglas dryly commented that probably the lady Mr Turner mentioned would find the Arctic a more pleasant habitat than Russia'.[17]

The inclusion of women in Russian expeditions provoked negative press comment in the 1950s. Under such headlines as 'REDS MAKE IT HOMELY' and 'CAVIAR, WOMEN IN RED ANTARCTICA', the female scientists' roles were domesticated. Outrage at the threat posed by Soviet bases on territory claimed by Australia was also defused by the implication that the Russians were 'soft', because not only were there women on their bases but caviar, carpets, wallpaper and dial phones as well. No room there for heroism! The press was enthusiastic, however, when the two PanAm 'hostesses' landed briefly at McMurdo on a commercial flight, though the term 'invasion' was used repeatedly to describe their arrival. They were wrongly said to be the first women in Antarctica, and were referred to as 'the girls'.

Both the term 'girl' and the notion of a 'feminine invasion' continued in press reports into the 1980s, though the first ANARE women were accorded adult status. The Australian media called female expeditioners from other nations 'girls', perhaps to deny their double threat as women and representatives of other nations. And journalists' interest focused on things such as the women's underclothing, rather than their science projects. When possible, women were photographed with children. Beth Gott's farewell, for example, was headlined '... AND MUM SAILS SOUTH',[18] while Elspeth Wishart and Linda Clark were the 'PAIR [who] MUST LEAVE FAMILIES BEHIND FOR SEVEN WEEKS'.[19] Gillian Deakin, a doctor who spent 1986 at Davis, is pictured in a laboratory, with the caption denying her professional status, 'Antarctic lures a Florence Nightingale in long-johns'.[20] A 1999 winter flight carrying medical supplies for a female doctor with cancer at South Pole station was tagged 'WHITE KNIGHTS FLY TO AN ICE MAIDEN'S RESCUE',[21] perhaps reviving the fear that women cannot manage in Antarctica.

A significant strand of resistance came from many former Antarctic explorers and expeditioners. Exemplifying the reasons for Mawson's dry comment, Vivian Fuchs as Director of the British Antarctic Survey and leader of the Commonwealth Transantarctic Expedition of 1957–58, described the conditions on British bases as 'still extremely tough'. Women would be 'unable to handle the heavy cases of supplies now designed to be handled by men' and worse, 'new buildings would also have to be erected for women, and their presence would change the whole psychological atmosphere of the bases'.[22] Similarly, the US commander of Operation Deepfreeze cited lack of facilities and the effects on the men as the main reasons for excluding women adding, 'Women will not be allowed in the Antarctic until we can provide one woman for every man'.[23] He later said he felt the men did not want women there. 'It was a pioneering job. I think the presence of women would wreck the illusion of the frontiersman—the illusion of being a hero.'[24] This is a persistent theme in male reactions to having women in Antarctica. It *was* tough then, and women who have undertaken comparable exploits recently are exceptional people. However, women do not shrink from hardship and, in earlier eras, were simply excluded from opportunities to demonstrate their mettle.

Male sexual fears and fantasies are woven through the discussion of women's presence in Antarctica. This has sometimes been disguised as concerns about their physical and emotional toughness, revealing that men may believe they could have additional burdens in looking after women. Gallantry is mentioned, especially by the early women voyagers, in descriptions of men's behaviour towards them. Some women say that they were allowed to pull their weight only with difficulty.

Lynn Williams exposes one myth when she reflects that, physically, the only thing that her grandmother would have found hard about Antarctica was jumping from the ship-side ladder into the landing craft during a swell! Beth Gott described the procedure in a letter to her children: 'You climb over the ship's rail onto a rope ladder with wooden steps, go down the ladder backwards, wait for the DUKW [an amphibian craft] to rise on the swell, and then jump from the ladder. It is unwise to go too far down the ladder, because the DUKW may rise up and crush your foot between it and the ship's side.' The love of outdoor activities and their great competence at these draws many women South. There is also a desire to enjoy the same activities as men, to do the same things such as driving the big machinery and taking the unique opportunity to learn a new skill and have fun. The issue of emotional toughness is more complex and is discussed in later chapters.

Does the presence of women disrupt the dynamics of the male groups, and is this welcome? The frontier mentality suggests that it is not. Before women wintered, the threat they posed was mostly symbolic, although some expeditioners reacted negatively to or pointedly ignored the visiting women. Others were pleased about the change, though anxious about possible ramifications. Beth 'got the feeling the women were tolerated, but not really accepted . . .'. Women can feel discomfort in a 'boys' club' atmosphere, which gives a sense of belonging to members, but tends to exclude others.

Isobel Bennett had 'no feeling of antipathy from the group of men who went down with us or those on the station—they just treated us as people', a wish voiced by countless subsequent women expeditioners. Hope MacPherson agreed: 'We were all welcomed and accepted. A certain amount of side amusement was had about our coming, but it was quite harmless. We had no untoward advances. There was no resentment, really, except perhaps from the cook as we took some cakes with us and he was pretty good.'

Susan Ingham concurred, and noted in her diary that with the intense partying over Christmas, from which the women absented themselves after a certain amount of alcohol was consumed, 'only one [man] was really obnoxious'. On their return to the mess, a call was heard: 'no bad language, the girls are coming!' It seems that from the very beginning, women's presence was appreciated as a civilising influence that could be seen to serve men's needs while downplaying women's presence in their own right.

The pioneering role of those first four who left for Macquarie Island in 1959 deserves recognition. Some men were strongly opposed to the women going. Hope recounted: 'On the first night on board, as a welcome, the captain said, "And this is the first time we have had the pleasure of women—or ladies?— probably women—on the ship and it will remain to be seen if it is a pleasure".' Three of the first four to visit the continent were Australian Antarctic Division (AAD) staff and were known to most expeditioners. Elizabeth Chipman speaks for many women, even today, when she says: 'While all the attention was very exciting and the chance to visit the Antarctic continent would be the fulfilment of at least one long-held ambition, our feelings were tempered by the knowledge that not everyone in the Antarctic community was thrilled by the proposal to send women to the ice.'[25] Many years later, when discussing how she and her fellow women were received on that first visit to the continent in 1975, Shelagh Robinson reportedly focused on the negative impact on the station of the women's visit. She remembered that even a husky was 'very upset' at meeting women for the first time.[26]

Patricia Selkirk and Suzanne Stallman reported negative attitudes towards them twenty years ago. Patricia remembered that 'A number thought Antarctica was no place for a woman and kept out of my way. But there were a greater number who were co-operative in general, interested in and supportive of the science I was doing.' Suzanne added: 'I felt they weren't particularly looking forward to having me, but there was no overt antagonism.' And as a mid-1980s solo wintering woman, 'GD' found that 'one or two elements in the camp were capable round the bar at night of saying negative or distasteful things about me.' The station leader ensured that the hostile expeditioners did not 'swing the middle ground' to their side. Even in the 1990s, 'Krista' found 'no one challenged my right to be there, not openly, but a few people would have preferred women not to be there. Because the Antarctic is the last frontier, it's where men go to prove that they're men.'

In the 1970s and 1980s, the press reinforced that view, reporting that the presence of women was a 'bad day for misogynists',[27] or more ambiguously, that: 'The introduction of women to the icy wilderness melts the last macho frontier.'[28] As more women journeyed South, and their presence became inevitable, attitudes shifted towards them being perceived as a benefit and a resource. Comments even in the 1990s suggest that women who smooth the social fabric, are helpful or join heartily in male games are valued. One station leader succinctly said: 'We had two women at Casey for the winter ... They both added positively to the atmosphere of our year and were good for the station.' He noted in his log how the women fared. For example, on 29 July, 'The two girls are beginning to show signs of wear from the combination of drink and foul language in the Club'.[29] He does not record any intervention on their behalf. Some women have praised men who have quietly stepped in to prevent unwelcome behaviour towards them, while others have been distressed by the lack of support they received.

Station and hut log books and annual reports reveal the gung-ho, raunchy tenor of some years, and of men's attitudes to women: some consider women's conduct is a key to their acceptance, and others recognise that:

> the problems in a mixed party arise not from the presence of women but from men's reactions to their presence. The women can, by their actions, change the reactions for better or worse to some degree but cannot prevent them. Only a more enlightened attitude on the part of the men can do that and this will be a long time coming, given the background of the average male expeditioner who has, typically, spent most of his working life in a male-dominated environment (e.g. building trade, armed forces). The attitudes of some of the men made it clear that they had difficulty relating to women as people.[30]

This same man also noticed that 'all of the women were offended at times by male attitudes, and/or actions, while many of the men felt unhappy because of the presence of women'.

CONTINUITY AND CHANGE FOR WOMEN IN ANARE

The official Australian approach to women has been more open than in most other nations. The director, Phillip Law, considered a female scientist for Macquarie Island in 1953, though ministerial permission was refused. Law finally acceded to pressure from female applicants in 1959. He was aware of the psychological pressures on expeditioners, and the effect of deprivation of female company, and reportedly said in a 1975 interview that: 'The presence of a woman has a very softening and beneficial influence on men, especially if she's a mature, motherly type of person.'[31] With this statement Law suggests that there may be positive benefits from having women—especially 'motherly' ones—on station. Up until that point, the main discussion, both in Australian and other national circles, was of the potentially negative impact women might have on male morale, and of the difficulties they would encounter ranging from the physical hardships to the lack of separate toilets. Law's successors at the AAD were less sure that the positive aspects would outweigh the others. A 1970 report said that the Antarctic Division had 'an open mind' about women going South, but further expressions of concern about psychological problems and accommodation difficulties delayed women's inclusion in expeditions to the continent, and as winterers. Key support for the position of women came from the Division's chief medical officer, Dr Desmond Lugg, who recommended appointing a female medical officer in late 1975. There was a shortage of male applicants, and a qualified woman was available. His arguments were successful. Australia *was* well ahead of all but the Americans and New Zealanders, and today the British still insist on at least two wintering women.

Despite admitting women relatively early to the national Antarctic effort, the Division is nevertheless still dominated by men. As the AAD is part of the Commonwealth Public Service, equal employment opportunity is now official policy. However, the first permanent female scientist was not appointed until late 1999, and there are still only two women in senior management in the Division. Female employees cite harassment as a deterrent to seeking long-term employment. 'There's social inequality, women are looked on socially as "worth a try"', 'Faye' suggested, and 'Juliet' and 'Faith' disclosed experiences of repeated or protracted harassment while working there. 'It's a very male organisation', 'a very masculine construct', women find, citing as evidence its emulation of a military unit, or its very rational, anti-emotional and anti-feminine organisational culture. And, although Elizabeth Chipman actively worked for the abolition of the typing pool and the double standard evident in work practices in the 1970s, some women in the 1990s still feel that they are all looked upon as typists. They feel stereotyped, especially if they were originally employed in low-level jobs such as laboratory assistant or clerk, and constrained by the 'old [male] hand' dominance at the Division's Kingston headquarters.

Such dominance, and the numerical superiority of men, can lead to a continuation of the status quo where men prefer people like themselves, who are most likely to be men also. 'Faye' suggested that: 'There's some resistance to more than basic EEO issues. They realise some women are equal or better to some men at the job!' Some women feel that the AAD is not sympathetic to family considerations in any aspect of its operation. In the words of 'Hilary': 'I'm continually asked to promote ANARE as a woman-friendly community, with women-friendly jobs, "come on in, girls!" and yet what we don't do is acknowledge that 80 per cent of women between the ages of 25 and 40 have under-school age children. We don't even acknowledge that those are women, or we don't acknowledge that those women will not leave their children. Or their wider nurturing responsibilities. So we continue to send down very young girls only.'

One woman voiced the view that 'some women just want it all, they don't only want equality, they want it reversed'. Public service policy may be ahead of some other sectors of the Australian community on equal opportunity issues, but there is still some lingering ambivalence about women in the AAD

and ANARE. As 'Molly' succinctly observed: 'The blokey environment comes from the Division, it's still an old boys' ANARE,
and the Division administration pays lipservice to EEO and anti-
discrimination.' Management studies confirmed this in the early
1990s:

> People involved ... are characterized by what could be best
> described as a strong passion and potent beliefs ... which ...
> often conflict with modern beliefs about, and the practice of
> effective personnel management and are sometimes in opposition
> to modern public sector administrative legal requirements.
> Additionally, common national characteristics seem to become
> amplified among expeditioners.[32]

Seven years later, Elaine Prior made similar observations in her
research into the Division's organisational culture.[33] She found
that some senior and middle managers were keen for change.
Reports from the last two or three years suggest that change is
visible in recruitment of women, and in the atmosphere on
stations.

LOCATING CHANGE IN A WIDER PERSPECTIVE

This overview of women's inclusion in Antarctic teams illustrates
four major notions that stand in the way of their progress towards
equal opportunity. The first is the protection of the frontier
where men can be men. Women are posed as outsiders who
might shatter the myth. The second concerns women's fitness
for the task: do they possess the physical and mental abilities to
withstand the rigours of Antarctic life? The need for special facilities is a sub-theme of this; the early women expeditioners
showed that rostered shower times and locks for bathroom doors
dealt with such problems. The third stresses women's domestic
role, which provides a place for them in Antarctica so long as
they behave like stereotypical women. Finally, there are the possibly disturbing effects of female sexuality. Very recent research

confirms that relationships generally, rather than the environment, are of greatest concern during Antarctic service,[34] yet who wants to return to male celibacy, pin-ups and pornography?

The inclusion of women in Antarctic work mirrors the universal struggle of women to break out of purely domestic roles, and enter the world of paid employment and activity in the public sphere. Women *are* in Antarctica. The rewards have been huge, but they are still constrained within bounds set by the dominant group, as Chapter 4 details, and the costs for some have been high. Women are claiming their place in increasing numbers, and they stress over and over that it should be regarded as normal for them to be in Antarctica.

Experiences in Antarctica may also be beneficial for breaking down some female stereotypes of men, as 'GD' found: 'When you grow up in a feminist era, all you hear about men is usually entirely derogatory, all the positive things about humankind are usually seen as feminine ones and all the negative ones of violence and aggression and the competitiveness and so on seem to be the male ones. Down there I was helped to reverse this. I matured there, learnt what men had to offer me, and to society in general, not meaning sexual things but in terms of particular skills which were different to mine. I'm not saying that women can't do it—they do—but the men had these skills.'

TWO

'I had this dream ...'

What accounts for the human desire to explore? In childhood, we read about the discoveries and conquerors of 'new worlds', in books like *Famous Voyages of the Great Discoverers.*[1] Australian children of my 1940s and 1950s generation inherited the stories of the fifteenth- and sixteenth-century European voyagers, extended through the Australian Broadcasting Commission's Argonauts' Club. Then there was the land-based exploration of Australia, a dull classroom topic with dotted and crossed lines on the map sometimes merely stopping somewhere inland. The excitement of new conquests was contrasted with the dutiful, even futile, mapping of our own land.

Discovery, conquest, political rivalry, greed, exploitation: these colour the stories of human movement and conquest. But tales of the human spirit—pushing back the known, leaping into the unknown—are a never-failing drawcard, whether they are viewed comfortably from the outside, or lead to a feeling stirring deep within: the call to go ourselves, to find new frontiers, fresh challenges, further limits. The Antarctic has been regarded as a mythical place for centuries—*Terra australis incognita*[2]— and the story of its discovery and exploration is an important part of that myth. Pyne suggests an explanation echoed by others who encounter Antarctica: 'The Ice, by contrast, was an information sink. The explorer was compelled to look not out, but inward.

31

The power of discovery depended on what was brought to the scene more than on what could be generated out of it.'[3] Recent commentators have suggested that this inward journey is as important as the outer one for many women,[4] and this was confirmed by the interviews.

A number of the women interviewed stressed that they were keen to tell their story in order to emphasise how ordinary and normal it is for women to work in Antarctica. That side of their collective story is clear. It parallels a solid record of outstanding achievements. These include all the recorded 'firsts' for women there: the first to visit Macquarie Island with ANARE, to step ashore on the continent, to winter in each occupation, to winter on each Australian station, to be a station leader, helicopter engineer and so on. The roles of diesel mechanic and winter overland traverse party member are probably the only ones that women have not occupied—yet. But just as important is the quiet conduct of work in sometimes difficult and dangerous circumstances, the personal achievements—both physical and emotional—and the courage to dream as well as the persistence to make those dreams come true.

RESPONDING TO THE CALL OF ANTARCTICA

Accounts of Antarctic exploration have inspired many of the women who go to Antarctica. The first woman to winter at an Australian continental station, Louise Holliday, had childhood contact with Captain Moyes, who accompanied Mawson to Antarctica in 1911. Growing up in the United Kingdom, Ros Codling remembers that during her childhood Scott was presented as *the* national hero, so 'it was part of my upbringing'. She attended 'a small village school when Fuchs was taking part in the IGY trans-Antarctic expedition. It was my last year of school, and the school raised £3 for purchase of a pair of mitts for the expedition. Every Monday morning we moved the pin on the map as they neared the Pole. At about 13 I was given an atlas by my parents, with a single page of Antarctica noting "much of this has not been seen by man".'

For Liv Arnesen, the first woman to ski solo to the South Pole:

> It has all been part of a dream. Instead of fairytales, my parents told me about the Arctic and the Antarctic. My father was interested in old polar history, and I visited Nansen's office and house when I was 12. That was the start. Then I read a lot about it. Polar literature was more exciting than other literature when I was young, and I looked for things that girls had done.

She wondered what it was like to be Roald Amundsen: 'Amundsen set a goal for many other Norwegian expeditioners.'[5]

But dreams are not always enough. In Liv's late thirties, she decided to realise her dream to ski to the South Pole. 'I could not get someone who wanted to do it as much as I did, so I decided to do it myself.' She knew the Norwegian man who'd skied solo to the pole and thought: 'If he can, I can!' She chose an entirely new route, in part to 'avoid the other Norwegian expedition close by and the sort of competition it could engender'.

There was a lot of negativity before she went,[6] which made her realise that 'it's the man's last domain in a way—people said: "It's too tough." It's a girl's mentality to wait for full support to realise a dream.' Mentally and physically strong from her long-distance skiing experience, she thought: 'If I plan the expedition to show them I can do it, there's no enjoyment ... Men have more raw strength, but men and women have equal physical and psychological stamina. But it depends on your motivation. There are different male and female realities.' For many, the experience would not be 'for the joy of skiing, being in nature, etc'. Liv said she knew a lot of climbers for whom it was a kind of work, which took away the joy and fun. 'I was looking forward to getting out and skiing each day. I felt privileged to be there—I had dreamed about it for 30 years! My motive was not to be the first woman to do it alone. The incentive was within, to be faithful to my dream.' However, being the first woman did help her to get sponsorship.

Reactions to her odyssey suggest 'there's something completely unrealistic about a woman voluntarily dragging a sled for 50 days without a shower. It's a male monopoly—women should stay at home—or they say "it's already been done". People say: "You're so lucky you can do what you want", but we live in our own restrictions.' Liv believes that 'our primary duty is towards ourselves, to choose, which also involves a renunciation'.

Liv's achievement is outstanding. She does not focus on the unique, but on her gladness that she has given a lot of inspiration to other women. Nevertheless, she 'did it for myself, to fulfil an old dream. The dream became so strong it demanded to be realised, so that giving up would be a denial of my own feelings. You get in touch with and get to know your innermost strength, which provides an unbelievable vitality.'

Vitality was a quality found in many of the women interviewed, even salving the wounds from any bad times. And that sense of a dream that demands realisation—that *could* be realised—called many of the women I met to seek to go to Antarctica. There were different aspects of the dream, as the following accounts show. Elizabeth Haywood explained:

> Oh, I think that for me, as for many women, it was some of the same sorts of things, the sort of beauty of the environment, the wildness of the place, the last frontier stuff, the mystery, the fables, the mythology of the Antarctic as well. I've read Ursula Le Guin on this subject—and even for women there is that sort of magic of what Antarctica means to human beings, and the challenge and the other-worldliness it represents.

Joan Russell highlighted the importance for her of finding out that a woman with her skills could go to Antarctica:

> It was a fascination since I was a child. When I was 12 to 14, my father was in the army, and every year at Christmas time, the cadet unit of which he was the RSM would go into camp at Point Lonsdale, one of the headlands of Port Philip Bay. And in '58, '59, etc. ANARE shipped out of Melbourne. My mother, bless her,

would watch the shipping schedules and tell us when the ANARE ships were going out. So I actually saw the *Magga Dan*, the *Thala Dan* and the *Kista Dan* ship out of Melbourne, and wanted to go.

'WOULD THEY SELECT ME TO GO?' FROM LONGINGS TO REALITY

There are women who have longed intensely to go to Antarctica, even without stories to tell them it was possible. Most have realised their dreams through participation in national expeditions in increasingly diverse capacities. However, the image of women at work in Antarctica has been infrequently captured by official photographers. Antarctic Division advertisements now encourage women to apply for Antarctic service. The story was very different for the early women, and it is on the foundation of their daring and their achievements that women have found a place in Antarctica.

While the early female scientists had specific projects they wanted to pursue in Antarctica, other women applied for advertised positions, often being knocked back at first. Initially applying to go in 1967, 'J' received a very patronising letter, 'so I thought no more about it' until 1992 when she gave up her job, did the special Honours course in Hobart on Antarctic Studies, and won a PhD scholarship. 'Jade' also ran into 'a lot of negative attitudes the first time I applied and was told my chances were nil unless I was a medico … times have changed'. Fiona Scott first applied in 1979, was top applicant, but 'was told unofficially and verbally that I didn't get the position because I was a woman', a response many women encountered in the 1970s. Midj applied five times to the Bureau of Meteorology before obtaining one of their positions in Antarctica, suspecting that selection bias was her main obstacle. In the 1970s, Suzanne also felt blocked by her superior officer, but then became the first woman to visit all four Australian stations. Diana Patterson was shortlisted and interviewed for station leader in 1980, and felt that her height

was a disadvantage. She was asked: 'Ms Patterson, you're 5'2",
with eyes of blue, what would you do if confronted by a big male
seal?' She succeeded for 1989, after three more attempts, but
had to undergo a trial summer first. It is difficult to pinpoint
when such overt discrimination began to weaken, though Jean
Ledingham, who first joined in 1977 when 'head office would
have fallen about, thinking it's impossible, if you'd suggested
there'd be women station leaders in less than 20 years', recalled
with pleasure that on a 1990s voyage she encountered one
woman who was unaware that there had been no women on the
continent before 1980.

Few had a clear idea of the type of person who was selected
for Antarctic service. There were some stereotypes, defined by
outstanding physical and professional competence. Some women
talked about their boldness in even contemplating working
there. Ursula, for example, wanted to go on an early traverse
program, but 'I saw it as something someone else could do, and
didn't apply it to myself', though she has since been a deputy
voyage leader.

Each stage of women's admission to the Australian program
has experienced a period of testing and waiting. With unspoken
doubts about their acceptability, some applied tentatively, were
knocked back, and honed their skills. For example, Robyn
Downey combined her longing to go to Antarctica with a lengthy
period of preparation.

I had always wanted to have adventures, I don't know why or how
or where it started, and always had the idea that there was this big
adventure out there for me and wondered what it was. I got into
TV at 16. I worked in the control room operating the panels and
used to look at the panels and think it was the sort of job other
people envy you for and want. And sometimes I'd think 'Why am I
stuck in this daft room? I want to have adventures!' Especially
when you see documentaries made by people like the Parer-Cooks,
you think: 'They've got into a job where they can go and have
adventures. How can I do that?' I had a romantic notion of what
adventures were from books, but got to realise eventually

somewhere in my early twenties that those sort of adventures don't exist any more, so I looked round to see what does exist now, realised there were scientific expeditions, and came to the idea that whatever it is, I'd have to retrain to get on to one of the scientific expeditions.

Robyn was working one day when a colleague brought in a photo album. 'It turned out to be on his trip to the Antarctic and I just looked at it and knew "That's it".' It took two years to find out what professions they took. 'I thought of things like chef, but I didn't really want be a chef; carpenter: no, I don't want to be a carpenter.' She was operating electronic equipment and they took radio operators, but 'I didn't have a lot of confidence then so didn't think I could do that'.

A couple of years passed. Then one day she was sitting at home 'with a guy who was rattling on about ham CB radio, and I was pretty bored just listening, and then he said he was doing it to go to the Antarctic. So I thought "aha!" I asked him: "What do you need to get a ham licence?" and I thought I could do that. If I got a ham licence, I'd find out if I was any good before getting into a traineeship.' Her first attempt was unsuccessful, and she was advised to do three matriculation subjects. She applied again to the training school two years later and was accepted. 'Then I went to Sydney Radio for another year and a half and eventually applied to go to the Antarctic and got in the first time! It was an ambition, a very long-term ambition. I did have a couple of stumbling blocks . . .' but she successfully overcame them, leading to two winters with ANARE.

Robyn's pathway took longer than most, but others also prepared themselves. Some doctors have been sent away after their first application to gain additional experience—for example, in anaesthetics or general surgery. Carol Pye, who was the Davis chef for the 1989 winter, was a secondary home economics teacher and applied seven times before succeeding. She undertook a Certificate of Catering and gained extra experience to strengthen her application. The first woman to become a station leader on the Antarctic continent, Diana Patterson, worked on

JUST TELL THEM I SURVIVED!'

her outdoor skills, participating in week-long snow-caving ventures in the Australian Alps.

For Denise Allen, the first woman to winter on all four Australian stations and, with Lynn Williams, one of the first female winners of the Antarctic Medal,[7] preparation also involved accumulating experience. Her interest was awakened as a university geography student. After trying teacher training she joined the Bureau of Meteorology and discovered that Antarctica was a possible posting. At that stage no women had wintered on the continent at Australian bases.

> I thought what a fantastic posting, so I aimed to get there. I had to do a few field postings out in Queensland and was the first woman in this era to do so, then I went to Willis Island, a coral island about 280 miles [450 kilometres] off Townsville. I was the first woman to go there. They have four officers there, it was a proving ground for me. Still very few women have ever been to Willis. From Willis Island, I applied and went straight to Macquarie Island, in December 1984.

Following two winters as medical officer, Lynn Williams was the first female field leader.[8] She developed her interest during university Mountaineering Club days. Her husband had wintered at Scott Base, and others in the New Zealand Alpine Club with a 'mountaineering type background' went to Antarctica. Her husband suggested that they try to go together, so Lynn carefully chose medical residency posts 'that would be appropriate to being selected'.

Scientists, too, have prepared projects that could be undertaken within the Antarctic science program. Isobel Bennett and Hope MacPherson, both experienced in rough field conditions and ship-based data collection, wanted to extend their biological survey of the inter-tidal zone. Isobel recalled: 'It all started with wondering what happened on the inter-tidal south of Tasmania ... Macquarie Island was the only possibility to study the cold water zone', which no one had previously looked at. Although 'Scott and Mawson have been my heroes all my life, it

was not from desire to go to the Antarctic so much but to continue my inter-tidal work' that led to her requests to the Antarctic
Division. Hope and the Division's biological secretary, Susan
Ingham, were keen to see the habitats of the specimens they were
cataloguing. The Victorian Museum, where Hope worked as
invertebrate curator, had contact with the Antarctic Division,
which knew that she wanted to get to Macquarie.

Pauline Reilly applied persistently in the 1970s. She wanted
to extend her major research on the Australian little penguin to
other penguin species. In 1971 she asked the Antarctic Division
how to get there. The third time she asked she was accepted for
a round trip, but 'something went wrong, and round trippers
were put off'. It took another four years before 'I eventually
received a call one Monday evening: "How would you like to go
to Macquarie Island on Thursday?" "Yes!!" They knew I'd say it.
I had to have a medical, have my teeth checked, etc. I spent six
days there seeing millions of penguins, there were four species
and I nearly went out of my mind with excitement. They all
behave so differently: Kings are very curious, friendly; Rock-
hoppers stood their ground, pecked at you; Royals pecked at you
in the breeding ground; Gentoos are the third largest, but they
fled!' She found there was little written about Gentoos, and
suggested further study. She was invited to submit a project,
which she did jointly with zoologist Anne Kerle. That led to a
three-month stay the following year (1978–79), and later to a
major book.[9]

Such women had strong, specific desires to extend their
scientific interests through Antarctic research, and many still do.
I spoke with botanists, zoologists, microbiologists, geophysicists,
meteorologists and physicists who had a keen interest in doing
research in Antarctica. For Patricia Selkirk, this evolved from her
research on bryophytes, which are 'very unimportant in the composition of vegetation here but important—in fact dominant—
in the sub-Antarctic and Antarctic. So it's an important place to
look at to study bryophytes.' Corinna Sullivan was attracted by
the opportunity to 'work in an area of physics I had not done

before—upper atmosphere physics'. Working with captive leopard seals at Sydney's Taronga Park Zoo led Tracey Rogers into a doctoral project: 'The obvious thing was to go to Antarctica.' As a Queenslander, she never had a longing to go there, but she has now been four times.

Cheryl combined an intense personal interest with her profession as plant pathologist, and prepared for three years to become an expeditioner-scientist. In her first week at Casey, she broke her leg so badly during field training that she was evacuated to Australia for surgery. Despite strong pressures not to return, she went back to Antarctica on the last ship of the season and, when I met her there the following summer, was draining the last precious drops out of the experience, reluctantly leaving on the final summer voyage. Debra Enzenbacher, a budding social scientist, was so keen to spend the winter at the US Amundsen–Scott South Pole station that she worked as a summer shuttle bus driver at McMurdo station, gaining the experience to apply for a winter logistics and cargo operations position. 'When I was getting things ready to go to the South Pole I found a diary from when I was eleven or twelve years old that noted that one of my goals in life was to go to the Antarctic.' She returned to her academic work and on her next two visits collected material for her doctoral thesis on Antarctic tourism.

Antarctica offers a professional challenge without the usual supports. For 'GD', this was a strong reason for going: 'I thought that being the only clinician there would be very exciting . . . I'd be allowed to do everything. There's nowhere else where you're able to practise medicine like that' in today's specialised medical world.

Caroline Caddy, a poet, and Christian Clare Roberston, a painter, combined a deep interest in science with their art and their very deep wish to experience Antarctica. Caroline hoped that her publications would vouch for her seriousness, as did Clare, who had held successful exhibitions. A stable job in Darwin first enabled Clare to trade the imagined landscapes she had been painting for the real ones:

As part of that quest I went to Iceland and Greenland which I found fascinating. But always in the back of my mind was Antarctica, and one of the things I was thinking even then was 'If I can prove that I'm absolutely serious about this, if I can get myself to the Arctic then people will take me seriously. If I can do a major exhibition on Iceland and Greenland, then I'll have the credentials to be taken seriously as a woman, as an artist—all those things that people tend not to regard as being of great concern in the Antarctic—they might be able to be overcome just by being able to prove myself.' So in due course, having done the Iceland–Greenland and Hawaii exhibition, I was in a position where I was able to apply to the Antarctic Division and everything came good.

EMBRACING ADVENTURE AND CHALLENGE

For some women, the specific call of adventure—more usually associated with men—was the reason. This was often coupled with an early exposure to stories about Antarctica. Others, like Lucinda, were simply 'always fascinated by Antarctica—the spirit of adventure' which, up until the time she went to the Prince Charles Mountains as a biological field assistant, was oriented to caving and sports. Pene Greet, a physicist who has now been five times, is a self-described 'keen outdoors person, so it appealed—the adventure and excitement of doing something different'. Almost identical words were used by another scientist who has thrice wintered.

In Pia's view:

Boys had adventures, and Antarctica is the epitome of adventure. It seemed such a wonderful place. I hadn't met anyone who'd been, until I was in my late twenties . . . I was sure I'd go and worked on it—I did my Masters in krill biology, enrolled in a PhD, got up my sea time. Then saw a job advertised—all seven guys in my lab group at Murdoch applied, had similar qualifications (late 1989). Then I got a job interview and rushed to the lab and they didn't get the interviews—they said it must be affirmative action, that I was the token woman. I was flabbergasted to get it, though I also knew I'd get it.

Or as Mandy Holmes, twice chef at Casey, more simply stated, 'adventure, travel' were two of the many attractions. She added that the second time she went, the opportunity to study during her spare time was also appealing. Several women listed specific aspects of the job, especially the opportunity to work on their own, as part of the attraction.

From talking to the women, it became obvious that challenge was part of the Antarctic experience, if not an acknowledged motivation for embarking on it. The first female field training officer, Ann Wessing, had a need to challenge herself. Others saw opportunities for personal growth and development. For Gina Price, the personal aspects were the biggest challenge; she loves people, 'so it was an enjoyable challenge' and she never doubted she could do it. Born in 1959, the year the four pioneer women went to Antarctica, she considers that:

> There are very fortunate opportunities in my generation to take up that challenge—finally we can do it, after a couple of generations of women who couldn't do it—we can go, when we want to go and spread our wings. I love the feeling of wind in the hair, Lillian[10] loves gulping the air. There's a sense of adventure, answering those needs and desires rather than feeling 'I've done it!' I like to push myself, not to get to the top.

Amanda Nimon, an Australian working at the Scott Polar Research Institute in Cambridge, was 'looking for something challenging. I'm afraid of heights so I did sky diving, and I don't like the cold so I decided to try to go to Antarctica! The appeal was the challenge—not many people get to go.'

THE CALL OF WILD, REMOTE PLACES

It is difficult to pinpoint how wild places attract people because the reasons are so diverse. Clare's fascination is with landscape, and with painting the underlying physical processes. A deep love of nature and the outdoors was characteristic of a large number of the women, often providing the major motivation to go to Antarctica. In some instances, this passion had led to their current occupation, especially the biologists and the field training officers, who also had backgrounds in science. It is difficult—and pointless—to try to disentangle the 'lifestyle' and professional aspects of this passionate motivation. For example, Anne Kerle grew up in country New South Wales and found herself in Melbourne with 'a need to get out into the bush'. So she joined the Phillip Island penguin study group, where she met Pauline Reilly, who aroused her interest in Antarctica. Ulla had already been to the Arctic when, as the first female radio operator on the *Nella Dan*, she visited Antarctica in 1981 and knew she wanted to return. It's something she 'can't put in words. I adore listening to the stillness and quietness, being at one with nature'.

The following comments give a glimpse of how a love of nature and the outdoors is a path into Antarctica:

I came to Tasmania for the bushwalking and the lifestyle, and went to Antarctica because of the job, and to see the wildlife and the environment. (Judy Clarke, biologist and Antarctic medal winner)

I go bushwalking a lot. If I had an offer of work in a large city, I'd say 'no!' but to go to a wilderness, to a place where not many people go, 'yes!' (Midj Jones, meteorologist)

I got involved with climbers like Lincoln Hall and Tim McCarthy-Snape when they were doing their first Australian ascent of Everest with Greg Mortimer. I got to know them and they taught me to climb. I always loved the outdoors. When they were dreaming up the idea of going to Antarctica to climb Mt Minto, I offered to be the cook. (Margaret Werner, Antarctic tour leader)

I was doing scientific research at the time, so it could be achievable. I didn't realise how difficult it would be; it's very competitive, there are not many positions, and it's difficult to find out how to fit into a project, with given skills. There was an extra appeal: my partner and I had done a lot of outdoor activities and ski touring, and it was very attractive to go to a cold, isolated wilderness. (Tracey Pitman, microbiologist)

I wanted to see and experience a place which is so different from home, a place relatively untouched by humans with abundant wildlife and great beauty. Who isn't interested in going? For years and years I dreamt of going, but by the time I actually went I had given up! (Robyn Carter, field assistant)

It was the end point of an interest in adventurous outdoor activities. I started out with girl guides in my teenage years, then bushwalking, mountain climbing and rock climbing in New Zealand. (Gwen Shaughnessy, biologist)

I have an interest in skiing and bushwalking, and have been trekking in Nepal, so Antarctica was an extension of that; it tied things together. (Adele Post, botanist)

Extreme environments are the main attraction for some. Born and raised in Denmark, Ulla was alone 'amongst 150 or 200 relatives' who 'always had a strange desire to go to remote environments', much to her mother's dismay. Clare, too, was 'always fascinated by extremes. As a small child, I wanted to travel further north, south, further up, down, around the next head-land. The whole idea of extremes is very central to me.' Carol Pye elaborated:

When I travelled, I always wanted to go to the end of the place—Stewart Island, John O'Groats and so on. I don't know why. I guess that I feel satisfied in practical tasks when I know it is successfully, thoroughly completed, so to go to a place and not reach its physical extremity if it's close or possible, or to reach a boundary, I feel I've not thoroughly explored and sought all the information that's possible and available.

Bringing together the centrality of the longing, regardless of gender or possible barriers, 'Jade' noted: 'I have been asked: "Do women have different motives for going?" When I was younger it was what I really wanted. You accept it may not happen, but it did. Spending a year in a wilderness is the attraction. There's something about the ice and snow. The place lived up to expectations.'

THE SIGNIFICANCE OF OTHERS

One senior manager suggested that 'some still view Antarctic work as serving their country', but added that this aspect may attract men rather than women. Motives are complex. Caroline raised a possible gender-based aspect:

> When you read about Scott, it's the glory thing. A lot of the ordinary seamen and people who went down as just part of the expedition who you don't hear about very much, most of them were there in those days for the same reason that you or I are going down there: that want to experience this new land, this unknown place, and the glory had nothing to do with it at all, just a purely personal experience.

Women certainly expressed a commitment to science and to the environment, as later chapters show, but not within a nationalistic framework.

Other people, however, figured in the personal journeys of many women, perhaps illustrating the distinction made by psychologist Carol Gilligan between an individual, 'big idea' basis for morality, associated with masculinity, and a more feminine one, grounded in relationships.[11] For example, Joan Russell, an articulate feminist, pointed out that it was critical to know of someone with her skills:

> I knew that I had almost no chance. Because I knew that it was scientists that went, and I knew that I wasn't a woman scientist. And so until Diana Patterson was selected in 1988, I didn't have any other model for women's involvement in ANARE. Then I realised that I too could probably make a successful bid for a position as a station leader, and I did and I prevailed. When I heard about Diana Patterson being appointed it incited me to put in an application.

While some women knew other expeditioners, three of those interviewed came from Antarctic families. Jenny Selkirk and Erica Adamson both have mothers (Patricia Selkirk and Heather

Adamson) who have undertaken scientific work in Antarctica. Patricia is a leading Antarctic terrestrial biologist, and Erica's father, Don, has a long record in sub-Antarctic research. Jenny's field is geomorphology, and she went twice as a volunteer before going for her own doctoral research. She found that:

> People often say 'You must have got in there because of your mother'. It's no different to doctors or lawyers—Smith and Son— or hardware shops—MacDonald and Son. Because it's women they think it's nepotism, or you're only there because someone paved your way for you, which is rot! You're not going to go because of your name if you can't produce the goods. No one would think two hoots about it if it was [a] man but because it's women, it's viewed as if it's got to be nepotism, or something other than the fact that the merits of the various people concerned are applicable and that just happens to be what they're interested in.

She grew up 'interacting socially in an environment where Antarctic interests were the normal things—the research interests of my parents and their colleagues ... I always liked it, hearing about it, seeing photos'. In 1989, on arrival at Macquarie Island, 'it really grabbed' her.

The interest was 'easy' for Erica:

> Both my parents are scientists, and my father has been in Antarctica in summer for years. I did science at Macquarie University. There are other scientists there working on Antarctic projects, and I saw it as an interesting place to go and things to do and a potential opportunity, which is how I got involved. When I finished my degree, a job came up at the Antarctic Division, which was perfect timing.

During her childhood, Jenny Mackenzie's father went for one winter and four summers. 'He's the reason I wanted to go. We are the first wintering father and daughter team!' Jenny heard stories about it from her father and remembers the bearded stranger returning. 'I also remember the slide shows, and stories and things. So I've always wanted to go down.' Several Antarctic Division employees had spouses who had been there, though none stated a simple 'me too' reason for wanting to go themselves. The late Evlyn Barrett cited an interesting personal connection, a neighbour who was engaged to a biologist working at Macquarie Island in the 1950s: 'We all had ham radio contact!'

A MEDLEY OF ATTRACTIONS

The idea of going to Antarctica was suggested to several of the women by others. They were often women with keen outdoor interests, working in areas involving possible Antarctic service, who responded eagerly to the suggestion to apply. The accounts show the diversity of interests and the enthusiasm with which women have pursued them.

'Helena' 'stumbled across it' after meeting people with Antarctic experience at university. Her response was a clear 'yes!' when the opportunity arose to spend a summer with a penguin project, which led to her PhD based on research on Macquarie Island. Her fieldwork included one eight-month 'summer'. She commented that 'most women volunteer. Opportunity is provided by word of mouth'. This underlines the role of networks in recruitment to Antarctic work. A position at the University of Tasmania Antarctic Co-operative Research Centre 'sounded fantastic' to Ruth Eriksen. She applied 'as it was an opportunity that would never present itself again. An aura of the unknown was bound to applying. The same job would have been less tantalising without the Antarctic possibility and I probably wouldn't have looked twice at it. It's a very routine research-based job, but with the opportunity to go to an area not frequently visited, about which not a lot is known, and that is wild and adventurous.' Ruth comes from a family of Norwegian sailors, so 'maybe it was a natural progression to work in oceanography'.

Morag Anderson's experience was different. She was 'stunned to be asked' by a former Honours year colleague: 'I'd never thought of it before. At the time, I didn't have a man, a commitment to a lease or financial commitments.' So the following

January she went to Davis as a volunteer wintering microbiologist. Others were presented with the opportunity quite suddenly, while several also cited escape from boring jobs as a reason for applying. Estelle, an archaeologist who has now been to Antarctica four times, was one of the latter, though she also had a very long-standing interest: 'The more I saw images, heard about it, the more I wanted to go!'

Participation in the life of a small isolated community attracted a handful. Tracey Pitman already knew about life there from her partner, and was intrigued by the prospect of 'a small isolated community, drawing together'. For Ann Wessing, Antarctica itself was the dominant attraction during her first season. Of subsequent seasons she highlighted social aspects and the opportunity to make friendships in that special environment. For Bridget, an Antarctic Division employee, it is 'the ethos rather than the place itself that appeals'.

Women have clearly heard the call of Antarctica, and a sense of adventure has figured in their accounts.

'COULD I BE AN EXPEDITIONER?'

Although the women weren't asked for their image of the sort of person who would be selected, this came up spontaneously—for example, in Peta Kelsey's sense that women need to demonstrate physical strength:

I had a background in outdoor activity. I've done a lot of canoeing and bushwalking and things like that. I hadn't ever thought of it, but I had a friend when I was at uni who applied to go, and he was one of these highly intelligent people who studied a lot and did very well and he said: 'You should apply for this, you'd get it' because when they asked him what outdoor experience he had, he had nil, whereas I could fill in bushwalking, and at that point I was into canoeing and I'd competed in the state championships and got a couple of 80 per cents, that sort of thing. People have heard of those sort of races so you put that down and they think 'she's strong enough physically'. So I applied in '82, and I didn't actually get it. But once this person had suggested I apply, it seemed like a really good idea, so I applied again in '83. I got down to Macquarie with AGSO in 1983.

Peta enjoyed Macquarie Island so much she applied again the week she returned to Australia, and in 1985 wintered at Mawson.

More commonly, women were concerned about the adequacy of qualifications, skills and, critically, experience. As already recorded, some went to considerable lengths to enlarge those in order to stand a chance of selection, though most were surprised when they were accepted. Jane Goddard admitted:

> I wanted to go for many years. I can't tell you what first put the seed in my mind . . . I just assumed I probably wouldn't have the qualifications they wanted and I hadn't channelled my life specifically towards that until I was talking to a friend who had been down there. He said: 'Look, you've got ideal qualifications for it.' And it suddenly all seemed far more realistic. It had just been a dream before that, then it became nearer to reality . . . It took me several months of thinking through all the pros and cons and I applied at the end of that year . . . I wanted to really think through all the implications.

Alison Clifton had 'always wanted to do it. I saw their advertisements but didn't think I had the skills.' It wasn't until a friend pointed out the selection criteria for station leader that she found a position to which she could aspire. Ann W. had always wanted to go to Antarctica, and she worked on expanding her mountaineering skills and on her self-esteem. Nevertheless, 'I felt I didn't quite deserve it, and was scared I couldn't do it. I felt others were more experienced.'

Antarctic dreams sometimes go a long way back, as Gina discovered. Halfway through her year as a physicist at Mawson, as she was about to photograph an Emperor penguin, 'I thought: "I've been here before!" as I remembered that I had a placemat as a kid with an Emperor on it!' On the other hand, others have gone without much premeditation.

REFLECTIONS

While Antarctica has been part of the European imagination for
centuries, tinged with images from Arctic exploration—a different
icy world—it is the British, Australians, French, Scandinavians,
North and South Americans and Japanese who have explicit links
with the explorers and whalers who reached the Southern Ocean
and Antarctica. The impact of this heritage is found in the cultural
backgrounds of many of the Australian Antarcticans.

There are other motivations for travel and adventure, not just
confined to particular cultural traditions. Climber Brigitte Muir
remembers from her first childhood scramble that 'the thrill of
danger and the unknown—as well as the attraction of the forbidden—made the summits even more of a temptation. Most of the
time, though I was far from rebellious thoughts, quite content to
do my best to please to receive the rewards of subordination, that
confidence in the self directly linked to the degree of acceptance
among others.'[12] From caving to climbing, she discovered 'that it
doesn't take a summit to make for an interesting time, that I
needed to go somewhere else, soon, and that I would always need
to have somewhere to go, somebody to meet'.[13]

In Brigitte's childhood, there was concern about the physical
dangers of adventurousness, perhaps some disapproval of young
women going off on dangerous activities. But go they did, and
although Isobel Bennett, the oldest of those interviewed here,
turned down an interstate job in her early twenties because of
parental disapproval, neither her subsequent wanderings, nor
those of any other of the women, caused more than parental
concern. Maybe those who did not dare to apply were more constrained—whether through self-censorship or outward disapproval
we cannot tell. For the women in this book, children were the major
factor limiting further Antarctic work, except for brief summers.

There is a growing literature on women's adventure travel,
both contemporary and from previous generations. Writers such
as Dea Birkett have tried to find out what motivated Victorian
'lady explorers' and enabled them to break with the restrictions

50

placed on them at that time. She found that a number seemed to have been impressed both by their fathers' freedom of movement, and the physical space created for them inside and outside the home.[14] And like some of the women interviewed, the early women travellers 'relied on the printed world of their childhood books to provide the ingredients with which they could construct, in their own words, their imaginary landscapes'.[15] Emboldened by these accounts and the images they formed from them, they did go out. They had private incomes, which was an important factor. Birkett suggests that 'theirs was an uneasy inclusion in the myth of exploration and discovery. They were continually torn between the two conflicting landscapes of self-fulfilment and duty'.[16] Their accounts are now being reprinted, or told for the first time by women researchers.[17]

Some commentators on women's travels are fascinated by the question of whether or not women 'move through the world differently than men. The constraints and perils, the perceptions and complex emotions women journey with are different from those of men'. Mary Morris quotes Lawrence Durrell, describing the extraordinary traveller, Freya Stark: 'A great traveller is a kind of introspective as she covers the ground outwardly, so she advances inwardly . . . The landscape is shaped by the consciousness of the person who crosses it. There is a dialogue between what is happening within and without.'[18] It follows from this that women might also discuss their travels in a different way, with more reflection about what they experience.

The accounts here of women's motivation for going to the Antarctic echo some of these writers' themes. They were inspired by heroic tales, and the mystery of the Antarctic itself was a powerful drawcard. Curiosity based on the chance to do research in Antarctica, and to live in a small isolated community, were further stimuli. And in talking about their experiences, some emphasised that they thought women do experience the world through different eyes to men. They felt that reflection was a vital aspect of their Antarctic sojourn, and that it was an opportunity to make an inward journey as well as an outward one.

THREE

'I just wanted to do my job well!'

I want rather a sense of the ordinariness and appropriateness of women in Antarctica, that they're down there working alongside men without that being remarkable. I am the most experienced woman ice diver in Australia but what I did is not particularly difficult, and I was lucky to be there. I don't want a sense of women doing awesome things, but want a sense that women *are there*. (Anitra, biologist)

Antarctica is a workplace, first and foremost, and many women were quick to point out it is a workplace for men *and* women, and that it is 'no big deal' for women to be there. By being selected, and re-selected, women have earned their place as fellow workers in Antarctica.

WORKING IN ANTARCTICA

To maintain the stations, especially during the harsh polar winters, annual teams consist of highly competent professionals: a chief expedition mechanic in charge of the powerhouse, two mechanics, two communications technical officers, two electricians, one or two plumbers, one or two carpenters, a chef, a medical officer and a station leader.[1] Meteorological observers and technicians are appointed by the Bureau of Meteorology

(Met). Rangers from the Tasmanian Parks and Wildlife Service (TasPAWS) are appointed to Macquarie Island.[2]

Regular data collecting for upper atmosphere physics (UAP) is undertaken at all four stations, by a wintering physicist or an electronics engineer. They also monitor data collection for the Australian Geological Survey Organisation (AGSO), except at Mawson where there is still a wintering AGSO geophysicist. The majority of winterers are Antarctic Division employees, at least on the continent. They may also maintain instruments or collect data for other researchers, and set up research for the summerers, such as initial observations on newly arrived wildlife. Wintering scientists, usually fewer than four, include expeditioner–scientists with contract positions with the Antarctic Division (AAD), university-based students working on their own and others' projects, and researchers from the CSIRO or TasPAWS. Most science is conducted in summer.[3]

Women have now occupied all wintering positions except those of diesel mechanic, electrician and plumber. Seven have been station leaders, in four cases, twice. The first female summer storesperson, Phillipa Foster, was appointed in 1981, and there have been female summer laboratory managers, field training officers and maintenance personnel, as well as two female helicopter engineers. Women also serve as voyage leaders and deputy voyage leaders, and as medical officers and crew on the chartered vessels taking expeditioners South.

Marine science is undertaken in dedicated voyages or in combination with the resupply voyages, and may now include winter ice-edge projects. On 20 August 1999, the *Aurora Australis* was at 66°36' S, 144°40' E in nine-tenths cementing pancake ice with an air temperature of –16°C. A party of four had just been dropped off to camp overnight while investigating a group of Emperor penguins on the fast ice. The ship had been depositing recording buoys earlier in the day in the large area of open water in the ice known as a polynya, the main object of study of this eight-week voyage.[4] Besetment in the ice is still a hazard, lengthening the voyage's normal six to ten weeks. Most voyagers are scientists and technical officers, who may undertake several voyages a year.

Helen B. found that 'on the ship it's so much harder than doing science ashore'. Ruth E. explained: 'You are using high-tech equipment, and it's hard work. You do twelve-hour shifts, seven days a week.' For Liza, the challenges included 'keeping highly complex equipment level and functioning—working with glassware and equipment [especially on days when the sea is so rough that you can't keep a cup of tea on the table]. Working at sea can be very difficult, for example, with hazardous chemi-cals—you get very good at what you do, if you work at sea you can do it anywhere.' Tonia elaborated: 'You're on the trawl deck collecting specimens once the catch hits the deck. They're taken from deck to the wet lab, where you process as many as possible and freeze and bring the rest back including all the zooplankton. Once you get to the site, it's full bore 24 hours a day, in twelve-hour shifts.' She worked with Pia, and one project examined the population structure of certain fish.

> We went to a series of predetermined sites, took a water sample then put the trawl net out (it takes at least half an hour to deploy) to a predetermined depth, fished for half an hour or so and pulled it up to see what you've got. When the fish came on board our work began—you put them in bins, weigh the whole catch, take their length and weight, slice them open to look at stage of reproduction, take stomachs and preserve them, scale them, take the otoliths out and preserve them in an envelope. It's quite fiddly work—one would cut and sample, the other keep their hands clean and label and store the samples.

Some voyages include 'round trippers' who have diverse inter-ests and projects. They include writers, journalists, artists, photographers and film-makers, senior academics, observers such as Antarctic Treaty inspectors, members of organisations like Greenpeace, politicians and others. Round trippers combine long days at sea with hectic days at the stations, and preparations can be lengthy in order to gain the most out of the brief icy encounters. They have little sleep while near the stations, and then work on their return to produce poems, paintings, reports, etc. Clare felt:

> As an artist on the ANARE resupply voyage, I was aware of being 'excess baggage' because all the non-essential personnel were repeatedly told that we could only go if someone more important did not need the space. However, as it turned out, the 'non essential' people have between them done more than enough to earn their keep, producing books, television series and exhibitions. Personally I feel I received what I needed and was able to give back something of value to the Antarctic Division, so everyone should be happy. It was a compliment to be taken seriously by the Antarctic people, because I felt insecure about the whole thing at first.

Staff of the AAD once had 'familiarisation' trips after three years' service. They may now apply to become voyage management trainees. The voyage leader and deputy are in charge of all aspects of cargo, movements of people to and from the ship, liaison with the ship's crew and general oversight of life on board. People without a task on the voyage need to be occupied and have their time structured. Bridget found that 'you get very single minded, work long hours and don't miss out on shore things much. The experience depends on what happens—when you're far out [Mawson] and other expeditioners are on board [Davis], it's hectic and complicated. There's limited flexibility.'

Hierarchies amongst expeditioners are based on occupation and type of stay. Pay and status do not necessarily correspond. If JAFOs[5] are the 'lowest of the low', 'diesos', who maintain the powerhouse—the lifeline for the station—have often been the highest. Of the ANARE expeditioner positions, the highest paid is the medical officer, and the lowest the chef. New workplace agreements currently regulate Australian-based and Antarctic-based salaries and conditions for AAD employees, subsuming some allowances and leave within a second salary tier. Employees of other organisations may receive some, or none, of the allowances. Saturday afternoon is common duties time—mostly cleaning—and expeditioners are also rostered to assist the chef on 'slushy' duty, and on night watch. Everyone participates in these duties, including volunteers, many of whom have taken leave without pay to go. One seasoned volunteer commented: 'I get white [hot] angry that it's mainly as volunteers that women go. There's not only not many women, but those who are there are often unpaid. Women are not very good at making claims; they're grateful for the experience.'

Conforming to general patterns, except for female doctors, women are heavily concentrated in the lower levels of pay. Those who are not paid are excluded from the winter dreams about spending the accumulating bank balances. As Morag found: 'They were talking about all the spending they'd do, and I was just watching my meagre savings disappear in phone calls to Australia!' Pay issues can become heated, especially on Macquarie Island over summer. The AAD argued that volunteering provided a wonderful opportunity to see the Antarctic, which is its own reward, although they will soon pay all their project personnel, including their many volunteers. Volunteers and postgraduates are responsible for a significant proportion of the Antarctic scientific output.

SCIENTIFIC WORK ON MACQUARIE AND HEARD ISLANDS

Susan Ingham's diary contains a graphic account of a day's fieldwork on Macquarie Island. During her second visit in 1964, she and Chriss Carrick set out to check on previously banded penguins.

> Searched Sandy Bay and rock platform for banded penguins, getting three each of Bauer Bay and Hurd Point yearlings. Lunched at south end of Sandy Bay, having taken an hour and a half on the penguin checks. Then the day began to lose its verve. It was necessary to climb up a creek valley and down the

other side to get past Brothers Point. The creek was moderately
steep; not too bad going. When we reached what looked like
the top there was another gently sloping valley to come. At the
top of this we looked down on an almost sheer tussocky and
scree slope, perhaps 300 feet [100 metres], down which we slid
as much as anything. This had taken an hour. The next two
miles to Red River are a real horror stretch: no beach to speak
of; big rocks, too steep to scramble over; standing in the water
with steep tussock, seal wallow and occasional Rockhopper
colony behind them. With all our care, we couldn't help going
uphill too far and having to make our way down again, and
being forced up again, time after time. Constant scrambling and
being entangled in tussock, and picking our way through and
past wallows, is very tiring. At one point Chriss and I collapsed
in opposite ends of the same wallow, she in one leg, I somehow
on my back. At another point Chriss almost pulled a muscle, a
cross seal got a piece of my outer trousers and I came down
hard on my seat. After Red River the going improved, being
stony beaches and negotiable rocks. However, we were too tired
by then to improve our speed. Finally saw Green Gorge open
before us, the hut in the distance, paddled across the creek on
the beach up to the hut, reaching it at 6.00 p.m. after ten
hours on the road.

For biologists, 'There's an urgency about the work because
you're working in limited biological cycles—the animals go and
you've blown it.' This leads to long hours of intense work, as
'Helena' experienced:

Sandy Bay hut was our base—8 kilometres from station—it's very
small, an aircraft engine packing case with two bunks, and no
personal space. We worked outside all the time—it was quite
taxing! We had none of the support that they have on base—we
do everything ourselves like repairs of lamps or radios, are outside
for all the work for very long hours, and walk long, treacherous
routes to sites—in all sorts of conditions—for example, stomach
flushing in high waves when everyone else had stopped work
because of the weather. We then have to clear up our samples and
gear, write up data *and* cook dinner and get up and do it again
next day, in abysmal weather.

Trudy Disney wintered for a project on the light-mantled sooty albatross. The project aimed to do a census of the breeding population of the birds on the island, establish a program for long-term monitoring of population trends, and measure hatching and breeding success.[6]

> The work involved a lot of walking with heavy packs of equipment, there was a lot of paperwork and you could get very cold staying in the one spot for a long time, and it was off the beaten track and so I was away from the station. We had little lightweight tents which we used occasionally, though I used the field huts as much as possible, you can work from the huts and they had food, etc. in them. I was away from base for about 200 nights, and there was a lot of time when I was working in the field from the station, too. One of the most difficult aspects of the work was making sketches to accurately describe viewing points for future bird censuses.

Trudy also undertook projects for others. She did monthly beach surveys of marine debris to monitor and evaluate the impact of anthropogenic debris and waste on marine living resources,[7] and collected skua pellets to try to assess the amount of plastic waste being ingested by the sea birds on which they prey. 'Pulling the soaked pellets apart for examination was smelly and time consuming!' And there was weekly monitoring of wind traps for invertebrates for the CSIRO, weekly seawater sampling for a Tasmanian scientist, and moss sampling for a TasPAWS botanist. She also assisted in the ranger's cat trapping program, 'resulting in eleven extra cats being killed'.[8]

Jenny Mudge, the first female wintering ranger, took up the story:

> Parks and Wildlife manage the island so the rangers are there to see that permits are adhered to. A lot of the work is cat and rabbit control. And in summer there's a lot of tourist work with the ships coming in. They come for two days and the rangers oversee the visit: deal with quarantine, that all conditions of the permits are followed, and also you tend to get into some guiding for them. A lot were more interested in how we lived there than [in] the wildlife except

for the special ornithological groups. I had studied up on the wildlife so I'd know it all myself to be able to answer questions, and then got asked ones like how much the fuel tank holds!

It was a very harsh winter, with eight weeks of snow cover:

We were without any water for that time as it had all frozen. It's hard in winter, with limited daylight, to get from one hut to another in a day. With the snow cover it was difficult to see the traps as they got lost in drift, so the total count for the year wasn't very high. With rabbits we are mainly using the myxo virus. I stayed out ten to fifteen days, then came in for about four days back on station. For a fair bit of the time I was on my own for up to a week. Whenever I could, I got involved in others' work, too: albatross banding, spent a day or two with the Royal penguin work, and a lot with seals—for example, branding them. I think the rangers should be involved in the work of others. The ranger is there to oversee work so you need a good understanding of what the bios are doing.

Time becomes crucial during the brief seal pupping period, with only a few weeks available before the pups are weaned. Doreen was a volunteer on a project investigating male fur seal copulatory success and mating choice.

There was genetic work, taking samples from pups and males to see who fathered the pups, which males/females are crossing territory to mate. The work involved tagging of pups, territory checks and recording who was there, three-hour observations on territories to look at male–female interaction. I was the main field assistant for the project; however, Simon needed a team of three or four to capture adult females. We used a big butterfly net, then held them down to tag and take blood samples. There was a more structured work pattern of being out by 9.00 a.m. till tea. There was also lab work examining faeces for fish ear bones, which don't digest so they're useful for diet analysis.

Geomorphologist Jenny Selkirk explained that she didn't need a lot of equipment for data gathering—'lots of visual things, you go and look at it'.

That's the good thing about geomorphology. Other people say they're going on a jolly, and I say 'I'm going on a reconnaissance survey'. You just go and look at the landscape really. The basic equipment is plastic bags and a trowel and notebook, a tape and callipers and clinometer. It didn't mean anything till I went back, saw, sampled, 'kicked the dirt', sank up to my knees in it, cussed it, and now I know what it means!

Living conditions on Heard Island are very basic, with hazardous rain and wind, and slippery, icy surfaces. There are historic remains on the island from its use by early whalers and sealers, and also from the first ANARE expeditions. For archaeologists Estelle and Angela, the survey work on these remains was routine. They just 'got on with it', though there were distractions, like walking in the wind along a narrow spit with waves crashing on both sides. Botanist Jennie went out in the mornings, 'if there were no blizzards'. She also helped to count the female seals gathered in large 'harems' presided over by a single male known as a beachmaster. She stayed on 'unless it was snowing and we couldn't see the plants'. Saturday showers were a highlight:[9] 'It was pitted corrugated iron so if a westerly blew, you got pummelled with black volcanic sand. You came in your gumboots and clothes, got it going, stripped quickly. It was freezing, but you always felt better!'

Gwen participated in an elephant seal survey. 'We arrived in late winter, when there was still some snow on the ground. Every day we went in twos or threes to different areas of the colonies and counted the number of pups at all the breeding sites ... it was cold—only round freezing, but it's jolly miserable because the wind blows all the time.' Shipping problems stranded them for an extra month, during which they obtained permission 'to see if there were any albatross on one of the other areas, which necessitated going on one of the glaciers', a previously forbidden activity. Lynn Williams admitted that 'I was very grateful for my mountaineering background at that stage!'

SCIENCE ON THE CONTINENT

Science projects vary between Antarctic stations, depending on local conditions. However, physics is undertaken at all four stations. The basic expeditioner-physicist positions involve monitoring equipment and data collection, calibrating instruments, and downloading data to send to other institutions. All the female physicists talked about the satisfaction gained from fixing technical problems—usually the task of other people back home. With a shortage of jobs for physicists, the expeditioner position often attracts highly qualified people, who also run their own experiments. Pene and Gina were doing related higher degree research when they first went South, and many others have included higher degree work while there. The Antarctic provides good conditions for observing the ionosphere, and while the UAP research is laboratory based, having instruments in working order when, for example, atmospheric conditions are right for a data-collecting campaign is exacting when you are the only person on the spot. Peta explained that you have to take the 'A factor' into account: 'that things don't happen just as you'd expect, and they take a lot longer'.

To do work that is usually very satisfying, in that environment, was the bottom line for person after person interviewed. Barbara Wienecke was selected from a huge number of applicants to spend the winter working in an Emperor penguin rookery with one assistant. 'I was out at the rookery most of the time, spending seven months on the ice, 47 kilometres from Mawson station, and exposed to the full brunt of blizzards.'

She 'never had a boring moment'.

At midwinter I got up at 10.00 a.m. It was black, the moon was up, auroras were raging. We spent five hours a day at the colony but had a maximum of three hours with enough light to work. In May we were quite busy, and in early June. We set up the camp, put on the first round of trackers, learnt to handle the birds, even learnt how to work and walk on the ice. We were looking at energy expenditure while the females were away for two months. We injected a fluid into the Emperors and took blood samples—this was not an easy task with a 30 kilogram bird not so willing to cooperate! The fluid tends to freeze, especially in a small needle, and there was an issue of how to keep the glue with which the electronic instruments were attached at the right temperature. In June we watched the movement around, collected lost eggs, and later dead chicks, to estimate breeding success.

It was 'very frustrating' when the time depth recorders (TDRs) stopped working:[10]

Operating in ambient temperatures of –36°C, it's amazing electronic devices work so well, with the birds swimming through the ice, too. Radio transmitters were deployed to get some idea of the movement in and out of the colony. Trying to use an electronic device that runs on batteries is very hard in a tent on the ice. The radio trackers started to drift in frequency too. It wasn't much but the computers were set to track only a pre-set frequency and a lot of time was spent checking the frequency. That's when you get cold, sitting round with no heat and 100 instruments to check!

There were 23 000 birds, with 11 000 chicks.

Wherever you look there's just penguins. I've looked every penguin in the eye, it's just fabulous! There's just something about penguins—the characteristics of each species are entirely different and so are individuals. We had one 32 kilogram female who didn't exactly volunteer to carry an instrument. She knocked a visiting mechanic to the snow, she was fighting! She gave us a hard time, and we had another beating when she returned.

Scientists who have to collect samples and conduct work outside are 'at the mercy of the environment'—for example, when there is no melt during the summer to expose plants for study. The regular sampling trips to the lakes around Davis, especially in winter, involve very real challenges. Tracey P. 'used boats to sample on one lake'.

This was very dangerous as the water temperature was −18°C. We didn't go out much when the air temperature was below −30°C as things went wrong much more under those conditions. We took quads or skidoos, and a field assistant if possible. We tried different plans, like going to a field hut till it warmed up. We had to be adaptable and resourceful and felt we were. Field trips were monthly. It took a week all round for a day's work. It was different in summer: there were helicopters, though that has its dangers— once we didn't have adequate shoes; you don't prepare as well when you have the helicopters.

Elanor admitted that 'sampling trips were a vast drain on one's energy':

After a day in the field getting cold and wet, it was absolutely exhausting to come back only to be in the lab until the early hours of the morning. I'd get up at 7-ish, be in the office by 8.00 a.m. Worked until at least 10.00 p.m., often 11 or 12 with an hour for lunch and the same for dinner (maybe). No smoko . . . I avoided that! Just cups of tea at the microscope. I worked seven days a week unless someone managed to coax me away, I was ill or just too damn exhausted to wake up! I sampled Ace [Lake] every two weeks and Rookery every four. I ran experiments in the intermittent weeks. And I went to Zhong Shan[11] three times to sample No Worries, their station tarn. After sampling, I had to rush back that day and spend until 3.00 or 4.00 a.m. in the lab, but would sleep until smoko the next day![12]

Able to plan her field collecting at Casey in summer when the plants were exposed, Erica arranged her schedule so that 'most of the work in the lab was over winter when the weather was too unpredictable'.

It was very cold and uncomfortable working outside then. There was a rush at the end of summer, a lot of lab work in winter. I really enjoyed working in my lab. It was a cosy, very small shipping container with a window looking out over the bay and the icebergs which could be seen moving. There was a sensational view to sea, and I got a big kick out of my work; there were a lot of interesting results. Also, you can catch up on a lot of scientific reading, writing, plotting graphs, etc. in winter.

63

Some of the work is very intricate. Sharon Robinson and Jane Wasley have a moss project at Casey during summer.

We collected 1 centimetre squares of moss samples using a small pocket knife from one site only. When the moss sample was lifted out, small stones were placed in the hole to retain the moisture around the remaining mosses which in time would creep up to the rock edges and grow over them. We are very concerned never to abuse the samples, to get the best use out of them and not waste any.

Adele summed up the frustrations and satisfactions of scientific fieldwork in Antarctica: 'It was doing science in awkward circumstances and being isolated. You could be doing something more efficiently back home. But being in such a pristine place studying plants was a privilege: it was priceless.'

DOING ONE'S JOB IN ANTARCTICA

As official Antarctic photographer, Jutta Hösel found her work always involved 'a battle with the dust'.

It doesn't rain in summer, it's the driest continent on earth, and there are vehicles going up and down, and no vegetation to hold it. The atmosphere is dry in the buildings too—a photographer's nightmare! I knew it and used UV filters on all the lenses, partly against the dust and partly against all the blue. It was a daily battle. When we came back at night we had a late dinner on ship, and I was so tired from carting the gear around I had to force myself to clean the cameras for one last time, and reload them.

Elizabeth Chipman later wrote that: 'No one worked harder than Jutta ... she spent long hours away from the station lugging her tripod, cameras and film stock over ice, rock and summer slush in order to record ... every possible aspect of living and working at Casey station and environs.'[13]

Jutta recalled:

> The Antarctic environment was most interesting, but my role was
> always to photograph the scientific experiences, the scientific
> happenings, the unloading, general activities. Somehow I tried to
> do both, which was too much. Casey was a special trip. There was
> a list of photos I needed and wanted. I went around and
> photographed the powerhouse—had worked it out to set up
> flashlights with a tripod so I'd have enough far-reaching light to
> illuminate all the equipment—and the camera was on a tripod
> when someone said there was a seal down on an ice floe. I saw it
> through the window, left all the equipment behind, and raced
> down to the water's edge and there was a Weddell seal on an ice
> floe. I had another camera but it was too far away to get a good
> photo.

A seal, an Adélie penguin near the station, a visiting Emperor
penguin or spectacular skies can still bring expeditioners out to
marvel.

Cold and isolation are not the only things that affect work in
Antarctica. Issues of personal space and interaction also dominated the interviews. For example, the mess is the most-visited
part of the station and the chef is responsible not only for the
food but for looking after people. Mandy explained that 'the
chef is the only person on station who has to physically work
with every other person at some stage or another. The mess is
like the hub of everything, and the chef is expected to be cheery
and happy and say hello to everyone, sometimes three times a
day, even if you have a bad day. Part of the job description is
to keep a happy, comfortable atmosphere in the mess.' Carol
added: 'I realised that people were chatting and hanging round
in the mess, but it was my workplace and I was at work, and on
display at it. That was hard, I just wanted to get on with my job!'
However, despite an extra task involving preparing special meals
for a dietary study, she said: 'It was my best year, probably. I was
in charge. I was "mum".[14] It felt it was a complete job from A
to Z. You had to shop, know clients well, plan and cook. Other
skills you had to have too—for example, using the forklift for

shopping,[15] the sort of experience you wouldn't normally have.' Mandy elaborated: 'During winter, some stations decide to have a special dinner every Saturday night. Sunday is the chef's only day off, so if Saturday dinner is late, it's often too dark for the chef to go off station on Saturday night.'

On the other hand, the medical officers may be under-employed; their potential patients have been medically screened, so accidents are one of the doctor's chief concerns. Jenny Mackenzie found:

> Some doctors ask, 'You can always get people off, can't you?' and you have to say, 'Well no, you can't, you could expect to be stuck and if there's a life and death situation, well it's life and death on the station, and they live or die according to what you do.' And they sort of go, 'oh ...' because every medical practice is based on management until retrieval, off to the specialist; we stabilise, and they're gone. In Antarctica you've got to stabilise them and then operate on them, and this is a different proposition altogether for someone with major trauma. You've got to cross-match the blood, get the anaesthetic machine ready, get theatre ready, get your guys [assistants] ready, etc. Meanwhile, you've got this guy's life while you're doing all the rest of the prep. There's a lot there. If you think of it too hard you get scared so you try to just make the preparations without trying to lose any sleep over it.

Louise suggested: 'It's terrifying if you really think about it—to go as a professional, and live with your patients. I hoped and prayed I could do a good job.' Jean Ledingham agreed: 'The medical aspects were terrifying. It was "one-handed medicine" then[16] ... I did an operation, with a general anaesthetic, on the stewards' table on the *Nella Dan*!' In Jane's words: 'Medically it's the ultimate general practice; it's the ultimate challenge, I think, because your limits are being an expert in absolutely everything, and no one of course is—no one can be—but it's the ultimate remote medical location.'

'GD' had to deal with 'a serious orthopaedic injury from a fall on the ship'.

This was challenging, it was hardly optimal therapy that I was providing, I knew I wasn't an orthopaedic surgeon but I had to do my best—that was the conditions we all went down on. That was the critical thing—for all the risks they were taking, they did have a doctor. I didn't. I ultimately knew I was supported by the others in that—they couldn't criticise me because I was taking a bigger risk than them.

Dentistry is done by the doctors,[17] and they are often involved in medical research and biology projects. As Lynn Williams explained: 'I had my own research projects, which kept me busy for half a week once a month, taking blood, spinning it down, doing the monthly physiology checks.' 'GD' said she 'always had something I had to do. And that in a place where it's highly efficient, with no shopping or housework except when rostered on, your day is very productive with no annoying non-essentials. I always found time to go out on other people's projects, especially the biologists, which was important to me. I loved to do it.'

The doctors have to live with potential patients, some of whom have not previously consulted a female doctor. They are warned about possible 'unnecessary' consultations. 'GD' recalled: 'I used to say if someone had a problem with me, infatuation or relating to me inappropriately, I made sure in my own mind that it was going to be *their* problem. I tried to maintain an element of professionalism. They can come to me and tell me things or not. Certain men had difficulty telling me things they probably should have—I felt it was up to them to overcome it …' Alternative tactics included Annette's 'very bad memory' to avert corridor consultations or comments on others' health.

Station leaders can make a large personal input, within the official job description. Joan Russell distinguishes management, which dominates now with the ease of contemporary communications with headquarters, from leadership:

Manager is a role, leader is about the exercise of power and authority. Managing was my job. Leading isn't a job. I'm a manager, yes. In terms of setting standards and maintaining

standards, both socially and professionally, I don't think there
would be any of my expeditioners who would deny that I took a
very upfront leadership role in that. And many of the reactions
which were enacted during that year [1990] indicate that that's
how people saw me. They saw me as the leader, and the setter of
standards, and the arbiter; many of them did not choose to bow to
those standards, but they all acknowledged that they were there.

For Louise, there was 'a huge scope for freedom in decision-
making, and creative management'.

How you do it affects such of lot of everybody else's life and well-
being. So if you find, by a sort of process of good luck, good people
and so on, that it's actually working, then it is very much a sense of
'I'm being effective here and it's being good for other people, and
the program is doing well, and we're achieving what we set out to do
and we're achieving it together', and there's a sense of community
satisfaction and community achievement, which is empowering and
gives you more sense of well-being.
   You're the only person on the station who doesn't have a work
program written down. You don't have a set of tasks that you're
expected to achieve; you don't have objectives against which you can
measure your performance. Sometimes station leaders want to be
seen to have done it all—'my year', 'my station', 'my people'. I never
used those terms, I always used 'our'. They only gain a sense of
achievement through usurping the achievement of others, and this
of course is resented. Most station leaders are chosen because of
their leadership and their drive and their personal positive
contributions to things. Yet your achievement is actually only
through the achievement of others, so that in a sense it is vicarious,
and you have to be willing for that to happen, to see that your good,
so to speak, your achievement, your success, can only arise out of the
achievement of others, and to that extent the leadership role is
absolutely one of facilitation. But if you can do it, and see it like
that—and I worked this out fairly early on—then the sense of
empowerment is huge, because it's not only your own, it's everybody
else's, so you get the 20-fold whammy if you can see it that way.

Intense group effort, coordinated by the station leader, is
needed for resupply. Angela found:

This is difficult, and you get a sense of achievement out of it. It's nice if station goals are set that involve the whole station, but people get on with their own jobs. They're not exploring or doing joint jobs these days. I had to see others' goals were met, but often they didn't have any either. It was frustrating in some ways—at the end of the year I felt I'd done all I could, that I'd been successful but there was no standard to measure it against! The station was clean and tidy at the end—the appearance of the station is important to a female.

This point was also stressed by Alison Clifton, the first female station leader on Macquarie Island.

Diana's view is:

First of all there is the organisation to keep the base running smoothly—common duties, rosters, science supports, facilitating work programs. The main job is facilitating everyone achieving the outcomes in all the specific projects. I think you've got to have a harmonious community with a strong work ethos. I see part of my job as creating that atmosphere, that ethos, so that people do fulfil their programs. And part of that increased productivity is that people are happy. So part of my job might be throwing a good party. And certainly at Davis the social side of things really contributed to that productivity. I loved the job—being in overalls, etc. It's an opportunity to observe a close-knit community, observe where the group is going and orchestrate to change direction—for example, organise a party, suggest some jollies, trouble shoot, counselling, which can be difficult—it's very rewarding. It's a simple existence in some ways, though there's a subconscious strain with respect to safety.

On styles of leadership, Diana, an experienced manager, thinks that 'women are stronger on a perceptive-intuitive style though some men can be stronger on this. I sense that I am more confrontationalist-direct'. Norwegian Monica Kristensen said that, 'as a communicator and parent I like to give a lot of freedom and responsibility to others, it's an academic style based on consensus, the stage before democracy'. Susan Headley found that 'female station leaders have a limited choice of management styles if they wish to be popular'.[18] Unlike male leaders, they are judged more on performance of feminine roles than on efficiency in their jobs. Angela felt that 'all the Antarctic Division care about is harmony on station, that's the bottom line!' She measured the success of her year by the fact that 'there were nineteen living bodies still talking to each other, and the buildings didn't burn down!' Safety was highlighted by other female leaders, too. Such concern reminds us of the bottom line in living and working in Antarctica.

WHAT IS SO SPECIAL ABOUT WORKING IN ANTARCTICA?

A number of the women maintained that it was no more difficult to work in Antarctica, and claimed that the conditions could be better than in other isolated places. However, the environment does provide challenges for outside work. For example, archaeologist 'Tamara' found working on Macquarie Island very physically demanding: 'It kept my brain occupied. The wet and the cold were a constant challenge and there were a few novel problems, such as keeping seals and penguins out of the trenches I excavated. Also a constant battle against flooding.' Other polar archaeology 'had been conducted in ice not waterlogged ground. Therefore I designed the research and then carried it out using general archaeological principles with some special case adaptations. I was not briefed as such. Much of my support came from fellow expeditioners. I tend to work better if I'm left to get on with it so this all worked out to my benefit.'

Like a number of the scientists, the communications officers and meteorological observers had experienced work in other isolated places. But just how relevant is prior experience to Antarctic performance?[19] On the psychological selection tests, a high score on 'sensation seeking' is common.[20] The desire to seek new experiences and to test oneself in a new and challenging environment was strong amongst the women interviewed.

'Tamara' outlined two recurring issues: the need for resource-fulness in working away from the usual professional supports, and the satisfaction of doing so under often-difficult circumstances. Resourcefulness was shown in solving technical problems. Some women casually mentioned that they had done courses like electronics, and therefore felt confident to face potential difficulties with their equipment. Peta and Wendy, both geophysicists, each successfully installed new equipment.

Equipment and materials can be adversely affected by Antarctic conditions. Things freeze, and it can be difficult to transport delicate equipment over rough ice. Tracey Rogers admits that 'the radio technician saved my life fixing things' during her first season. However, the second time, 'all the equipment I was using, I tested at the Zoo's walk-in freezer. The worst problem was things getting shaken to bits on the *sastrugi*,[21] a common problem for first-timers. I toughened things up and learnt how to fix them myself the second time.'

Like the doctors mentioned earlier, some scientists were overwhelmed by the dimensions of their task. Helen Beggs only had a single day's prior training on each project. After several days' changeover, she was on her own. 'There were a few notes, some manuals and that was it! I had real anxiety about it.' Another expeditioner-physicist, Gina, noted:

Nowhere else in Australia would you get so much experience with equipment. I ran nine experiments for five institutions, with more than a quarter of a million dollars worth of equipment. It was a real joke to send a 25-year-old Honours student to run this equipment, but also a wonderful challenge to a young graduate who had sat back in the lab and let male partners do it—this was not so at school (all girls), but I regressed at university. Women don't come across the opportunity to diddle with tools usually; boys are more comfortable with electronics and diddling.

Rapid learning and a sense of achievement were both important aspects of the experience. Helen's account is low-key: 'Yesterday I fixed the LSO-11/02 computer which stopped dead just before I went on my jolly. That was a good feeling.' Ann said:

It was a challenge and privilege to get the job. Then the hard work began, with most of the first months off station with small groups. It's very physically tiring, training 80 people, plus other station responsibilities, training the Search and Rescue team when everyone is under pressure at the end, checking equipment, ordering new equipment and advising the station leader on preparation of the team, as well as assisting with fieldwork. Going and teaching things when it's excruciatingly cold, and you would much rather curl up and be warm, or when you're really tired— keeping up the enthusiasm, motivating people who don't want to be there, confronting those who are being difficult . . . The job always presents challenges; everything is new.

Initial enthusiasm can also pall. Helen wrote in her diary:

Day after day I battle hurricane force winds and bad visibility to travel the kilometre by foot or quad to the lab to change a chart or film. I risk life and limb for physics data . . . Every day I have to battle the tedium of doing the same old routine work with not a scrap of physics in it. Just data gathering, scaling, calibration, paperwork, logging, around and around and around week after week seven days a week with a few days each month off when I manage to get away on a field trip.

IS IT HARDER TO BE A WOMAN AND A PROFESSIONAL IN ANTARCTICA?

Research shows that women feel under pressure to perform well at work.[22] Women in Antarctica are very visible and clearly exhibit this anxiety. As Jennie said: 'There's a lot of pressure on the women to perform. For example, others notice the physical fitness of the women: it's generally higher than the men's!' Elanor felt she probably put excessive expectations on herself as much as feeling they were imposed by others, while Angela R. admitted she felt she 'had to be better than the men': 'When I had a sense of failure, even if I was getting reassurance externally, I kept feeling I should do better.' It seems a 'fear of failure' afflicts substantial numbers of women. We long for 'respect and recognition, the desire for acceptance, and the wish to be loved ... [coupled with] the belief ... that such longings are doomed never to be satisfied'.[23]

There is work pressure on all expeditioners. Lynn Williams advised:

Competence at your job is really a very important part, in a small group like that it's not going to be an easy year for you if you can't perform your job, you may be good at other things, but individual job performance is probably the highest rated thing by the group. If you're incompetent at your job, nothing will save you. If you're not cooperative and at least doing the minimum in the other duties, that's a recipe for disaster.

Leslie maintained: 'Women start from a basis of having less credibility and have to work harder—you have to prove yourself in Antarctica.' Lynne also felt: 'There was always a lot of pressure to be a hard working successful scientist when you went to Antarctica. I have yet to determine if this was just pressure that I put myself under or if it was real pressure. I suppose because it cost so much for the Antarctic Division to keep a scientist in Antarctica, I felt under pressure to produce the goods.' A number mentioned that some station leaders in particular were disinclined to accept women's competence until it was proven there.

Some women experienced external pressures to perform. Phillipa Foster found that:

When I started at the Division, some thought that women shouldn't be there. As a forklift driver, I anticipated that. They feared I couldn't do the job. I perceived I'd passed the test they set of unloading a truckful of timber with overhead wires in a very confined space. It was really a test of manipulative skills, and they wandered off after a while and I got on with the job.

73

Melanie gave a reminder of how it feels when you simply don't have the knowledge for a task:

> I think it's all judged in the male arena, down there—if you can do a traditionally male job, then you've succeeded. It was particularly evident—there's a lot of machinery and equipment that we used, and what the males don't understand is that typically girls don't grow up with this stuff, and they find it difficult that grown women don't know the difference between one tool and the other. Sometimes I get the sense that women start to compete in that way, too, against each other.

Gwen added: 'There's going to be this relative incompetence because of lack of familiarity, and women are going to feel inadequate about it and men are going to seize on this.'

Ruth 'was only aware of being a woman on board when you feel you have to prove yourself—the crew are sure you don't know what you're doing. You work harder, solve problems on your own wits for two months and have to earn respect. That's important—you're there for two months and you need respect.'

For scientists, gaining respect from non-scientists can be particularly difficult. According to Morag:

> Some boffins are hopeless, with few practical skills. Being female and a boffin together put me on the lowest rung ... Scientists are seen as freeloaders, with no role at station, and their work is not understood. For example, I had a problem with my work, but couldn't get help with it except some for the technical aspects. I needed another's offer of help, as I was cautious about asking for help. I admit to making several mistakes with it. The technicians were not helpful and made me feel really stupid. Because of the lack of appreciation of scientists, I approached asking for help really cautiously, though resented having to ask for every bit of help instead of having any offered.

It can be hard to balance self-sufficiency and assistance-seeking. Some women perceive unsolicited help as belittling. Ruth was put down by the ship's crew members, in the face of her competence, demonstrated by running her laboratory for weeks at sea. 'Whenever I did something complex or technical, the crew's favourite saying was: "Does your mother know you can do that?"' More experienced, Angela McGowan felt: 'Some of the women who didn't want to show any kind of weakness would think that asking for help is letting the side down.' She and others found that their willingness to ask for help made life much easier.

Louise Crossley analysed the underlying dynamics and contradictions:

> Many of the values are based upon male strengths, and one of them is straight physical strength. There's still a very profound sense that unless a woman can pull 44 gallon drums around she's not pulling her weight, and yet there is a corresponding degree of chivalry that prevents you actually doing that kind of thing . . . all the men there are so competent at what they do, and because I was a woman station leader and didn't have a particular competence, becoming respected is harder for a woman. But once you've got it, it's easier in some ways—you see, men are more critical of bullshitting men and arrogant men . . .

That is a perspective helped by experience and age. It is harder when you are young and female in Antarctica. As Pene reflected: 'When I was 21, I thought I could change the world. At 25, I wanted to make an impact. By 30, I still felt I wanted to do something that would make a difference. At 35, I just decided doing a good job was what I wanted.'

FEELING GOOD AND BAD ABOUT WORK AND SELF

Elanor's Antarctic experience was a valuable one: 'Workwise, it was a success and I have a lot of good data. I also know I worked as hard as I possibly could. Hence I feel proud about that. If I learnt anything at all from my time working down South, it was to be prepared for every eventuality. If something could go wrong it would, and you had to learn not to give in easily.' Jennie also emphasised the positive aspects: 'It's unlikely to have helped in a career sense, but in the sense of being a better researcher, yes—you have to be adaptive there, pick things up quickly, and you don't have research back-up, especially for Heard Island.'[24]

External factors can impact strongly on one's self-evaluation in Antarctica. 'Elaine' noted: 'When work is not going well, you can't get away from it; it's constantly there.' For the station leader, who is under even more scrutiny than most, 'any sense of personal incompetence was heightened because your stuff-ups were magnified too, they never go unnoticed, and the potential for long term spin-off was substantial . . . in that context, because it's such an enclosed society, there isn't anywhere else to go, you have to live with it.' However, Louise C. suggested: 'It increases your sense of self-esteem in some ways, but it certainly makes you less adaptable to the realities of the world—and the kind of high you get makes your expectations higher in some regards but they're not actually all that easy to fulfil!'

CELEBRATING WORK, AND ONE'S OWN AND OTHERS' SKILLS

The opportunities available in Antarctica foster learning on many levels, something Gina enjoyed: 'If you chose to see it as an opportunity for learning, it was great. The previous year there had been two PhD students and an Antarctic Division engineer. I was the only one in physics the next year so it looked like one woman was to replace three men!—but they set up the equipment.'

A number were specific about what gave them more confidence. In 'Davina's' words, it felt good 'having done it and realised you could get help from others, over the phone, plus realising you were not expected to know everything! I left one experiment that wasn't working, I was worried but wasn't expected to succeed with everything. Training here helped me technically.' Helen K. acknowledged: 'Yes, it's made me more self-reliant, definitely, and it's sort of shown me that I can do the things that maybe I wouldn't ever thought I could do—just getting out on my own, being able to cope with being by myself—I'm not the sort of person that would go out walking by myself, ever, but down there I really discovered that I could be by myself for days at a time and it didn't particularly worry me.' Lynne added: 'Field trips were always quite demanding, you needed to be well organised—but they were fantastic—very rewarding. I feel a lot more confident. I hadn't had much experience with being in cold weather but now I know what to do in Tasmania: it's fantastic to know this.'

And there was the pleasure of being with other highly skilled people and learning from them. Tracey R. underlined the reciprocity in this: 'They're working eighteen hours a day unloading a boat—that's super teamwork, another highlight of Antarctica: the teamwork that happens. The scientist who has some time and goes out to help them unload, as long as you don't get in the way, that's great.'

A good time, according to those I spoke with, is when you know that work is going well, and when there are exciting things to do in your spare time. Meeting the challenges to one's own and others' satisfaction is exhilarating; equally, feeling one has not succeeded leads to long-term pain and loss of confidence and self-esteem. Doreen provided a thoughtful summary: 'It's good to celebrate women's experiences as so few go [to Antarctica], but I look forward to the day when it's normal that women go there. I want to be judged on my own merits and capabilities, not as a female, but [on the basis] that it's normal for women to do things with certain skills—I've got a lot of satisfaction that I was accepted to go for my skills.'

FOUR

'Everything you do is noticed there!'

The unknown holds a fascination for humans, and remote places have an irresistible attraction. But what is it *really* like to live in Antarctica? Part of the picture is available from large-screen documentaries and the World Wide Web.[1] Obviously, it is mostly cold, although sunny summer days of +3°C bring out the T-shirts. The extremes of light probably affect people more than the extremely low winter temperatures, and the high wind and changeability are hazardous.

As those who regularly collect biological samples during winter know, temperatures can plummet to −38°C. Lynne, Tracey, Morag, Ellie, Erica and Fiona are among those who have driven over icy terrain in the winter darkness for sampling. Heavy outer clothing covers multiple inner layers, though equipment may necessitate the removal of a glove. They speak with pride about their fortitude, and Lynne found that 'we got respect from having to go out and work, not just play, in the cold'. Women have worked at all the remote field sites, on islands and inland on the icecap. And some women have participated in the hard-won exhilaration of long dog-sled trips.

Physical conditions are challenging throughout Antarctica, with local variations. New Zealand geologist Nerida found Davis quite easy after her season in the field beyond Scott base in the Transantarctic mountains:

Once we were camped in tents at 2600 metres, close to a cliff edge, near the top of Mt Feather. During one of the blizzards it would have been about minus 60°C including wind chill, with wind gusts of up to 80 knots passing over the tent. I thought: 'will I survive this? What should I do if the tent starts to blow away?' We were at a high altitude so it takes longer to cook, you have to think more about cooking, cleaning yourself, going to the toilet, the safest way to get a sample on a cliff face, and you're always worried about the others in your field party!

AUSTRALIA'S ANTARCTIC AND SUB-ANTARCTIC STATIONS

Each ANARE station has unique features due to its particular location, terrain and climate. Macquarie Island is in the sub-Antarctic, north of the Antarctic Convergence, and is ice free, whereas Heard Island, just south of the Convergence, has a permanent snowfield and icecap. Both islands are in the 'furious fifties', with high winds and frequent mist, rain and snow. Visitors rhapsodise about their wild beauty; they are treeless, yet able to support green vegetation. Macquarie is milder, with no 24-hour winter darkness. It is possible to go out alone there, as Kirsten points out: 'When you need space there, you can throw a pack on your back and go. That's really important when you're in a crammed hut.' As Jenny M. noted: 'You can walk away from the silly, petty things.' Many consider Macquarie is incomparably different to Antarctica. Helen K. described Macquarie as like another home, while Doreen added: 'It's cosier, more interactive, it can be really comfortable if you're with a good group.' However, more accidents occur in its wet rugged terrain. More people work in the field there, and it is necessary to walk everywhere, whereas vehicles are used on the continent.[2]

Of the three Australian continental stations, Davis and Mawson are within the Antarctic Circle, while Casey, the closest to Australia, is just north of it, though lower temperatures have been recorded there. The area has low rocky islands and peninsulas, and the icecap rises steeply behind the station. Rapid weather changes occur. The sandy beaches and hours of sun have earned Davis the title 'Riviera of the South', and in summer there is a large area of exposed rock. Its many lakes are a major feature, especially for scientists. Mawson is at the head of a horseshoe-shaped bay, and high mountain tops are visible from the station. It is the oldest, most distant and windiest station.

Early expeditions were small, sometimes as few as eight to twelve people. Today the winter numbers average eighteen on the continent and, until very recently, fourteen on Macquarie Island,[3] while particular projects, such as the continental station rebuilding in the 1980s and early 1990s, doubled the number of men on station. This male dominance, and the general culture of male construction crews, meant the social environment could seem more intimidating to women, even though their numbers were increasing as well.

Australian continental stations today are large, modern constructions. Each station generates its own power, has satellite communication (ANARESAT) and treats its own sewage. Buildings include living quarters, workshop, store, 'operations',[4] balloon shed (meteorology), powerhouse, laboratories and so on. The living quarters are spacious, with dining, recreation, sleeping and bathroom areas, and over winter expeditioners can spread out. Some see these quarters as too comfortable, too formidable a barrier between people and the Antarctic environment. During her Mawson winter, Robyn Downey had a 'caravan'[5] towed close to the living quarters, and slept there to experience the full force of the blizzards. Macquarie Island, affectionately known as 'Macca', has older, smaller buildings—like those of the middle period for the continental stations but sharing improved communications. Summer field camps are simple—field huts (often old shipping containers), fibreglass huts and tents—and communication with them is still basic.

Old-timers remember nostalgically the cramped first-generation quarters, where the 'real' dongas[6] afforded each person a tiny, unsound-proof personal space. The expeditioners lived very close together in those conditions, a little less so in the improved

Pioneering women in their Mae Wests about to go ashore at Macquarie Island for the first time, December 1959. Left to right: Mary Gilham, Isobel Bennett, Susan Ingham and Hope MacPherson. (Courtesy Isobel Bennett)

Susan Barr and 18-month-old daughter Ingvill, Svalbard, 1982. (Photo Trygve Aas)

Judy Clarke painting nesting Adélie penguins to distinguish the males from the females, Mawson, 2000. (Courtesy Judy Clarke)

Left: Roger Kirkwood and Barbara Wienecke weighing a 28.5kg Emperor penguin, Taylor Glacier colony, Mawson, 2000. (Courtesy Barbara Wienecke). Right: Karen French releasing a meteorological balloon, Davis, 1995/96. (Photo Midj Jones)

Left: Melanie Fitzpatrick ice climbing, Casey, 1992. (Photo Mandy Holmes). Right: Station leader Joan Russell, shoulder deep in tussock, coming off the Brothers Track, Sandy Bay, Macquarie Island, February 1994. (Courtesy Joan Russell)

Judy Chappell and Astrida Mednis tagging seals, Lied Bluff, Davis, 1996. (Courtesy Judy Chappell)

Gina Price with husky pups Patrick and Brendan, Mawson, 1991.
(Courtesy Gina Price)

Maria De Deuge runs beside the husky team, Mawson, 1991.
(Photo Richard Teece)

Elanor Bell emerging from a hole in the ice during the midwinter swim, Davis, 1996. (Courtesy Elanor Bell)

Joan Russell at the Peterson Island apple hut during the first seasonal elephant count, December 1990. (Courtesy Joan Russell)

Gina Price carrying out duties as an upper atmosphere physicist during a particularly spectacular show of the *aurora australis*, Mawson, 1985. (Courtesy Gina Price)

An aerial view of Mawson Station, January 1997. (Photo Elanor Bell)

Adélie penguins, Davis, 1990. (Photo Morag Anderson)

Icebergs in summer, Davis. (Photo Morag Anderson)

Icy Cave in the Sørsdal Glacier. (Photo Morag Anderson)

A green iceberg, 1996. (Photo Melanie Fitzpatrick)

second-generation buildings. Fire is an ever-present risk, once depriving the winterers of a kitchen and mess. The term 'donga' is still used for the living quarters, though only at Macquarie Island is there any resemblance to the original 'donga lines'. In 1989, the Casey 'tunnel rats' were reluctant to move to the new station from the cold, corrugated iron-enclosed second-generation quarters. Erica related:

> It was our home and we loved it dearly despite its many discomforts, it had a sense of history, of adventure and challenge. You would walk into the tunnel and it would be −40°C. You rugged up and ran down the tunnel to warm your hands on the toaster at breakfast time ... We felt we were 'doing it proper'—not 'doing it tough' but really living in Antarctica: it wasn't cushy.

Life on station is different now, though life in the field has changed little. The links between the new, large stations, better communications and increasing numbers of women have all led to the mistaken notion that women have 'made it too soft' and spoilt the heroic dimensions of Antarctic work. Meredy pointed out that: 'You can't blame change on the women, change is inevitable. We need to accept what it's like now.' Women certainly don't expect life in Antarctica to be physically easy, and many have been vociferous critics of the new stations, especially on environmental grounds.[7]

Scientific activities and recreational opportunities on stations vary. Scientific data are collected at all four stations, especially meteorological, seismological and ionospheric data. Macquarie and Davis are the major centres for summer biological research, with Davis accommodating greater numbers of researchers; the saline Davis lakes also allow sampling in winter.[8] Mawson has been a continuous centre for cosmic ray recording since 1955, and is the major place for upper atmosphere physics (UAP). Emperor and Adélie penguin research, together with geology and botany in the Prince Charles Mountains and glaciology traverses of the Lambert Glacier, take place from Mawson, but there are fewer newcomers in summer. Glaciology is also conducted from Davis and Casey,[9] and geology at Law Base in the Larsemann Hills west of Davis and in the Bunger Hills, between Davis and Casey. A variety of other projects are also conducted at Davis and Casey, including seal and sea bird studies, terrestrial biology, environmental impacts and archaeology. The population of Davis may exceed 60 at peak times.

'Summering' scientists may spend eight or nine months on Macquarie Island. Jane, an experienced volunteer biologist, commented that 'a lot of attention is given to wintering, not to summering, yet with nine months of summer, some summerers are there longer than winterers. Living in the field is less luxurious, more intense, and tougher—for example, you cook and clean, fill the water tank, then come back to where it's all done for you and you have to participate in rosters.' Joan[10] said that living in the field could be compared with life in a concentration camp—isolated and tough, with some very real risks in terms of survival. The summer maintenance people stay up to six months, while the lengths of other summer visits vary.[11]

The size and composition of summer groups markedly affect the social climate on station. Pene noticed that, 'after being the only woman at Mawson over winter, I enjoyed sitting on the stairs at Davis and watching all the women there (sixteen over summer). It leads to a *very* different atmosphere.' She also acknowledged that some of the young women 'brought their university values with them and there can be a lack of understanding of other people with whom they are living'. There is little sense of a whole group during summer, and the field programs create their own culture. The frequent ship and helicopter movements add to the sense of urgency: to study the wildlife during the brief breeding season; to gain access to rocks and plants when the ice melts; to complete projects during the capricious good weather 'windows'. There is a 'work hard, play hard' ethos, and old-timers (now including a number of women) often set the pace. Prior experience can lead to better access to resources, and women may have an edge in getting technical assistance, though some have also experienced favouritism to others, or direct enmity, that has hampered their work.

Towards the end of the season, patience wears thin, especially if planned work has not been achieved. The wintering group may stand back from unnecessary involvement with summerers, holding themselves in reserve for the coming winter. Ricarda, like many, felt when the last boat left: 'At last we have the base to ourselves, the hangers-on have gone, the party-goers. There's a sense of loss, and relief, when they go.' At the end of their term, they may resent the newcomers, especially if they have had a 'good year' together. Researchers, especially those concerned with human existence in confined environments such as space-ships, space stations and submarines, have studied the changes in group life of those wintering in Antarctica as a comparison. Of particular interest to them has been the effect on group morale and individual performance of the so-called 'third quarter phenomenon' when the worst of winter is over but there are still some months before relief.[12] There are three studies of wintering that include women.[13] Late winter can be a very diffi-cult time if things have not gone well, and newcomers will probably be welcomed. A lone woman may be delighted to meet another female, as Louise Holliday recounted: 'I met Ulla and we talked for an hour solid. I felt I'd known her all my life! I enjoyed the female communication. I hadn't realised that women talked differently to men, and we exchanged more in the hour than I had done in the previous year.'

Over winter, some groups resemble families in their closeness and the quality of their interactions. People share a sense of belonging, care for one another and create understandings, even a cultural 'dialect'—jokes, phrases, behaviours, meanings—that makes the group distinctive. Individuals develop positions and roles equivalent to those in a multi-generational family, though the absence of actual children and older people is felt strongly by some. There are rituals, especially the midwinter celebrations when there has been an expectation of a bawdy performance of *Cinderella*. Cross-dressing, 'girlie' posters and magazines, regular blue movie nights and 'page three girls' in the daily station news bulletins have been part of the tradition, and all have become contentious in recent years. The more familial environment on Macquarie Island has been fostered by the smaller wintering numbers and the older station buildings, though numbers are not the only factor. People live more closely together than at the modern continental stations, in a more cosy, creative, 'make-do' atmosphere.

To spend a summer at a remote field site is an 'intrepid', 'genuine' Antarctic experience. There may be grumbling by the summer residents about the converted shipping containers parked outside the living quarters known as the Red Shed; these become transformed in the imagination when hooked together and towed inland on traverse! There are several particularly attractive features of field camps: companions may be hand-chosen, allowing more personal space despite cramped quarters, and there is an absence of the politicking and bureaucracy of station life.

The microcosm of station life

Apart from the isolation, there are several factors that character-ise station existence. One is the fact that you live and work with the same people, 24 hours a day. There is no escape, except for field trips or 'jollies'. A second aspect is thus the relative lack of freedom, despite the hugeness of Antarctica, for the continental stations have strict limits beyond which you cannot go alone and without notification procedures, for safety reasons. The dangers are real, but increased bureaucratisation of ANARE and the ease of communications with headquarters have often been blamed for these limitations, and an 'us–them' mentality can develop between headquarters and stations. One female leader suggested that a short, welcome period of relief could be obtained by a feigned communications failure! Those wanting change welcome the improved communications and the normalisation of station affairs within the ambit of the Australian Public Service. There are strong lingering resentments of this, a feeling that Antarctica is and should remain 'different', with its own 'rules'. Certainly, the third factor is that, as a consequence of both the physical and administrative restrictions, privacy is almost impossible. You encounter others in order to eat and, given the lack of social and intellectual input from the outside—especially over winter—people-watching readily becomes a major pastime.

Gossip is rife, exacerbated these days by station-to-station communication, especially between old friends. This often leads to comparison of leaders and fellow expeditioners, and of how good a time is being had—which usually means the partying and easygoing leadership. As such communication mainly takes place between men, it can have a very destructive impact on women, who become the objects of idle chatter, sexual speculation and male competition. It is also very difficult to overcome early perceptions by others. 'Elaine' found: 'You get one go at it and that's that. You stay the person they pick you to be, [you're] not allowed to grow. I felt negatively judged.'

A persistent irony about Antarctic life is the lack of personal space, a problem felt acutely by many. Even the large stations resemble a fishbowl, especially in the enclosed isolation of winter—though, contrarily, complaints surface about people who withdraw to their rooms, with their personal videos and hobbies, failing to participate in communal life. One of the irritations of tourist visits is their inquisitiveness about station life. There is a visibility and level of scrutiny that few women have experienced before, as discussed below and in Chapter 5.

THE LAYERING OF CULTURE ON ANTARCTIC STATIONS

Except for the British stations, where staff spend two continuous winters, there is an annual turnover of people. The human presence in Antarctica is transient: we come, we go, and we must bring with us all the necessities for human existence. This includes our cultural baggage. Our experience of Antarctica is filtered through layers including the immediate group, national culture and international stories of Antarctic exploration. So far, women's voices in Antarctic stories have been mere whispers. However, as Kerrie pointed out: 'This does not mean it is a man's world. There's a long way to go till there are more equal proportions of women there, but there's no reason why we shouldn't be there.' Woman after woman echoed this. However, it does mean that the Antarctic culture which women enter has been *established* by men, and this has consequences for women. They have simply not been there in sufficient numbers to develop an alternative, although change is evident.

The various layers of culture considered in this chapter are the group, ANARE and Australian culture. Interviews with women who have worked with other national Antarctic programs suggest there are common features but also some variations—for example, with the social composition of Antarctic groups and differences in gender relations.

'My tribe': The station crew

Each group coming together for a season in Antarctica comprises a unique collection of individuals. 'Recidivism' and networks of expeditioners[14] mean that some people come together amongst old friends, while others anxiously wonder who they will meet. A group largely composed of newcomers may have more space to develop its own ethos; experienced and older men tend to play a dominant role in other groups. 'Belle' noted in the mid-1990s that: 'A few things are led by really dominant males who intimidate both men and women.' Encouraged by management to see themselves as a team, but lacking sufficient training in communication and group processes to realise this goal, 'a lot of male behaviour is forming a hierarchy, especially when women are present. There's bonding over general issues rather than particular relationships—the group mentality of men living up to the male stereotype' as Gina observed. Pene continued:

The boys are a group whose standards and interests will vary from year to year. To be accepted by them you have to conform to their ideas, not do anything different, or upset their group interactions. The group works because all of its members will admit to only very simple needs of other members, mostly male companionship. It would seem that, for most of the boys, all their social requirements are fulfilled by the comradeship provided by being one of the boys and they will not admit to any other social needs.

Those not conforming can have a lonely, difficult time. Differences of ethnicity, class and sexual preference, as well as gender, are all reasons for not belonging. Pene explained: 'Women are superfluous to the male hierarchy, and are treated differently. They don't get the support and emotional back-up. Men don't recognise or talk about that need for emotional back-up.' Gina found that the men 'really looked after each other; if one was "down" the others would notice and act', but she—like other women—found she was not included in this care. 'You could be feeling low and go to the mess and no one would notice. That felt isolated.' Women talked about having to go and ask for support, while the men appeared able to 'enjoy it in public'.

Some women felt that their mere presence breached the solidarity. 'Jade' said: 'I would walk into a room and the atmosphere would change, the conversation would stop. They were talking about things women were not meant to hear. Some men were more comfortable being with women than others and this was not a division on work lines. Age was a factor.' 'Faye' suggested that the more 'couth' men want to be at stations with women, and many men now would not like to be at an all-male station. Women stressed over and over that there were 'only people in Antarctica' and that gender was not an issue. Familiarity with men, as brothers and co-workers, helped. Only one of the interviewees was an only child, and the majority had at least one brother. Most had worked in male-dominated occupations, though for scientists, knowledge of men outside the university tended to be limited, just as many of the men were unfamiliar with women except as mothers, sisters, wives and lovers—not as fellow workers.

Communication problems can arise as a consequence of unfamiliarity with the culture and lifestyle of other expedition members. Pene has thought a lot about this: 'Men and women communicate differently, have different communication priorities, exemplified in the phrase "you just don't understand what I mean". The men in Antarctica are establishing a pecking order, so the conversation is driven by male requirements of establishing that hierarchy, and personal egos.' Like Louise Holliday, Trudy realised she had 'really missed other women when the new women came after the winter'. Michelle, who spent a summer in the field with four men, including her partner, remembers that, back on station, 'there were four or five women together at one time, and we were giggling and carrying on and it was lovely, that female chatter'. Debra wrote down the things she thought she'd miss most, and was a little surprised to find that 'actually, I missed women most'. Experienced leader Monica also missed other women's company, where she found 'the mutual openness that you don't often have with a man'. There are also women who prefer men's company and may be less comfortable with a group of women.

The bonds formed between expedition members, especially those who winter together, are complex. New, and different, friendships are a highlight for many. But there are pressures to conform and to maintain group loyalty. Expeditioners talk of 'my pack'. Ros Bowden, who interviewed women in the 1980s for the ABC's *Coming Out* show, found a 'group loyalty' or 'collegiate' phenomenon which she felt prevented even those who were harshly treated from talking about the bad times to outsiders. The reality, however, is that many of the relationships are not sustainable elsewhere, and breaking out of that code of silence has been critical to dealing with the damage that may occur between people and to people under expedition conditions. The silence was broken at the Women in Antarctica conference in 1993, providing relief similar to that felt by women finally believed when they speak about domestic violence.

The ANARE tradition

The 'ANARE tradition' is encountered in some form by everyone who goes to Antarctica. On a 1997 visit, an early winterer found: 'I recognised those expeditioners as the same sort of people I lived and worked with 40 years before.'[15] The ANARE Club, and former expeditioners working in the AAD, reinforce notions about ANARE that were forged in its first decades. Elements of it persist in today's pre-departure briefings and training, despite anti-harassment lectures, often loudly criticised or subverted by male 'old hands'. One staff member admitted that 'there are dinosaurs everywhere. Women who go to the Antarctic need to recognise this, and they need to equip women better who go, train them, give them skills and knowledge to cope better. Women think "it will change over time", "the second time will be better", "some day it will stop". With different recruitment programs it will be better, eventually.' Entrenched attitudes are hard to change, especially when subtly reinforced, and meanwhile it seems that the responsibility for preparedness and understanding is placed, unequally, at women's feet.

Images like the 'loyal buddy' and 'brave explorer' hold strong appeal, and even the anticipation of hardship is exciting. The images come from another era, before women were admitted, when bases were little more than primitive camps and behaviour could be crude. This was before equal opportunity, anti-harassment and personal safety in the workplace became legislated public service concerns. In the present communications era, the regulations and restrictions enhance the attraction of earlier times to many expeditioners. Janet noted some consequences: 'The men on the project talked down to women; they were trying to model themselves on the heroic era and it was inappropriate.'

Today, the explorer mentality and content of stories handed down from previous expeditions is considered very 'boys' own', especially (though not exclusively) by women. Caroline, speaking

of the hirsute topiary of 'silly haircuts' that mark special occasions, observed that 'something pushes us into doing it, like
kids playing with fire'. She suggested that it may have a different
tenor now that the expectations and rules of the all-male groups
have been affected by women, and they in turn have been
around long enough for the 'we'd better be on our best behaviour' ethos to have weakened. Another man from the pre-women
era who also travelled South again in 1997 commented: 'I was
also to see the effect that women had on expedition life. We had
fifteen women on board . . . Whilst the social life on the ship was
a lot less bawdy and raunchy than in years gone by, there was a
great deal more organised entertainment which was enjoyed and
participated in by all. So, whilst it may sound as though life was
somewhat inhibited compared to years ago, it did not detract in
any way from the fun and enjoyment of the voyage.'[16]

Excessive drinking, often the result of peer pressure, is recognised as the most common ingredient in unpleasantness.[17] It
lessens inhibitions and promotes horseplay and lewdness.
'Katrina' wondered why they needed to be so crude, and suggested: 'It's for camaraderie rather than sex, boys' own stuff,
wanking rather than doing.' Women talked about having to
censor themselves—to 'suppress my personality'—and no doubt
men who are different also do this, though some women suggested they were at least within the over-arching bonds of
masculinity. Extroversion may be a defence against the scary
emptiness of Antarctica, and an attempt to protect or assert
oneself in an unfamiliar human environment, and alcohol easily
promotes this. Stereotyped behaviour also occurs. It is a form of
distancing, noted in the all-female German group as well as all-
male and mixed ones. Ceremonies and practical jokes may ease
tension.

'Traditions' like the midwinter *Cinderella* performance offend
many contemporary sensitivities. However, attempts to stop the
performance may lead to conflict between stalwarts who wish to
keep such traditions intact, and those wanting to discover new
ways to celebrate midwinter. Blue movie nights and 'historic'

pornographic displays and magazines also provoke controversy. Some women have fought for the removal of all pornography, against strong opposition. Some women were not at all bothered by it, whereas others found it offensive and sometimes threatening. Julie, who works with BAS, felt 'women don't like pornography on base. It's a workplace—you would not have it in the office here. Also, it presents women as sex objects. If it affects one woman out of 20 it's not right. It also affects the image of the base with visitors.'[18] Women have succeeded in having the page three pin-up girl removed from the version of the daily news sheet in the mess, but it may resurface in the 'club' version, adding to some women's discomfort there.[19] Joan suggests:

> The reason we had pornographic objects and pictures around the station was not because anybody was getting off on it, or felt more at home with them, or actively felt pleasure from their being there, but that it symbolised to the majority of expeditioners, who were male, that this was a male space. Women were there as grace and favour members.

Excessive drinking and heavily sexual humour are offensive to men as well as women, though it is more often women who protest. And, notwithstanding legislation against harassment and pornography in public places, and the ANARE personal code of conduct, introduced for all expeditioners in 1987, protest against sexist and larrikin behaviour is unfortunately associated with the 'new' Antarcticans. It may be resisted as breaching the tradition. The image of the tough, self-reliant, risk-taking man mythologised and exaggerated in the notion of the 'Antarctic legend' also conflicts with the reality of work in Antarctica today. It surfaces in subversive and potentially dangerous ways, the more so when these are officially forbidden, such as covert recreational crevasse ascents and descents ('slotting') and the use of some vehicles.

It can also take more than a very broad sense of humour to feel comfortable with off-colour practical jokes which target specific community members. These are more than simple childish games, and underline the object's alienation from the dominant

group. And, while sub-groups usually form round common interests, more compatible values or particular individuals—usually
women—there are pressures over winter for the group to see
itself as an entity. This is emphasised through the concern with
harmony, which Meredy defines as the basis for genuine fun in
Antarctica. It can become peace—'at any price', women noted.
It implies giving in to the majority. Some women have been
poorly evaluated in formal assessment—and shunned—for
opposing things they find unacceptable.

In 1960, Phillip Law listed the qualities of a good expeditioner
as 'one who was good at their job, unselfish (willing to pitch
in and help in general station work), tolerant, capable of self-
control, optimistic, possessing "stickability" (in carrying a work
program through), and with a sense of adventure and curiosity'.[20]
Organisational ability, skills in communication and conflict res-
olution, perceptiveness, hard work and a readiness to learn from
others were high on Mandy's list, and others stressed tolerance,
a sense of humour and flexibility. Fairness, a light hand but the
courage to make unpopular decisions, team-building and motivation were added to the station leader profile.[21]

Strong echoes of mainstream Australian culture

Underpinning ANARE culture is mainstream Australian culture,
with its mateship, anti-authoritarianism and apparently easy-
going egalitarianism. There are also remnants of the
Anglo-colonial explorer tradition, which embraced some elitism
within expeditions. ANARE proudly boasts of its democratic
tradition, though leadership styles vary. Australian forms of
anti-authoritarianism add to the belief that bureaucracy has no
place in Antarctica.

However, there is an implicit class system in both Australia and
Antarctica. The structural rules of the workshop are different to
those in a laboratory. On station, the hierarchy may be ambigu-
ous and styles of leadership may strongly clash with expectations
of authority and roles in decision-making. Lifestyle associated

with class is a basis for sub-group formation. Power resides with those who are seen as most vital for the group's survival, which can place scientists, or 'boffins', low on the pecking order. This may be enhanced because the professions in general have been more 'feminised' than the trades, perhaps increasing resistance to women as tradespeople as well as lowering esteem for all professionals. Volunteers, all working for science, may have a particularly hard time. Women, who are most likely to occupy science-based positions in Antarctica, can be doubly demoted as female 'boffins'.

A 'wine and cheese' versus 'beer and chips' divide may arise, and several women said they had experienced station life as an 'intellectual desert'. Women can greatly enjoy learning new physical and manual skills, or letting the 'tomboy' side emerge, and some tradespeople become involved with science projects. Friendships with people one does not normally meet are often cited as one of the positive features of Antarctica. An aspect of the dominance of a blue-collar male culture, as 'Hilary' pointed out, is that 'there's a strong element of "let the legend live!" in ANARE. We don't talk about feelings, and we don't talk about missing people when we're down there, of issues that imply vulnerability, or being anything other than a good Aussie bloke'.

True to the cultural stereotype, mateship is celebrated on stations on ANZAC Day.[22] In 1997 Pene wrote:

So today is ANZAC Day. There is a whole day of 'celebrations' and activities. It drives me bananas! So, as in 1990, I'm just not participating. At least this year I knew to bring some food up here to work so that I don't have to go back to the mess, because then you can't avoid the activity. I just can't condone ANZAC Day activities. And everyone seems to need alcohol to have a good time here. The station leader didn't try to organise anything for International Women's Day! 'Ah,' some might say, 'but it isn't a public holiday and not seen by many as particularly relevant to Australia's nationhood.' Well, I bet a lot of other Australians don't see the relevance of ANZAC Day to being an Australian now, either!

Traditional Australian culture defines male and female behaviour, attitudes to the other and interactions. But women are catching up with men in many fields in contemporary Australia, especially if you do not look too closely behind the statistics— for example, women now constitute 44 per cent of the labour force,[23] ignoring their particular occupations, job security or pay. Equality between the sexes is widely advocated, but how far does this penetrate into people's beliefs? It is frequently pointed out in relation to ANARE that many of the men come from occupations, and working environments, where women appear—if at all—in subsidiary roles. Combine this with a strong sense of mateship, fostered in a particular way in expeditioner training and the experience of being together in a harsh environment, and with the reality of the womanless stations when the ANARE myths were forged, and the Antarctic 'men's club' is easily understood. Women are admitted on male terms, though they have indisputably won their places on their own merits.

IMPLICATIONS FOR WOMEN

Antarctic culture has not only been forged by men, but remains heavily masculine in its basic structure and atmosphere. How women fit into this culture, and its effects on relationships, are discussed in Chapter 5. Some implications for women of the physical, social and cultural aspects are raised here.

Speaking of the 1960s and 1970s, Jutta noted: 'It's really incredible, but in those days, and it's not so long ago, a lot of people used to say that "Women cannot do these things"—put a rucksack on and rubber boots and go off walking. Once you were there nobody doubted, you [would] just do it.' Susan Barr, who has worked in the Arctic for several decades with independent expeditions, as well as spending one season in Antarctica, found that: 'Being a woman in the field has not caused any problems, rather just a few peculiarities, like being asked whether I can manage a gun, where no man is asked about that.'[24] She added: 'But being a woman in this field, in the professions, in institutions on the mainland, is not quite so easy.'

Women in Antarctica, as elsewhere, have had to struggle for recognition as competent professionals. Mandy explained:

> Sometimes, as a woman, you get landed with the mother/sister/ wife syndrome for being in the kitchen. I could scream for being seen like that. It's hard for people to treat you as a professional, and it's not seen as a serious trade like a plumber. People say "my mother cooks". They don't realise that it's a four-year apprenticeship and five years' experience and other things before being eligible to go South.

Others, like Michelle, have found station leaders 'patronising and restricting'. Competent women, with outdoor and technical skills, are beyond the experience of many of the men in Antarctica, and women's youth may also count against them. Men may be reluctant to let them go outdoors, as 'Jade' found: 'Old timers have a definite attitude to new people. They don't want to do things like skiing themselves, but don't want new people to do them either, and are disparaging of them.'

Discussing the general stress on performance in Antarctica, Jane Wilson observed: 'It doesn't matter what gender you are, you earn respect for what you are. Women are under more scrutiny initially, not given as many opportunities in Antarctica—for example, going out in Zodiacs—but ultimately this breaks down though you still have a struggle, too.' Another hurdle is there for scientists: 'You need to show you have life skills to be accepted as a boffin.' 'Charlotte' was put in place by a 20-year-old male companion: 'At the end of the trip we got home and were feeling very pleased with ourselves, and I remember him saying: "Well, you did really well for an older woman!" I thought "aarrgggghhhh!" and all my sort of rampant feminism came to the fore! But I held my tongue because I thought: "Well, fair enough, I did, and you did much of the work, so I could hardly complain!"'

As Mandy noted, there is a tendency to consign women to traditional female roles, something which may or may not be appreciated by women. Station leader after station leader commented in reports and logs on how well women were playing a social role for the group, leading one woman to comment on the need for more women 'to share the nurturing'. It bears out Phillip Law's perception, mentioned in Chapter 1, that women would be helpful to men in Antarctica. Pia noticed that: 'It's much harder for women. It's an all-male environment. You have to be one of them, but also their mother, sister, counsellor— trying to be professional and scientific and mothering too!'

Women seem to be expected to carry a far higher emotional workload than men. In fact, the general emotional vacuum on station was one aspect that weighed heavily on a number of women. Debra acknowledged that 'men are mentally more closed', and that 'you pull into yourself anyway in winter, and men seemed very hard to reach'. A consequence of this is the apparent lack of concern for how people are surviving emotionally. Louise C. said: 'The traditional culture of Antarctica is such that it's so male. There is a lack of interest in the inner storms you weather and that sort of thing, so that the culture, even more than ordinary Australian culture, encourages that internalisation of the inner storms—there's a sense that it's kind of wimpish.'

There is, in a word, a silencing of a whole human experience. It even extends beyond the Antarctic itself, as 'Hilary' found.

When I got back, the language that you're given to talk about the experience is very restricted, so people say: 'what was it like?' and there is an acceptable response to that. So you talk about the dramatic scenery, you talk about the scale of Antarctica and how it blows you out, the colours and all of those things, and that's about as emotional as you can get about it, talking about the colours, and even then it's a bit sort of sus. And you can talk about the stations, and you can be practical, you can even talk about rubbish on the stations. But what you don't talk about is the remarkable interpersonal stuff that's happened on your voyage, and no doubt that happens at stations.

Others have said that they talk about whether or not it was a good season, not how they experienced it.

There's no privacy in the fishbowl

While the lack of privacy affects all expeditioners, it seems particularly important to women, who are very visible—perhaps more for what they symbolise than for themselves: expected to be there for others but with very little consideration of their wants and needs. Estelle admitted that 'an aspect of going to Antarctica that I hadn't anticipated was that even though you're in the remotest place on the planet you have the least personal privacy. It was quite humbling. Being with people I didn't know and with few outlets was stressing.' Bridget explains, 'there's not pressure you wouldn't experience here, but here you can get away from it'.

This sense of being trapped is both very real—especially in the cramped quarters on ship or field camp—and also intangible. It is personal and emotional as much as physical. In Ruth Eriksen's experience, 'on one [marine science] trip, there was a sense of no escape if there was a personal crisis or conflict'.

A small, enclosed community will always magnify things. Apparently selfish behaviour, like over-indulgence in a food item in short supply—for instance, peanut butter or chocolate biscuits—can become a big issue in the group, and last for weeks. In the words of one scientist: 'It's a hard place to live, small issues become big things, misunderstandings get blown out of all proportion.' She thought that this was at the root of gender misunderstanding, too: someone is very tired and perhaps stressed, someone else makes a comment, and the woman over-reacts. It's hard, given the dynamics and the different ways men and women tend to 'socialise, talk, do things', to step back from bad feelings that have been triggered on both 'sides'. Many also believed that the group was too small to deal openly with even low-level conflict. Diana Patterson suggested, however, that tolerance could exacerbate a situation, with an offender not

97

getting messages about the effect of the behaviour on others. To challenge a member of one's small group, when there is no escape for months, nevertheless requires self-confidence, experience, courage and a belief that one will be supported. Experiences teach that this is not necessarily the case, as a number of women tearfully recounted.

Another aspect of living in a small community is the way in which some interactions invade personal space, summed up in the phrase 'getting inside your head'. This seems to occur particularly in male–female interactions, and is a form of both distancing and provocation. Corinna found that it was 'smothering. They repeat the process with one personal question after the next. They don't give you the space a courteous person would. Basically, they force themselves on you and try to go somewhere (in your head) which is definitely out of bounds to almost all of the outside world except those you yourself invite in. It feels very much a *violation*.' She added: 'You're the one who's got to deal with it when you're really not the problem.' One result can be, as Joan put it, that a woman suffers intense 'marginality and alienation. At every level of my being. Every single level of my being.'

Working and playing together

The experience of teamwork in Antarctica can be a high point. With the present stations, occasions for teamwork have diminished. It occurs for major events like the annual resupply, a huge logistic feat when everyone helps unload the ship in a race against the weather. Phillipa, an experienced logistics manager, described the operation of a construction group.

If men are having a big pour of concrete or something, it's hard work but they love it. They get right into it and they talk about the big pour, and 'We've got another, I reckon there'll be ten truckloads.' 'You reckon ten? I reckon there's twelve in that pour' and they banter more. They'll turn it into a fun thing. Whereas because women don't do that kind of work, you don't see women being like that so much. I used to love it, and on a number of occasions would drive the BAG trucks, and do pours, and it was always just really good fun, because you'd usually do a pour on a really good day anyway, so the weather was wonderful, and you'd have the boys up at the batching plant, and they'd be all covered with dirt and cement—it's the shittiest stuff in the world, it's a filthy, dirty, stinking, rotten job. And they're all laughing and chatting and having a cigarette. Then 'Let's get it ready' and they'd get it all mixed and all ready. There's a kind of loudness and it's unrestrained; there's an energy about the work that they're doing because it is physically hard work and demanding— you've got to wear masks and you've got dust in everything, you can't touch anything without concrete dust on it, and women aren't generally involved in those sorts of things. And I just love jumping up and climbing up to the back of the AGI and putting the water in, and 'Yeah, turn it on!' and pouring in the mixes 'cos there's all this stuff you put in it, and working the AGI, and 'Whoa, slow it down, slow it down!' You interact with a lot more people—and that's the other thing, the teamwork. And many many many of the women going there do not work in teams and that's absolutely it, it's the teamwork stuff. And I do envy men that, because I just loved it.

Because of her profession, Phillipa is one of the few women who can gain admission to this sort of Antarctic team. As Angela Rhodes noted:

In Phil Law's days, with the boys together, who all did things together, they had a lot of fun. Now the stations are so complicated you need self-starting specialists, who get on with the job. They talk about team development, but they're not selecting those people—I had a sense of a bunch of individuals on the station in my year. There are not many jobs that can be interchanged.

Cooperation is required for the search and rescue (SAR) team, the fire team or the theatre team in a medical emergency. Apart from the doctors, women have found it hard to be included in the SAR or fire teams, and miss out on the bonding that goes on at the additional pre-departure and in-field training of these

groups. For women, teamwork mostly occurs through participation in others' work. However, as summer field leader in the
Prince Charles Mountains (PCMs), Louise Crossley was able to
instigate the cleaning up of an old field base, using helicopters
to return the junk to the station for shipping back to Australia.
Everybody agreed to participate and:

> worked like absolutely bloody dogs ... When we finally got back
> to the camp, somebody who had been there all day had cooked
> this fantastic dinner, and we sat in the sun outside the mess with
> a beer. There was that sense of relaxation after the hard work,
> and a sense of satisfaction that was palpable amongst everybody
> ... It was something that I had wanted to do and had initiated it,
> and had thought: 'Is this OK, is this the right thing to do, is it
> fair to ask them to do it?' and then the outcome was so positive
> for everybody, there's that kind of empowerment where the
> outcomes are very good, and there's that sense of communal
> satisfaction.

In some years there is a group to organise the social activities,
and some years also have a peer support group, almost inevitably
including women. Social events have been the highlight for
many, especially the midwinter or Christmas festivities, or special
Saturday dinners. Elanor commented on midwinter: 'The day
itself is the highlight of the entire year, full of unfettered good-
will and fun. That was probably the only time I truly felt we were
a fully interactive team.' The new stations with access to television
have reduced the necessity for group social activities.

The ultimate event was an Antarctic wedding, held at Davis on
3 September 1994. The bride, Denise Jones, has wintered on all
four stations, and met her husband (Colin Blobel) there. She
recalls: 'The ceremony was a big station effort—the chef had
broken a leg so they all joined in. We had champagne, orange
juice, croissants at 10.30 a.m., and it flowed from there. I wore a
full wedding dress, Colin wore a suit and all ... It was a good
day. In the *Yearbook*, 90 per cent of the expeditioners put down
the wedding as the highlight of the year.'

Ultimately, being seen to do one's job well is the major criterion for acceptance in Antarctica. Women have gained acceptance as competent workers. A number set themselves very high work standards there to be above criticism, a fact which was noticed by some of the men. But is that enough? ANARE's oral tradition contains stories about strange blokes who are remembered affectionately, both for their work skills and their oddity, or the obverse, for one has to do something outlandish in order to become an 'Antarctic legend'. But, as one woman pointed out, it is only women's actual or alleged sexual behaviour that admits them to the legendary ranks, and there is a definite sense that there is less tolerance for women then men who may not conform to the group expectations. Some women still feel that there is an inner club from which their gender forever debars them, while others don't want to be part of a 'boys' own' culture anyway.

Monica attempted to pinpoint the effects: 'If you feel uncomfortable in male society, what is it? Not harassment, it's just different—for example, men's shoes are much bigger and they smell different. You're surrounded by masculinity and that can become exhausting. It depends on a woman herself how she reacts.' For Melanie, among others, it was:

an oppressively male environment . . . just the repeated messages that females don't belong here, and all the subtle stuff that comes through, the jokes, the harking back to the period before women were down there, it just made me feel that I didn't belong there. It's a whole atmosphere, a whole mood; it's not a specific sentence someone said or act someone did, but their whole behaviour pattern that creates this mood that tells you that you shouldn't be there.

But women *are* in Antarctica. Despite the Antarctic remaining, to many, the last bastion of the male hero, and despite women's history of being excluded from most fields of public life, they are changing the nature of the Antarctic experience irrevocably.

FIVE

'If you pat one, pat them all!'

What is it like being a woman in Antarctica? Does living in such unusual circumstances create specific problems or issues? According to 'Tamara': 'If women want equality here or in the Antarctic, there should be no more or less interest in their problems in Antarctica. Making a special issue out of it can work against women South who, being in a minority already, have a spotlight on their foibles and human-ness.' Other women simply said: 'Not a problem! We're all people there.'

Like Astrida, women can 'feel more like a woman down there as a result of the interaction with the men'. Looking back, 'Rowena' 'certainly did feel special because I was female', while Helen B. found 'the red carpet still happens for women there; it's very nice'. There are reciprocal obligations, as 'Geraldine' noted: 'There are physical differences and sometimes you need to accept this; you recognise other people's skills and talents and they recognise your own and you can help each other out.'

There is mutual watching between expeditioners and, despite the heavy, unisex, outdoor clothing,[1] people learn to identify each other by gestures and body language. You cannot be anonymous in Antarctica and, as Angela McG. explains, 'being a woman is somehow different to being just "someone" there'. This has several dimensions: the pressure of male attention;

being treated differently; and the sexuality of 'man-watches-woman', who is vastly outnumbered.

Of the 1970s, Elizabeth Kerry commented: 'You realised it was a bit unusual for women to go and that you'd be watched and noticed and some would disapprove of women being there. I didn't experience any antagonism.' More recently, 'Cara' found: 'It's a bit annoying at times; you get lots of attention and can't escape. You have to tolerate it, take it as it comes, joke about it. You need to get acceptance as a person. Some expeditioners like to get a rise out of women if they can.' 'The men watch what the women do; they notice how much time a man spends with a woman'; 'during my month on station, people would start talking if I spent time with any of the men'. This behaviour is so widespread that Lynn Williams suggested treating the men the way you would the huskies: 'If you pat one, pat them all!'

There is a strong sense that women have a social obligation to the men. 'The social hurdles for women are different to [those for] men,' 'Winsome' observed. Men expect women to be there for them, as 'Helena' noted: 'I experienced intense pressure. I told one good male friend and he then observed and backed me up. There's no privacy, or sense of space; the men believe women are there to emotionally service them. You have to back off. A lot of men are not aware of this pressure.' Most of the women *are* aware of it.

Some of the pressure is about women's ability to perform. Gwen said: 'It's more when you suddenly sense that you're being treated by men like a woman that it dawns on you there is a difference—for example, when they are condescending towards you.' 'Jade' 'felt low when I was made to feel different'. As discussed in Chapter 3, women may feel vulnerable because they lack experience with mechanical things, but they also feel they have to over-perform in their normal work.

Inevitably, in such a small, isolated, male-dominated community, there is a sexual overtone to the scrutiny of women. There appeared to be a fear of the development of sexual relationships underpinning the reluctance to allow women to stay on station and to winter. Such concerns have been associated with mixed groups in other remote situations. Denise Allen reported that: 'On being selected for Willis Island in 1983 I received a half hour lecture from senior Bureau [of Metereology] staff regarding only four staff members being posted for six months and they didn't want four and a half coming back!' There is even current speculation about sexual relationships on the space station.

Anitra expressed this concern about sex dramatically: 'Women are still regarded by many as "sexual hand grenades" waiting to go off!' Or, in Meredy's words: 'A female in Antarctica gets slotted into a pigeonhole. You're fair game, they think you must be looking for something so they test you out.' Denise Allen, a Meteorology staff member, talks about being called the 'weather girl'. 'But they were really referring to "whether she will or whether she won't" as a subject for male speculation. Such a woman will be the subject of intense rumouring and competition between men. I have observed men having difficulty coping, showing anger, disappointment or feeling rejected, when unattached women on a base became attached.'

As 'Geraldine' said: 'Men often speculate right at the start who are the "free" women and I think women speculate about the men too. I know a couple of men had a bit of adjusting to do when I was obviously involved with my partner and they weren't in the running any more. Often men are not satisfied with a platonic relationship, a non-sexual one. They withdraw when there is obviously a "sexual other" in one's life.' However, when Denise Allen wintered with her partner in 1992, she found 'other men became more approachable and felt more comfortable with a friendship developing once they realised I was part of a couple. Being selected as a couple was accepted more readily by others than those who developed relationships during the year.'

Stories of sexual pressures are passed to newcomers. Two young female scientists, each in strong relationships in Australia with men who had been to Antarctica, summed up the anxiety that can build up. 'Schifra' was 'a little bit scared at first, I hadn't

Pene Greet, Meredy Zwar
and Fiona Scott, Davis
wintering women, 1997.
(Courtesy Pene Greet)

Liv Arnesen at the end of her solo expedition to the South Pole, Christmas
Day 1994. (Courtesy Liv Arnesen)

Debra Enzenbacher, South Pole Station winterer, 1987– 88.
(Courtesy Debra Enzenbacher)

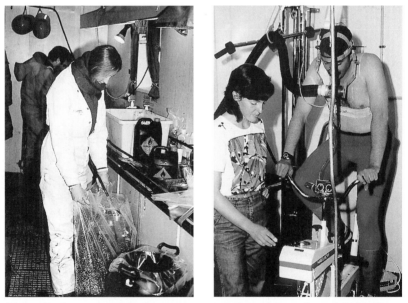

Tonia Cochran preparing specimens in the wet lab on board *Nella Dan*,
Marine Science Voyage, Prydz Bay, 1987. (Courtesy Tonia Cochran).
Gillian Deakin doing clinical testing for her medical research program,
Davis, 1986. (Courtesy Gillian Deakin)

Jane Wasley assists Sharon Robinson take a moss sample, Casey, 1998 /99. (Photo Annie Rushton)

Jennifer and Patricia Selkirk (daughter and mother), Jessie Nicol Creek Valley, Macquarie Island, December 1989. (Courtesy Patricia Selkirk)

Left: Elanor Bell drilling a core to take a water sample, Ace Lake, Davis, 1996. (Courtesy Elanor Bell). Right: A penguin butter sculpture by Meredy Zwar (with partner Mike Manion) made for the midwinter dinner, Davis, 1997. (Courtesy Pene Greet)

Medical officer Gillian Deakin moonlighting as a cement truck operator when it was all hands on deck to lay the foundations for the new Operations Building, Davis, 1986. (Courtesy Gillian Deakin)

Elanor Bell doing slushy duty, Davis, 1996. (Courtesy Elanor Bell)

Station leader Louise Crossley at field training, Macquarie Island, 1999. (Courtesy Louise Crossley)

Morag Anderson as a punk, Easter fancy dress party, Davis 1990. (Courtesy Morag Anderson, photo Ray Pike)

Denise Allen and an albatross chick, Macquarie Island, 1985. (Courtesy Denise Allen)

A polar pyramid tent in use during field training at O'Brien Bay, Casey, 1995. Left to right: Gary Kuehn (field training officer), Ross Anderson, Suenor Woon. (Photo Robin Burns)

Morag Anderson at Platcha Hut (a typical field hut), Davis, 1990. (Courtesy Morag Anderson)

The first ANARE women on the continent, Casey, 1976. Left to right: Jutta Hösel, Shelagh Robinson and Elizabeth Chipman. (Australian Antarctic Division photo by Glenn Foote © Commonwealth of Australia, 1976, neg 29220)

Elizabeth Chipman at Casey, 1975. (Australian Antarctic Division photo by Glenn Foote © Commonwealth of Australia, 1975, neg 29226)

heard anything very positive, mainly from two men in my department who've been. I was a bit worked up about it and on the
defensive for the first couple of weeks. I think for a woman you
have to be fairly strong emotionally, avoid intimidation and stand
your ground and have plenty to do.' 'Belle' had 'heard stories of
tradies traipsing around after women. I expected that so gave out
strong "go away guys" messages, but I haven't seen any of that.
We're still in a minority, but there have been no problems like
that really.' However, she too thought that 'one of the things
that can be hard about being a female down there is the attention you receive'.

YES, SEXUAL RELATIONSHIPS DO HAPPEN IN ANTARCTICA

In the early days of ANARE, the director, Phillip Law, advised
men to forget sex and to work hard. He considered the absence
of women a hardship, but that work and adventure would go
some way to compensate. This hardship is evidenced for many
male expeditioners by fantasies expressed in the log books in
field huts. There are, however, some men today who would still
prefer women-free stations. In the Aussie mateship myth, opposition and antagonism by men hinges on women's potential to
disrupt male solidarity and to introduce the distractions and conflicts associated with sexual interest, competition and
relationships. Not only do women intrude on the 'easy' relationships between mates, they distract them and may provoke strife.
   Statistically, Antarctica provides women with a good chance of
partnering. In the first decades they were there, most women felt
that a relationship was not possible, because of their position in
Antarctica and also because of the general mores of the time.
Yet Hope Macpherson, for example, thought that relationships
'are bound to happen! Put two or three women and a dozen
men in a small place for twelve months, and you are bound to
have problems—even here'. She felt, however, that it was a
'modern attitude not to deny sex'. In her generation, 'women

had an obligation to watch their behaviour', but now 'there are no restrictions'. Pauline Reilly, who celebrated her sixtieth birthday on Macquarie Island in 1978, suggested: 'Handling sex requires maturity. It had been a big problem for my generation. It's a different ball game for the younger generation: it's all expressed in an open way. I had long yarns about sex with one or two of the younger guys, because I was older. You need to not judge people. I was thankful I was not placed in the position of being younger.' Nevertheless: 'There were the usual innuendos and passes, but it was not a problem.'

Few spoke of their fantasies, but one early winterer asked: 'Have you thought about the effects on female sexuality of all those men doing very manly things?' Now, there is almost an expectation amongst women as well as men that women will have a sexual relationship during an expedition.

In addition to available, importuning men, women highlight two aspects of partnering. One is the pleasure of sharing such a peak experience in an intimate relationship. There is the special nature of a relationship formed in Antarctica, and of sharing the memories of it with your partner. One-third of the women I interviewed had been in Antarctica at the same time as their current partner, though fewer than half that proportion had started the relationship there. Sixty-five per cent had a partner who had been in Antarctica at some stage.

The second reason for partnering in Antarctica is to handle the various pressures. Since men are numerically dominant in the pack, and given the small numbers of women, it is likely that particularly close relationships will be cross-gender ones for most women. Women say that the need for intimacy, and for some protection from the sexual pressures in general, prompts them to select one man. A close friendship and the need for closeness often lead to sex. 'Rowena' simply admitted: 'I developed a relationship of convenience there. I'm an emotional person, he was nice and you need someone to be close to.' Many have experienced this. 'Wanda' elaborated: 'There's isolation, emotionally, and it's lonely; it's necessary to draw a support group around you—friends, people you feel more comfortable with—and with women and men that's likely to lead to a sexual relationship, but you have to put it in perspective of life in Australia.' She began a close friendship towards the end of the season when she was very tired, lonely and in need of companionship: 'It was appropriate for Antarctica but not necessarily appropriate back home.' Pene advised:

> I have really tried to emphasise how much you have to be careful when choosing to go into a relationship. You have to see that person every day until you leave whether the relationship continues or not. I also like to note that you have to consider the person you are taking as a partner. Is he going to be able to cope with the pressure the other men will put on him? Your partner needs to be strong and able to stand up for himself in the group. He needs to be able to live on station without being one of the boys.

What happens after returning from Antarctica can be difficult for both men and women when one has been more involved than the other. To find a wife or girlfriend meeting the boat has deeply hurt some women, and a close Antarctic friend is threatening to the wife or girlfriend left behind. Nor are men the only ones to leave old relationships during their time in Antarctica, and some women have gone South determined to resolve a relationship. The women who have occupied the Expeditioner Family Liaison Officer position in the AAD are very familiar with the toll on relationships when one partner goes to Antarctica.

One woman thought that 'you can have good friends with men on a relatively normal basis—if both are grounded. If there's a problem of communication, they can push you and you can get confused—women probably get more hurt than the men, they think it's real but they betrayed themselves.' A friend with whom one can 'be oneself' is valued in Western culture. Some women in Antarctica have been lucky to find a man who is sufficiently supportive and trustworthy. Pene said: 'It was a very supportive relationship.' Nevertheless, it can affect the position of both in the group: 'Because of it we were less part of the group than we would have been as individuals. More emotionally independent. We both got criticised for not socialising enough, not going to the club.'

To contain competition between men, and control women, promiscuity—especially female promiscuity—is frowned on and unsettles the group; and the sexual activities of a married woman, real or rumoured, raise fears about the behaviour of wives back home. The tantalising possibility of sex, but the statistical unlikelihood of satisfying it, upsets and frustrates men, which can lead to negative feelings towards women in general.

There may be resentment of the possibility that every woman who goes to Antarctica can 'get it', and with choice, whereas few men can. Those who do may be envied and even ostracised, depending on how discreetly they behave in public, and how both partners relate to the group in general. 'Davina' confirmed this: 'When our partnering became general knowledge it was a big upset on station and half a dozen men came singly to me and said: "You shouldn't have done that." If I'd partnered one of them they wouldn't have said that! This was one of the biggest upsets for me that winter: one of the men didn't speak to me for the rest of the year and a few did not speak to my partner.'

Mateship may be reasserted when a woman dares to change partner on station, though this will depend on the esteem in which each is held. It is commonly stated by men that an established couple—one formed before embarkation—is appreciated as a reminder of normal society, so long as they are not flagrantly affectionate in public or too withdrawn, and a discreet couple formed down South may also be appreciated if each is liked. 'Katy' commented: 'Others don't have bad feelings about a pair unless you're rubbing their faces in it. As long as you're pretty discreet, sex is OK.'

Both men and women criticise flirtatious or promiscuous women. General 'girlie' behaviour—the so-called 'queen bee' or 'lumpy jumper syndrome'—is particularly frowned on. Kathrine suggests that people 'need to be conscious of flirting, because you're a mixture of generations, a mixture of backgrounds, it's just something that you need to think about, be conscious of'. Some women maintained that they had no control over the messages they gave out, or were unaware of them, though 'J' vehemently responded 'Bullshit!' to this. 'Helena' elaborated: 'Younger women often thrive on the attention they receive, but there's a real cost. It becomes an addiction, and they need to continue getting reinforcement from men, which can lead to competitiveness among the women instead of the minority sticking together. Also, it's superficial and small reward, as they actually service the men's emotional needs. Women often provide emotional support to the men, but it's not reciprocated'—hence the feeling women get of becoming burnt out.

WHOSE PROBLEM IS IT?

A community is more 'normal' when women are present, something which is noticed and appreciated by many men. However, rather than acting as a 'civilising' influence, some men think that women bring out male negative behaviour, and this is considered the fault of women rather than of men's lack of self-control. Distancing or 'othering' of women also occurs when women are abstractly idealised and then placed on a pedestal, and treated with excessive 'care', which can be experienced as claustrophobic. There may be attempts to restrict participation in outside activities and tasks, and sexual possessiveness which may not involve asking for favours, but simply keeping others away and thus restricting free association. The simple twofold categorisation of women as 'damned whores or God's police' persists.[2] Then there is the 'queen bee', a woman who is possessive of all the men in her 'hive'. Men may also behave in a similar fashion towards 'their' women against newcomers. Both these cases tend to be group phenomena and, while possessiveness is involved, the 'owner' turns aggression against others of her or his kind. Susan Headley's thesis on Antarctic women provides a valuable analysis of the ways in which station culture has maintained male rule over women, who are regarded as communal property.[3]

Human beings can exercise choice, however, and have responsibility for their behaviour. Neither the unbalanced male:female ratio in Antarctica, nor the remoteness of the location, is an excuse for harassment of others, or for reduced responsibility for one's acts. Monica Kristensen suggests that 'women can change their behaviour. If they perceive themselves and act as a victim, they become "soft" and timid. It's not harassment but a role they step into.' They can also deliberately provoke men. Women are not passive and may actively encourage sexual games, though all women are not potential seductresses just because they are women, just as all men are not incipient rapists. Isolated incidents can become inflated. Yet it seems there is a strong tendency always to blame women for the problematic aspects of male–female relationships in Antarctica. The nature of Antarctic small-community life and its masculine ethos is inclined to spread stories of sexualised female behaviour in ways that permit, or foreground, male 'exploits'. Kathrine explained that 'men flirt too, and yet it's always the woman's problem. You still see a guy say: "He deserved it, she was asking for it" and yet you never hear in that situation of a guy being told he was chasing her. If men chase, and that's acceptable, is it not then acceptable for women to flirt?'

Other women also expressed concern at the one-sided allocation of blame and the double standards for sexual behaviour. Jane W. asked: 'Does women's sexual behaviour affect morale, but men's doesn't?' And 'Beatrice' pointed to the context as well as the effects:

> I could never claim to have been harassed because I was a woman, but many of the things I experienced were exacerbated because I was a woman—for example, being linked with a man, accused of doing it, romances, etc., true or not. The guys didn't experience this to the same degree because the same assumptions here of the girl being the 'slut', 'tart', 'troublemaker', 'seducer', were offset by the man being a 'stud', etc.

There have been proposals by the Antarctic Division to alleviate some of the male–female tensions that focus on female behaviour. One of the most controversial suggests that women should be told about male reactions to their behaviour. What is it like to be a man there who has probably prepared himself for celibacy, and then finds women are available? How do married men react? Do they know the anguish they can cause? Has no one thought to discuss with men what it is like to be a woman there?

Another suggestion commonly heard in Antarctic circles is that women should modify their behaviour. This is a difficult issue, implying self-censoring and stressing the ramifications of individual behaviour for others. Susan Ingham and Isobel Bennett each felt strongly that 'we were very much on our best behaviour'.[4] Four years later, Beth Gott was warned that the 1963 foursome were 'on trial' because a previous woman had 'gone slightly ape encountering all the women-starved men'. Similar admonitions accompanied the first women visiting the continent, and Elizabeth Chipman recalled: 'The hierarchy also made it plain that we were responsible for upholding the highest traditions of decorous behaviour and implied that with us rested the fate of all women on future Australian expeditions.'[5]

Nowadays, as one female station leader observed:

Some of the younger women are not necessarily conscious that women are still a long way from where we could be. They think they can be what they want to be or do, but no one can; we have to make compromises. There's a lack of awareness of one's impact on others—for example, the preparedness to modify behaviour and attitudes. One [woman] got off the ship at Macquarie Island who demanded that the posters come down and then came to parties in fishnet stockings, G-strings and T-shirts. Men need a modification of their behaviour too. Community living requires group consideration.

Remembering that the majority of group members are men, there is a tendency to target and limit women, rather than men, for the sake of the group.

111

Women today are divided on this issue. There is the feminist position that women have a right to be themselves, and to be safe. Against that is the reality of the sex imbalance and the widely different experiences of Antarctic men with women outside their usual associates. Lynn Williams pointed out: 'Oh sure, there were restrictions. You're always on duty as a doctor, too—don't forget party nights are a time when everybody's going to trip over on the way home and knock themselves around, so you've always got a certain amount of constraint, which is just by never being off duty.'

A number of women adopted the realistic position that: 'Women have a right to dress as they like but common sense dictates otherwise.' Ruth Eriksen felt: 'You need to be careful about dress.' Mandy spoke about general behaviour: 'You don't *have* to modify it, but in the interest of a harmonious community, I think it is advisable.' As a personal strategy, Denise Jones found: 'The pressure led to me trying to appear less obvious—for example, I stomped down corridors and hardly ever wore a dress so that when I did, they'd say: "See, she has got legs!"' Similarly, Trudy considered that 'women can't flaunt their sexuality in a small group situation'. Others, like Denise, try to suppress it. Women and men have to decide how they want to behave, and 'Renate's' view is common today: 'Your behaviour down there is a personal issue, and it's not up to me to dictate to others.' However, there is still a tendency to make judgments about a woman more readily than about a man, and some women as well as men were censorious of other women's behaviour.

IMPLICATIONS FOR WOMEN

When we consider women's sexuality in Antarctica, further aspects of the alienation and silencing discussed in Chapter 4 are revealed. Many women feel constrained in the ways they are able to express themselves down there, especially the ways they express their sexuality. The 'blokiness' of the dominant culture is one aspect of this, for there seem to be rules and games that pressure women to conform to male expectations and terms. It's hard to pinpoint, but humour, the round-the-bar atmosphere, the prohibition on expression of emotions have all been given as examples of this 'culture'. Women are approved there if they adopt more 'traditional' roles, which tend to emphasise their role as serving men in various ways. This can result in women feeling they have lost the autonomy to be the person they really are, and that they have to silence important parts of themselves in order to be acceptable. They cannot be expressive and emotional, for example. Then there is the sense of loss of rights as a person, especially the right to safety, which happens when harassment occurs. Many of the women who have experienced harassment have also felt that their right to protest has been denied, either through finding that they cannot gain redress because that would disrupt group harmony, or that they would risk future selection if they complain.

'Approved' female roles

Women are seen as a resource for men, whose continued acceptance depends on fulfilment of expected roles. The mixed groups in Antarctica throw together people whose life experiences one rarely encounters at home. Women underline the fact that this can be a wonderfully enlarging and enriching experience, with long-term friendships formed that may never have happened elsewhere. However, it can lead to conflict based on ignorance, misunderstanding and the micro-dynamics that take place in such an enclosed and limited social environment. The dominant group—men—and the dominant subset within that—tradesmen—not only bring with them a strongly gendered culture, but a limited experience of the dominant female subgroup, scientists. Women who are competent in the world of work expect to be met as workmate rather than 'other'. They encounter men unused to female leaders, or women who both use *and* maintain computers and other complex equipment, or enthusiastically go into the remote field for weeks on end.

The common dominance of a particular male culture on ANARE stations can be a problem for men who do not fit the mould, too. Males vie for position with other men, and the lowest ones, or outcasts, can be pilloried and scorned, which causes pain and anxiety. Women are outside this hierarchy, a fact with two major consequences. They may feel excluded, unable to step through the intangible barrier of gender, or they may be repulsed by the situation.

Outside the male status games, women may enjoy a certain freedom, which includes the opportunity to participate in activities they would not come near at home, like driving heavy equipment or learning trade skills, and they find willing male 'tutors'. For some women, the Antarctic brings out the extrovert and the larrikin, the opportunity for promiscuity and to participate in 'boys' games'. 'Hilary' explained:

> It reminds me very much of being at College in first or second year uni, it's that phenomenon on the station, and on the ship. It's that kind of heady, irresponsible, 'this is time out of time'. You get away, you've left home almost and you head on down there and for girls particularly, you join in, and you're doing boys' things with the boys, you're part of something bigger and more exciting than you'd ever been part of before, or which you could have expected to be, because it still is a frontier, and girls have been excluded from it for so long.

Women need a sense of acceptance and belonging in the group, although this has consequences for their sense of self. As Anitra explained: 'Down South it is so important to feel accepted, liked, a member of the group, so the threat of being put outside that is too hard to bear. So women especially need to be gratified by relationships, human contact.' 'Renate' described an important dimension of this:

> One of the problems is having people to go off station with and feeling comfortable with them—it's an important way to deal with

the isolation. To not be able to go off on your own, and having space, is really important. That can get really difficult. It's positive that people want to 'play' with you but it's hard to be on your own there, or sometimes to go with a group of your choice. That can't be done spontaneously—everything has to be approved which is necessary for safety but it can be a bit stifling.

It's even worse when the 'playmates' want to 'get inside your head and stomp around', as Kirsten and Corinna described it.

Women have to subdue significant parts of themselves to conform to male expectations. For some, this comes naturally. Women 'are able to cooperate well, pick up on subtle things that make a difference'. This is appreciated by other women—or, conversely, really missed when women are perceived not to behave towards others in this way. The point is that it is *expected*. Many women tend to adopt one of three roles in Antarctica that they believe 'protect' them: those of sister, social worker, and one of the boys.

Brothers and sisters

'We're your family now' is a comforting phrase used to create a small safe space for letting go, and many people experience the group in those terms. It is a safe label, expressing mutual obligations between members, though we do know that nasty things can happen beneath its cover. Familial-like participation comes easily to many. Denise Jones said: 'Each time I've gone, I've learnt a bit. I come from a large family and think that helps— you have to be a bit more thoughtful. I didn't work out strategies in advance, but stood aside for a while and watched what was going on.'

Meredy found the sibling relationship to be the safest one:

You don't want to become personally involved with their problems; it's OK as long as it doesn't become too heavy, then it's manageable. You can't be too cold and aloof. You have to try hard to keep your community together; if you want your group to get on, you have to put effort in. I had to be the person they would

115

come to talk to, be neutral and not too close to someone: a brother–sister relationship. Others may not understand it and become jealous so you have to be really careful. You have to give and take, not be the one to make demands—for example, you need to make slushy duty fun so it's a day away from their normal job. They're not kitchen staff with the chef calling the shots.

Meredy worked hard and was recognised through the award of an Antarctic medal.

The sister is often described as a 'little' one, which does not only imply physical size. 'Bibi' explained: 'They had ideas about what one did on station, and were very patronising towards the youngest. They treated me as their little sister and I was not trusted to do things—for example, go off and walk alone. It was OK, but as a woman and the youngest it was not on. They were not happy for me to go; they assumed I was incompetent despite my experience.' Some women like such protectiveness, while others resent it: 'For almost everyone on station I was either a good friend, or someone to be protected in a daughterly or sisterly role. I was aware of that, especially in retrospect, aware that there were a lot of people always there, making sure I was OK and looking after me—a lot there were looking after me. It was really, really lovely,' said Erica, also in her early twenties. However, her mother Heather was criticised by a construction worker on the way down as 'a fool and a bad mother' for letting her daughter go, implying that there was some risk.

Gina suggested that men were more comfortable with women in a setting defined as 'family'. For women used to working as a minority amongst men, slipping into a familial role can be a step backwards into traditional gendered relationships, downplaying work competence or individuality, or simply the easiest way to de-sexualise the situation.

The social worker

A defined caring role within the group is another way to incorporate traditional female roles into the definition of self in Antarctica. Like the 'sister' role, it involves even-handedness, which is a way to put yourself outside the close attentions of any single person except as 'helper'. The role recognises and even exploits gender differences, to fulfil the need to find a legitimate task for group acceptance. It is a role that some women resented being forced into, and some found it was not necessarily free from sexual innuendo. After all, many men fall in love with their nurse, counsellor or confidante!

Sometimes women suspect that men invent woes to claim their attention, which has happened to some female doctors. It can be draining, and the listening is rarely reciprocated. Women may also be unwilling to open up, because of the vulnerability inherent in their minority status, and the fear—sometimes realised—that confidences have not been kept. Women do the emotional work for men: male confides; woman listens, counsels; male goes off relieved; woman worries. According to one summing up: 'Women give men a lot of support in Antarctica—it's the biggest benefit they've given to the cultural ethos; men have somewhere to seek support from. Women can be isolated there.'

Some women are outgoing and form a sub-group where they feel comfortable, getting pleasure out of 'looking after' others. 'Rowena', for example, described herself as:

> outgoing, very social. Friends are more important than work, especially there. I felt my role the second summer was to support my friends, over winter my closest friends were trades ones rather than academic ones. You work long days. After work you want to be with the people you're most comfortable with. I am normally happy, and a social organiser!

Nevertheless, she felt: 'If you're not careful, your true personality can get suppressed. If you don't fit into the mould, it's hard, you're very dependent on people there.' It took a long time to dissipate the anger at feeling she was letting herself be controlled by others, and that it happened because, as a woman, she stood out socially. In addition to finding this role burdensome, some resent the ascription of nurturing to them as if it is natural for all women, and available to any man.

One of the boys

The desire to be 'one of the boys' is another way to express group membership and downplay gender differences. It has boarding school or holiday camp overtones, but also reveals a longing to fit in, to be accepted by the dominant group and cast off the burden of one's gender. Participation becomes central, especially around the bar, sharing drinks and jokes, not objecting to the language that might be used, wanting to be part of what has been presented as the full Antarctic experience. It is an attempt to participate in the male camaraderie, and to overcome the differences that gender seems to impose.

Thinking of oneself as 'one of the boys' equates the concepts of 'male' and 'normal'. As Leslie suggested:

> There's a real macho thing, which makes it hard for women. You're expected to be one of the boys and you have to take a lot of teasing. There's a Catch-22 as women are looked down on in a way if they do that. Women still have a really hard time. They're expected to take a lot of rough and tumble and bullshit. Men think social rules don't apply there.

Pene suggested further implications:

> Being one of the fellas is one of the distinct ways of coping down there, and is acceptable to both men and women. It doesn't upset the power dynamics. If you play that role you can't take a stand on issues, especially on women's issues, or determine your behaviour. You must be happy to have the group determine it.

To see oneself as 'one of the boys' may mask uncertainties about how to handle one's sexuality, and observations suggest that those using this strategy are often flirtatious, perhaps deluding themselves about their desire to be ungendered. Gina observed: 'It's ironic about being "one of the boys" and having relationships! Does it mean they're playing the male game? To

118

play it their way you have to let go of a lot of your femininity—even to aspire to be one of the boys.'

The dilemmas and contradictory elements involved in being a woman in Antarctica are suggested by 'Bibi':

> There's not a problem if women realise there's got to be give and take: I was warned about it the second time. I was incredibly aware of what I did, my behaviour. I wanted to be on an equal footing, one of the guys, their little sister, and made an effort to be sociable with all of them. They didn't see me as a sex object; they couldn't do that. I was just 'H'. If you had a nickname, you felt you'd made it, were one of the boys. It was a warm fuzzy feeling—you were really accepted, they'd swear, tell dirty jokes—it didn't bother me, I felt they could say anything.

However, she found 'it was difficult not being a woman over winter, so I shaved my hair off! This made me neutral, of no gender. The guys didn't want to have sex, they were a family over winter especially. Those who came in summer wouldn't have had sex with a winterer—summerers are fair game for a grope, affairs, etc.—there were none, however, when I was going to winter.' She got through winter by saying: 'Don't tell me about discrimination, I'm me, and that's that', gritting her teeth to stave off messages that it was too hard, that she *was* different to the boys, that her perceptions and feelings were no different. It became safe to acknowledge 'the hard stuff' at the conference [1993] 'but not back there' one woman suggested.

Another perspective—a view with which a number of others would agree—was offered by Cheryl. 'I like male company, I quite enjoy it—I would always have a good time and have never been anywhere in the last nine months in Antarctica where I felt threatened. It depends on my attitude as well, I've seen others who have been offended. I don't agree with some of the behaviour. It's not necessarily offensive though, if you know where they have come from.' Yet there is a contradictoriness in this position for many women, as Wendy admits: 'I felt one of the guys and the odd one out too!'

Suppressing part of oneself

The sense of being an 'outsider' can be reduced during summer—for example, by being in the field with one or two hand-chosen assistants. This provides a psychologically more comfortable space away from the daily gaze. You can bury yourself in work, and arrange your working schedule to avoid coming to meals regularly—for example, through late rising, taking food to the workplace or eating late at night. This can lead to criticism for being anti-social, and restricts social activity, which could be very difficult over winter. A number of women spoke of always being on guard socially, of having to know the right time to leave a party and of things they could not do in Antarctica. Others longed for more time to themselves, or 'reinvented' themselves as extroverts to gain some personal distancing. This does not always achieve the desired result and may simply be part of the fun of the new environment.

For many, there is a distortion of the self, as 'Belle' related:

> Some of us are wary of showing our 'feminine' side as you end up with heaps of attention. For example, I wore a dress to a party once this summer with reactions varying from blatant stares, sleazy comments, to a kiss on my shoulder. Since then I stick to my usual station dress of King Gees. I've also heard men complaining of another of the women who feels the same way as me that 'she's a man'. She projects herself this way to avoid the attention. I think it's something you can cope with over summer but for this reason, I wouldn't be keen to winter.

'Chrissie' prepared herself, asking in advance: 'What's the worst thing that can happen? That this guy could turn ugly. So you feel yourself, deliberately, being physically unattractive. Then you're ahead of the game, you're not sending conflicting sexual messages.'

The need for such suppression goes beyond sexist behaviour and overt harassment. In Anitra's words:

120

I had friends who'd gone and thought I was aware of what it would be like. I had the expectation that certain things there would be difficult for women, from my feminist consciousness. The mistake was in thinking the manifestations of sexism would be obvious—for example, bum pinching in the dinner queue. That up-front stuff has mostly been quelled: it's part of the Commonwealth Public Service, the world's more sophisticated. Jokes are still there. What I didn't anticipate is that it's still there, only more subterranean so hard to recognise and dismiss or deal with. I was frightened after a couple of weeks in an environment that said: 'This is our environment. You fall outside the status quo, you are wrong.' I feel I am feisty and strong, yet in the face of being confronted with being told I was wrong, my sense of self crumbled. You start to feel bad about yourself but can't put a finger on it, or recognise it as not-you, and do something about it. It leads you to under-estimate yourself and your own strength to deal with it. I turned to emotional jelly in the face of it.

She could participate with 'the boys'. 'I had a motorbike and could talk about it to them, didn't flinch at pornography which led to my being considered "not a bad bloke for a girl" which became really important but was not my real self.'

'Francesca' has pondered deeply over what goes on, and said:

You're confined with them in a really limited space and you're spending the whole time in other people's energy basically with not much time for yourself. And you're continually dealing with other people's minds and whatever's coming out of them. You just lose your identity—I certainly did. I lost the gauge on what I thought of so many issues and I felt a bit that my opinions were undermined and I started questioning them by the end of the season. Their ideas were so conventional—like normal society's ideals—that I just started questioning a lot of my feminist ideals, a lot of my lesbian ideals—just wondering if I got it wrong. It really gets to the bottom of things when a situation can do that to you—you're just not sure of yourself any more.

Silencing can occur between women, in part as they try to survive as a group in that environment. 'Roslyn' found: 'At training there were some women in a tight circle on the bunks,

121

chatting when I came in. They said "hi" to me and went on talking. It made me feel left out, and that maybe they knew something about me. They were a group, part of the family, and knew how it worked. They had it figured out how they'd "do" the year.' As the year settled down, 'I felt on the outside as I was doing it differently to the others. I felt a bit victimised, left out, excluded from the club. I made attempts to make friends with the women, got on reasonably well with one but wasn't prepared to conform with the rest of the women.' Women do not assume they will automatically be friends with other women, but feeling let down by a woman, or shut out, can be traumatising.

Human society continues to silence those who do not fit the mythical statistical 'average'—what is regarded as 'normal'. Psychological domination is part of structural violence. It involves the exercise of power over others,[6] but the underlying processes that determine normality, power and threat are complex and determined by specific situations.[7] It is easier to recognise and deal with overt violence, and silence gags the whole situation that can arise in Antarctica, making it very hard to change. The lasting distress from some people's Antarctic experiences arises from different forms of silencing: of the pain they experience there, and the inability to discuss it or be heard by those they expect to act on their behalf, as well as the ways in which some feel they have to silence important parts of themselves in order to survive in the group. Speaking out, a fair hearing, validation of feelings, mediation and follow-up counselling are the minimum support required, or the damage will continue. Unsilencing leads to release. 'It's them', 'Elaine' discovered. Silencing is ultimately not healthy for the silencers either, as Freire suggests,[8] for they deny aspects of themselves as they deride others, and false 'solutions' arise.

Harassment, or when it all goes too far

Harassment is one of the most difficult issues faced by women today, and while there are laws to deal with it, the issues raise fears and antagonisms within and between the sexes. Second-wave feminism has sought to increase women's choices, and to remove one-sided behavioural bans. Women have a right to be safe. Yet should a woman wear a low-cut, short dress at the bar on Saturday night? Is it inviting undue attention—or simply feeling good and wanting to enjoy one's body, especially after the daily weight of the outdoor, unisex clothes? Is harassment the due consequence if a woman doesn't watch her behaviour—a form of punishment, even, for being a woman? Again, the contemporary message is clear: relative deprivation should not excuse harassment.

How does admiration change to assault, unwanted touching, menacing words? And how can it be kept 'in control'? Equality implies joint accountability. To exploit the minority status of women, or to establish one-sided rules, is unfair. Better understanding of others' views and meanings, and development of skills to deal with unfamiliar situations and some of the strange interpersonal responses that can occur on a station, may contribute to a safer and more tolerant human environment. There is a viewpoint that harassment inevitably presents women as victims, as not managing. This is far from the truth, as 'Cecily' stressed, for so many 'go and have a good time and do a good job'. As 'Tamara' suggested, 'I do not necessarily see women as innocent victims of harassment and think they're quite capable of playing one man off against another in a sort of sexual power-trip. This can have a considerable impact on the small social world of a wintering party.' However, 'J' stated the bottom line: 'No matter where it happens, if you're treated in a way which derogates your dignity as a person and as a woman, verbally or physically, it is harassment.'

Harassment occurs in Antarctica, as elsewhere, and it occurs between every combination of people. It can be subtle and hard to detect. There are also various levels. Monica simply said: 'People fall in love with you on most expeditions. It is harmless—like a rash of measles—and you prefer some company to others.' As 'Hetty' found, the shipboard 'lech' who follows you around can be 'very uncomfortable but it's not dangerous'. Obviously people do fall in love, and that feeling may not be reciprocated. The silent lovelorn suitor is noticed, perhaps making both the objects of merriment, and is the cause of potential irritation or even threat. In Antarctica, some women have been afraid to reject too forthrightly, fearing for the mental balance of the man and the potential devastation to the little community. They have had to put up with it for months, feeling unable to share the problem and enlist the support of others. This is the unwanted attention of harassment. And yes, women can stalk men—and have. It is unacceptable, but rare, and far less likely to include a physical threat.

Some incidents can be perceived ironically. 'Cecily' experienced one guy

> who'd always get drunk and then proposition me. One night he tried again, and I said: 'Look, this is just not going to happen' and he said: 'Oh, why not?' 'To start with, you're married, and you've only been married for about two or three months before you went down' which to me was an obvious reason. And he said: 'Ah, yes, but I'm an arsehole'. And the thought that went through my head was: 'Oh well, what more do I need to say?' and I walked off.

Imagine how you would feel if someone wanted to be your best friend, was incessantly jealous, took everything the wrong way and wanted you to do everything with and for him, in a place where you could never escape. 'He was always hanging around and knew my routine. Others were aware and warned me off one night when he was in the laundry ceiling, there was a manhole in the bathroom over where I'd showered. I don't know what he would have done. He should have been sent home at the end of summer, and again at the end of winter.' However, when confronted by another woman whom he also harassed, 'he went to the station leader who took him under his wing!' One peeping incident occurred when another woman 'went out into the field with one of the older men, and he was making me uncomfortable and giving me cuddles in my sleeping bag in the evening. I caught him in one of the field huts watching me in the shower. I left the next day.' She confronted him about it. Like the previous incident, it was not reported at the time, but 'certainly it did affect my relations with him and it annoyed me, it was a bit of a low point because it sort of left a bad taste in my mouth'.

Field huts can either be a refuge with a hand-picked group, or a hazard, especially on Macquarie Island where there is much more mobility. 'Once I'd booked a hut, had a miserable day, and found three blokes there, smoking, with girlie magazines. I was cold and wet, and had to change my clothes.' This was not an issue with the scientists with whom she was normally in the field. Here: 'Conversation stopped, I could feel the giggles as I changed.' While she 'decided it was their problem', she was 'glad in a funny way' when two scientists she knew arrived, decided the other three men's behaviour was unacceptable, and insisted that they all move on. 'Rowena' also found that, after one incident that happened in public, 'his [the man concerned] mates gave him a hard time. The majority of men there are very decent, they know right and wrong'.

Yet physical assault and attempted rape have both occurred, though they are talked about in hushed tones, if at all. 'There were a lot of power games. One woman had a hell of a year, and was nearly raped. They nearly broke her door down at one stage during winter.' The emotional effects of such attacks involve a sense of violation, fear for personal safety, and loss of confidence and esteem. For 'Faith': 'It took a psychologist, with help from my doctor, to make me finally admit that I was being bullied and harassed ... I ended up thinking I was going completely mad.' Others do admit it, but do not know what to do, either through lack of knowledge of the formal mechanisms in place to deal with harassment, or because the whole situation makes this near-impossible, actually or psychologically.

Recourse on station is limited, especially as incidents can involve popular members of the group, opinion leaders or the station leader. One station leader 'dragged me off and told me how attracted he was "but nothing could ever happen because

I'm station leader"', though he did continue this 'game'. Such situations show the extent to which harassment is about power over another. And while reprimand and counselling can be delivered, there is no escape. For the affected woman, it may take years to work through the damage done, including a deep sense of offence if her fellow expeditioners did nothing about the situation. The behaviour does not have to be physically threatening to be extremely unpleasant. The exclusion and silencing that women can experience arises from sexist behaviour and assumptions rather than harassment. Up to one-third of women have experienced this in some form in Antarctica.[9] One manifestation is setting up one's fellows as a sport. Deliberate rumours about a relationship seem more credible than the reality of a friendship, especially to those unfamiliar with easy camaraderie between the sexes. And cases are also known where one person, or couple, has been targeted in order to 'set them up' and try to precipitate a sexual relationship as a 'punishment' for being somehow different. An aloof young woman—probably a scientist with little worldly experience, perhaps pseudo-confident or awkward and apparently imperious in her requests for help with her work—can be courted, her suitor egged on by his mates. Whether or not a bedding takes place is almost irrelevant.

Psychological harassment is also hard to manage. 'Britta' found that some men were advising others:

> not to be friends with me, taking me aside and telling me I had to say hello to each by name each day and do the washing up at night in order to be acceptable. I said 'get stuffed' and walked away. But then there was the stopping and staring when I came into the kitchen, not talking to me when I spoke at table. The station leader later accused me in other situations of inviting harassment through my behaviour, but there's no way he should have given the OK for me to be treated like that. He countered that if I wasn't so aggressive, and said this and that, it wouldn't have happened.

The ultimate expression of male power over others seems to be the use of threat as a way of entertaining others and subduing someone who is different—in 'Britta's' case, a strong feminist. This use of power is also found in seemingly minor incidents. One archaeologist on a private expedition said: 'I am small and cute and was treated like a child. This was offensive but not harassing.' But even the talk, the male teasing, putting down and affectionate abuse are not familiar to many women and make them uncomfortable.

'I felt intimidated by the atmosphere' was a comment made by many women, and by some men too. Another expression of this is the public display of pornography. As leader at Casey in 1990, Joan Russell acted on a request for its removal. Perceived not only as a bureaucrat enforcing unpopular rules in Antarctica, but puzzling to many of the men because of her honest admission of lesbianism, and her strong personality and approach to leadership, Joan was provoked and socially avoided by many for the rest of her stay.[10] It ultimately took a very fulfilling season as leader at Macquarie Island to recover. As she put it: 'I had the sensation while being issued with my Antarctic kit and clothing by Don Reid in the Division store in 1989, that I was passing across the counter to him successive layers of my self, like latex sheaths on coat hangers. When I handed back my gear at the end of 1990, and received in return the various stored "layers of self", I found that some no longer fitted me.'

Keeping the peace

Small groups in extreme environments tend to arouse strong passions. One piece of advice passed on by experienced staff and expeditioners to departing Antarcticans is to divide one's emotional reactions, whether to news from home or incidents on station, by ten. There is a strong belief that, to 'keep it happy', people should refrain from controversial topics and avoid the expression of strongly held opinions. 'Francesca' found:

> You come back, and all anyone wants to hear is how fantastic it was. They don't want to hear that you found it oppressive and

cried and wanted to come home. So you don't want to admit that it happened. The big message that nothing happened means that it must have been you. It's gender harassment. You just lose your identity; you lose the gauge on what you think of so many issues and I felt a bit that my opinions were undermined and I started questioning them by the end of the season.

Is group survival so fragile that some views and emotions must be restrained? It can be hard to ask for help, too. 'Alicia' remembered: 'I was crying for days, and no one came up and put their arm around me!'

The most important thing on a station seems to be to keep the peace, at any price. Certainly conflicts have to be contained—and preferably resolved—on station, but they are often just suppressed. It can seem like primitive mob rule.[11] Women, always in a minority, are most likely to have influence in the group when their behaviour and views are approved by men. The biggest problem is the perception of intolerance and unwillingness to listen to others, which may include a silencing of protest about negative behaviour towards women.

Poor communication and conflict-resolution skills appear to lie beneath much of the dissatisfaction, disappointment and distress over the interpersonal aspects of living together in Antarctica. There is also a sense that the AAD has over-compensated in recent pre-departure briefings, so that in Meredy's words: 'It almost got to the stage where men didn't want to talk to you or get too friendly in case you hit them with sexual harassment.' Then, as 'Faye' admitted: 'There are not the usual intervention resources that you have back here. A lot goes on the skills of the station leader.' And it requires self-confidence, courage and belief that you will be supported in order to challenge a member of the small group with whom you have to go on living. Some station leaders don't like a fuss and wouldn't act. 'I didn't want to make the "nuisance" even more angry by putting in a sexual harassment claim, or upset everyone else,' said 'Melinda'. Trust that confidences will be kept is also needed—again, not easy in enclosed, isolated groups. 'I didn't report him, of course, and I didn't make

any fuss about it' is considered 'strong' and 'pro-social'. It also
reflects the view that incidents are going to happen, they happen
everywhere, and women should be able to deal with them: 'It's a
hard place to live. Small issues become big things, misunderstandings get blown out of all proportion, and this is the root of gender
misunderstanding, too.'

It is more likely that complaints will be lodged after a woman's
return to Australia, away from the group pressures in Antarctica,
though there is still some fear that any complaint will lead to the
complainant acquiring a reputation as a troublemaker and
prevent the possibility of being able to return. There is an
impasse, because the person on station to whom one should complain, the station leader, is the one who assesses performance in
every sphere on station, and these assessments are used to evaluate future suitability as an expeditioner. 'Wanda' did think that:
'If it's over, you can complain. Women put up with subtle
harassment for peace on station rather than articulating it.'
'Jade' agreed, but also thought 'it was really hard to complain,
it seems so petty, it's subtle, and seems out of context back here'.

Trying to keep things 'sweet', ignoring problems and issues
between people on station, does not guarantee the peace. Such
things have a tendency to fester, especially over winter, affecting
morale. Some unresolved issues may deeply affect personal well-
being and performance. Ignoring interpersonal issues doesn't
make them go away, rather it can make those for whom they are
important feel very uncertain and even self-doubting. The majority can silence people who are different simply by ignoring their
issues. This process is a form of emotional bullying. One way to
deal with dissent is to establish a lowest common denominator
for what is acceptable. This probably leaves everyone a little bit
dissatisfied, but since the majority have the biggest say in determining this common denominator, they are advantaged. Such
group processes can cause deep distress in an isolated small
community.

Pornography provides an example both of the diversity of
views, and the difficulty of resolving differences in minority and

majority opinions. Some people genuinely don't notice, or mind, pornography; but what if one is deeply offended? Exercising the right to request its removal risks rocking the boat. There is a problem in weighing one person's rights against those of the group, but one-way pressure to conform is not a just solution. Yet persistence in standing up against something believed to be wrong can produce severe social consequences, as a number of women have found.

Feminists are accused of being troublemakers, who go down determined before embarkation to call 'foul' whenever men engage in so-called 'normal' bar-talk about women, appear to overlook women for coveted activities or look too long at women. Feminists respond that condoning sexism and paternalism, even tacitly, isolates and de-legitimates women. Feminist values may not be understood among the usual companions of many expeditioners. However, equality of opportunity regardless of sex, race or creed surely fits the traditional notions of tolerance and a 'fair go'. If Antarctic stations have been idealised as simple, easy-going places to live, free from the 'hassles' of normal life, then as Louise Crossley pointed out in her summary of the 1993 conference on women in Antarctica, why can't they lead the way in providing a safe, comfortable environment for men *and* women?

Gaining perspectives

Some women, often young and 'post'-feminist, can shock men and women alike with their behaviour. If problems are blown up ten times, so too is the sheer exuberance of an isolated station and the midnight summer sun. Cries of 'I had so much FUN!' can be heard and, perhaps following stories of male freedom in winters past, there is the opportunity to let go, eat more, drink more, work very hard, and play more. Multiple partnerings can occur, and life can be lived on the edge; like the mating animals, there is an urgency about the short summer light. A side of women can emerge that is rarely seen by men—one that both attracts and confuses them. Joan Russell reminds us that women can say yes now, too, but it seems we are not yet quite ready for women to claim the same space and privileges as men, least of all in Antarctica. But why are women's difficulties so frequently misconstrued? And why is it so hard to be heard, thus denying the healing power of speaking out?

This book only gives a glimpse of the effect of Antarctica on the lives of those who venture South, and the impact of that experience on a lifetime. The memories fade, even the bad ones. But some lives have been negatively affected by the experience, with anger, loss of self-esteem, poor employment outcomes and fruitless attempts to go South again to 'do it better'. Nevertheless, the negative effects have not spoilt the experience of the place for most: 'I experienced a sense of major grief when I left,' said 'Elaine'. 'I was really angry, yet I just loved the environment. There is nowhere else in the world you can sit beside an albatross chick and have your lunch!'

SIX

'Tell them I survived!'

Despite the obstacles, the story of women in Antarctica is mostly one of celebration. Words like 'daring', 'courage' and 'resilience' are repeatedly used. Not only have women claimed a place in Antarctica, and recorded outstanding achievements there, they have also withstood male opposition and a number of negative aspects of the prevailing culture. Many women have experienced few or no problems related to their gender and minority status. Others have faced significant difficulties, but have managed to overcome them and grow from the experience. 'Faith' considered that:

> Gender, power, equality and harassment are life's complex issues. The most difficult part of solving an individual's situation is simply to get that person to admit to themselves that the issues actually exist. My experiences were very painful at the time. But they have helped mould the person I am today, and I am thankful to have grown from these weird and wonderful pathways. They do not detract from the wonderful and life-changing experiences Antarctica has given me.

Many women have demonstrated an ability to deal with complex, unpleasant situations, believing that the positive aspects far outweigh the negative.

It is vital to present a realistic picture of what life is like in

Antarctica, to show how women have dealt with the challenges presented to them. Discussion with other women suggests that one of the difficulties in male–female communication is that women sometimes just want their experiences heard and acknowledged.[1] And while change to the persistent problematic aspects of Antarctic service is crucial, as discussed later in this chapter, an interest in and acknowledgment of experiences is a separate and critical issue for many expeditioners.

For numerous women, the formal expeditioner debriefing did not satisfy this need, leaving them frustrated yet often unwilling to use the counselling services now engaged by the AAD for expeditioners.[2] Nor is this limited to ANARE. In her story about the all-female German wintering team, Monika Puskeppeleit observes that 'not many people in the polar castle were interested in how the nine women overcame the outer and inner isolation of the polar storms'.[3]

Some women said they had faced few, or no, lows during their time in Antarctica. For others, the negative experience was a personal one that coincided with the Antarctic stay and may have been exacerbated by it. Deaths of family members are particularly difficult to deal with. Those left behind, marooned in Antarctica, are unable to participate in the mourning rituals and interpersonal readjustments that occur at such times. And death or serious illness and accidents back home may be especially threatening, reminding them of their isolation and vulnerability. Women thought that most others on station could not acknowledge their loss or reach out to them in their grief. Female station leaders referred to their concern about dealing with expeditioners' grief, and some female doctors talked about the importance to them of counselling expeditioners.

If some women experienced little to disturb their southern sojourn, others had some very difficult times. Even in the midst of enjoyment, something can trigger a change. For example Barbara Smith was finally able to fulfil an urgent dream. She had a very good time for the first months, then suddenly 'a black cloud seemed to descend', the effect of which lasted for over twelve months. There are two explanations for this. One focuses on the individual, and the interplay between expectations that—while they may partly be fulfilled—can become dulled by the reality of an Antarctic summer, together with the accumulation of stresses. The other refers to the morale curve, which is related to the stage of the season during a posting away from home:[4] the period when tensions accumulate but return is still distant can be particularly difficult.

LOW POINTS IN THE EXPERIENCE

As anywhere, a number of factors can negatively affect an individual. The list discussed here includes aspects of the isolation in Antarctica, relationships with other people, work and interpersonal factors exacerbated by the location, and personal responses.

Physiology

Female physiology may cause some nagging concerns. Women have all dealt pragmatically with specific plumbing arrangements, like un-cubicled showers and urinals—for example, by arranging to shower during the working day. Some women enthusiastically use the 'Sanifem' or FUD (Female Urinary Device), a little funnel that, with practice, enables women to urinate standing up. Others talk of toileting difficulties for men *and* women when outside in high winds, and of the tedium of solid waste buckets whose contents are returned to the station for disposal. Michelle noted: 'I was sick of shitting in plastic bags, and wanted a shower.' Such a fieldwork routine can be wearisome when other things pall.

Ann mentioned that: 'Having periods and being out on a trip when it happens was also a low! You feel tired and drained but it's not a huge problem—it depends on the length of the trip. There's less fresh food, more additives and preservatives and this leads to more PMT. There are general problems from the diet, especially the canned food.' One measure to deal with menstrual problems is use of the long-acting contraceptive Depo-Provera, a personal solution with some risks. The Head of Polar Medicine at the AAD ensured that the disposal of sanitary items on station was discreet so that any eager swains could not detect the stage of a woman's cycle from the burning waste.

There has been no research into the effects of the environment on women's hormones. Some women have suffered menstrual distress while in Antarctica, and some mentioned libidinal disturbances. For several, dealing with pre-menstrual tension was a major low point. Others talked about the general physiological effects of being there, of the body craving more light over the long winter, of the lack of sensory stimulation, and of lengthy periods in the field when you never *see* your body as you change clothes very quickly inside your sleeping bag.

Work

A number of factors can combine to cause difficulties, including interactions between work, relationships and the environment, as 'Alicia's' account illustrates. She was 23 when she wintered: 'young, a volunteer and ill-prepared'. Her work was unclear.

> Initially I had been brought in to go down as a technician. My boss was of the firm opinion that I would get bored down there without my own work to do so he and my Honours supervisor put together a project for me, tailoring it to my previous experience, and suggesting I enrol in a Masters. It involved testing the water, as they needed to know about the effects of a new sewage treatment system discharging into the bay near Davis and the factors affecting the survival of the faecal bacteria. They gave me very little support or interest, however.

One important piece of equipment, which she believed was on station, 'was RTAed[5] on the boat I went in on—at the order of my boss, I suspect. Poetic isn't it?' She also needed assistance to build some equipment, but 'I approached asking for help really cautiously, though I resented having to ask for every bit of help instead of having any offered. I think pride may also come into it, an unwillingness to admit that I was not completely and utterly capable of doing everything necessary to achieve my work.' And experiments did not go well:

> By the time you get to setting up the same experiment that has failed the previous two or three times, there is a great inertia. Each time the wall/barrier gets bigger. I was obviously having motivational problems by midwinter. Instead of getting help, of all people the station leader made constant jibes and references to it. When work is not going well, you can't get away from it, it's constantly there.

The baseline study was useful for subsequent research, but 'the peripheral aspects didn't work—my thesis bit. It was "all too big" '. Her work for a Masters never got off the ground, but she had to keep going with the other tasks.

Towards the end, 'the OiC had the temerity to admit that yes I had done a good job in my social work. A couple of other guys expressed admiration while I was down there for the way I was. It really was the first time in my life that people had expressed my worthiness to me so openly. So the old ego being stroked felt damn good.'[6] Nevertheless, the aftermath of her work situation, and some strongly negative interpersonal incidents which alienated her from the dominant group, proved hard to shake off. After eight years, she felt 'you take it in and absorb it into you', assigning her problems to 'youth and naiveté', which was nevertheless thrown into painfully stark relief during an Antarctic winter.

Surprisingly, aspects of work proved a low point for many in Antarctica. It is possible to gain more independence and enhanced confidence because you *did* manage there, making decisions and taking initiatives. But the process can have negative repercussions. For example, 'Schifra' recounted:

> My supervisor expects a lot of you and doesn't appreciate the different aspects, like the loss of motivation, feeling you want to hide, the hardships. When I emailed her about my computer

problems, she didn't have much input, just said 'carry on'. So I basically made the decisions . . . it was good to be a little bit more independent, though I didn't think so at the time. I feel proud I managed to fix the problem . . . little things like that can make you feel a little bit better about yourself.

A frustrating element of work for volunteers in particular is not seeing a project through, handing over the data on their return and not even knowing whether the findings are published. 'J' needed 'more to do and more responsibility'. Others find motivation sags if they sense that their supervisor lacks much interest in their work, even while enjoying the opportunity to be in Antarctica. The lack of interest is another form of 'deafness' to people in Antarctica, which may exaggerate other aspects, such as the cost of being a volunteer.[7]

Misunderstandings and teasing about scientists' working hours can be tedious rather than painful. Repetitive teasing, however, goes beyond taking the edge off a day. It can be experienced as distancing from the group, and can gnaw away at self-esteem. The implications of making regular observations across 24-hour periods, or at night, are not always understood and, over summer, cramped accommodation exacerbates other sleeping problems. Corinna had to do most of her work at night. 'I don't think that the station leader really understood that I had to work all night and to sleep during the day. Where I was accommodated it wasn't quiet.' Biological specimens often have to be examined soon after collection, following long hours in the field. The scientists are invisible, working in laboratories at night, but they are noticed having breakfast as others come in for smoko. Such work patterns affect opportunities to participate in group social activities, which can be resented as a reluctance to socialise. It enhances a 'stuck-up female boffin' image.

While everyone's performance is 'on show', women feel that they have to get it right first time round, or be dismissed as incompetent. Judi Hansen, when working from the US McMurdo station, said low times arose from those pressures which 'I put on myself to produce—for example, up nights on end to process samples when the rest had gone to bed having offered to help and been rejected'. She also felt bad because they only had half the diving suits required there, 'including mine which no one else could use. I got ear infections and couldn't dive, and became tearful because I wanted to "go" 110 per cent.'

Self-motivation is a key selection criterion for Antarctic service, so it is little wonder that some over-do it, as 'Pippa' noted: 'Work didn't always go very well, and when that happened I put more time and energy into it, overdid it a bit.' Jane Goddard reflected:

> They tend to select people who are fairly high achievers in their field. There's a real sense that everyone down there, in a way, is evaluating everyone else down there too. You do need partially to be thick skinned and you need to believe in yourself because you could so easily be undermined by silly little comments and things that people say, just from living in a close environment and having often intense relationships—that closeness with people that can really make your reactions and your emotions far more extreme and fluctuate more rapidly.

Relationships

Jane's comments illustrate the kinds of issues that can affect relationships. A number of women commented that they had gained perspective over time, taking away some of the sharpness and, with it, some of the pain, and they repeatedly spoke of the overall wonder with which they regard Antarctica. Nevertheless, relationships figured highly in the kind of distress that can last for years afterwards. Relationships with others are a crucial node in the process of evaluating, telling, absorbing, rejecting and readjusting elements of self and experience.

Even those with previous experience in small groups or communities, and the aggravations that can arise in them, named some aspect of relationships as a low point. Yet very little research has been done on interpersonal dynamics in Antarctica.[8] Inevitably, in the enclosed atmosphere over winter, small things can be blown sky-high, and one person's endearing foible over summer becomes homicidally irritating day after dark winter's day. Both men and women can become the butt of group jokes, which may turn into bullying rituals. Even one person daily intoning 'How's our cookie today?' accompanied by a hollow laugh, when he is one-fifteenth of the group members, constitutes a provocation, and can feel like an assault on one's sense of self.

Repetitious platitudes, or behaviours like a pointed refusal to sit with a person for months on end, disrupt the possibility for social interaction. These are all ways to make a person feel very alienated.

Obviously, groups differ, and two consecutive Antarctic seasons on the one station can be very different because of the mixture of people, leadership and specific events. The whole Antarctic experience is extreme. One woman suggested that there were test questions:

'How good is she?' It was subtle in conversation, but there nevertheless. They do it to men too. [A work colleague] humiliated me badly in front of the station. That was something else, the one-upmanship. It became a survival tactic to do it, and do it well. If you can't do it, you feel no good. I was confident before I went, but not since, not even doing professional courses.

'Wanda' suggested a broad diagnosis:

Women are still on trial fairly much. They're accepted as part of expeditions, but on the community level you're on trial—there are two sets of standards. It's OK for men to be outrageous, drunk, promiscuous. Women like that are crucified and have a very hard time 'getting back'. There are a few alcoholics ... Women put up with subtle harassment for peace on the station rather than articulating it. They are more conservative in their actions (these are easily misinterpreted), dress, etc. There's so little privacy, and few opportunities to relax entirely, and often very little emotional support. It's easier if there are more equal numbers—there'd still be relationships, etc. but it would be a more normal situation.

It is hard to discuss these issues openly and expeditioners are quick to defend their own, or others', behaviour. The strategies women adopt are discussed below. Bitter disappointment with the behaviour of other people, including in some cases betrayal of trust and intimacy, and selfish or hurtful behaviour of other women too, happens in Antarctica, as elsewhere. In Antarctica, it is particularly hard to resolve the situation and to find appropriate support.

The effects can be long-lasting. 'Beatrice' admitted:

> The hardest aspects seem to have been the way some people treated each other there, the things they said, and the sense that I could not resolve things in the way I prefer. There's a sense of unfinished business and that people let me down very badly, that there had been some interpersonal things that were so outside my values I am finding it hard to readjust. I allowed the whole situation to get me down. I think it was sheer depression. I cried myself to sleep every night for months and months and was physically and mentally exhausted. I didn't have the energy to devote to myself let alone other people! I can see it wasn't my fault now but at the time I made the situation worse by torturing myself, trying to get on with people who weren't interested and trying to help out friends who were also unhappy. I was desperate!

In retrospect, however, she has found that the friendships formed there were a high point.

Isolation in a harsh environment

There are strains for all, away from family and friends, and these tend to accumulate. When things go wrong at home or on station, when even phone calls are inadequate, the isolation is highlighted. It may be difficult to have private phone calls if you live in the summer caravans, or to have any contact when in the field. This can make a low time even lower, and throw into relief the superficiality of relationships around you. Wendy pointed out that you can feel low because 'conversation had to depend on anything that happened prior to coming, or on the station because of the lack of outside information'. There is a vulnerable protectiveness about people, which also makes it hard at times to attempt to confide in others. A partner can ease that loneliness and need, but the situation can also strain such relationships under the microscope of 24-hour contact and scrutiny. A misunderstanding with a partner there was rated as a very bad experience. One of the difficulties of months in the Antarctic is that friends and family at home recede, and they have trouble relating to issues on station. Distancing can also occur on return home, leading former expeditioners to seek each other's company.

Isolation and, on the continent, the boundlessness of the landscape itself, enhance feelings. And there is an inner loneliness, reinforced by the isolation from one's usual contacts and support systems. 'Francesca' found:

> The hardest thing about being lesbian in the Antarctic
> environment is the assumption of heterosexuality. This is no
> different from mainstream (malestream) Australian society, nor
> are the attitudes to women in Antarctica different from
> mainstream Australian society. The fundamental sexual power
> game, though, is challenged by a lesbian in a male environment
> that expects women to be available and become male property.
> When you challenge this, men become affronted, their egos suffer
> a blow and *you* have to cope with the consequences of their
> rejection. In Antarctica half the time it led to the usual baiting
> behaviour that plagues every feminist—men wanting a reaction to
> a critical remark to show that you're just a man-hater, etc., etc.
> [However] the other half of the time it seemed to make things
> better because the rules of the game changed and suddenly you
> could relate to a man without the sexual game-playing being there
> at all.

You can 'suddenly feel isolated', as Michelle confessed, especially when there are complications with work or transport. However, the physical environment was rarely a source of negative experiences. In fact, the place itself was the attraction for most women, and 'it did not disappoint'. However, the conditions inevitably create frustrations. The explanatory concept, the 'A factor', is invoked for diverse eventualities such as finding a vital piece of equipment was not shipped; the extra time that even simple jobs can take—especially if you're moving inside and outside and have to change layers of heavy clothing; and the fact that machinery performs differently, blizzards or late thawing can interrupt outside work and any liquid freezes.

However, many women found that being unable to go outside in bad weather was more distressing than the weather itself. Robyn Carter 'used to miss home and felt low when confined indoors for too long, due to bad weather, or when stuck at Davis for too long'. Women lamented men 'who go for the money, and are not interested in the place, they don't go outside all winter, which is sad'. And, as Elizabeth K. suggested, 'you get back to simple pleasures, you could be yourself again, it was a special society'. Nor was the environment experienced as monotonous, though some noticed sensory deprivation from the lack of new people or things, and others longed for a meal of one's choice with a handpicked small group. The lack of personal space is also distressing at times. On a voyage, 'there's nowhere else to go'. 'J' summed it up, saying: 'The common perceptions of Antarctica as a huge empty continent are inapplicable to the living spaces available to expeditioners.' No wonder some bivvy out under the stars whenever possible, while others ski, walk or arrange 'jollies' with a small group.

A few admitted feeling ill-prepared for and anxious about outside activity. It can even be extremely difficult to walk in a blizzard, holding tightly to a rope line, especially if one is small and light, or walking on ice. But rather than fazing women, the conditions were seen as a challenge, offering something exciting to explore, new skills to learn.[9] 'Charlotte' was one of the very few perhaps honest enough to confess: 'The physical storms were bloody terrifying. There's nothing more terrifying than a blizzard, because you just don't know which end is up.'

The cold can make life difficult, and some were surprised at their enjoyment of it. There is a tendency to play down its effects, even its extent—for example: 'Casey doesn't get very cold, only −15°C.' The different light conditions can be harder to adjust to, both the continuous light in summer, when you forget to go to bed in the absence of normal cues, and the wintry darkness with weeks when the sun is barely a glow on the horizon. The pleasure at the return of the sun evoked more comment than its disappearance did. The consequences of winter, particularly the physical confinement, were greater hardships for most. However, several women were prepared to admit their terror during the sometimes huge seas in the Southern Ocean.

Feelings about oneself

The personal baggage you bring to Antarctica, and the interplay of diverse people thrown together in a confined and isolated setting, can be a volatile combination. Difficult situations can lead to or feed self-doubt. There are also other aspects of going South that create inner storms which often dissipate slowly. The situation may exaggerate underlying tendencies to internalise problems, to become one's own harshest critic, and that in turn may be more characteristic of women than men. When it happens in Antarctica, it seems more devastating. 'It's three and a half years since my last return and just now the demons are starting to abate,' Anitra found. 'Tamara' added: 'I think only time helped in moving on, letting the experience go—and finding something that had similar challenges and rewards.'

'Beatrice' summarised the overall effects: 'I have very mixed feelings about my time down South. Workwise it was a success; however, personally it was a bit of a disaster. I came out of winter hating myself and totally devoid of self-confidence. This is slowly improving but is something [that is] very hard to come to terms with. You discover a lot about general human nature and your own suppressed personality that can come as a surprise.' Like others, she can see the positive side: 'As a first-timer you are not always equipped to deal with the resulting conflicts, emotions and offshoots of this, but I am sure there has to be a positive to even the most negative discoveries that can be applied to life in the "real world" or during other expeditions.'

A few have been deeply scarred. 'Elaine' said:

> I've been angry at myself. This dissipated at the conference—for
> not being able to do it, to cope. I felt destroyed by the time I
> left—something died ... It's a kind of a death—even if it's not
> bad—because it's such a tremendous watershed: you're grieving
> for the death of a bit of yourself and you're not prepared for it.
> It's such a confined environment—work, social, family roles
> overlap. You can't play, those props die and you come back naked.
> You flounder, and can't go back. The boxes, the edges aren't
> there so you lose a sense of who you are.

'Juliet' 'felt so guilty at my lack of self control. I couldn't last
three weeks without physical contact. I felt completely worthless'.

WEATHERING THE STORMS

Women develop survival strategies to prevent or ameliorate situations like those described above. For first-timers, there are few
guidelines, so women must combine the skills they bring to the
situation with rapid learning in Antarctica. I will not clutter this
section with psychological theories about coping,[10] which are
flawed in that they ignore the cultural and environmental
context. Rather, the insights that women have shared highlight
the varied events, responses and resources and provide some
clues for those who come after them. And, as Kerrie Swadling
reminds us: 'It is just such a fantastic privilege to be there.'

Work

Top of the list of survival strategies is being well prepared and
feeling good about one's work. The two are interrelated. It has
to come largely from within, because very few have found others
willing to give meaningful feedback. This confidence, and doing
the best you feel you can, can help to overcome the attacks that
some jobs seem to attract, especially in science. Ruth Eriksen,
and Heather and Erica Adamson, for example, invited others

into the laboratory, showed them the equipment and explained the nature of the work. Involving other expeditioners in field assistance is another strategy that can help break down barriers and change attitudes to scientists, who may otherwise be regarded, 'as a woman out there in the field, as a scientist, as a bit of a joke'. Scientists sometimes have to overcome the criticisms of some procedures they use. Kirsten strongly recommended that 'it is even more important for people to see you genuinely care for the animals and their well-being. Sometimes you're doing nasty things to them and you have to be able to justify what you do in your own mind and to others.' Ruth Lawless was one who was scrupulous about this, and told her assistants to stop if there was any procedure that they were not comfortable with. As mentioned in Chapter 3, Sharon and Jane were also extremely careful with the way they took moss specimens, in keeping with their beliefs and values.

Another valued quality in the Antarctic is the ability to improvise. 'Sue' nominated 'improvisation and technical skills' as survival strategies, again involving awareness, foresight and preparation.

It is not enough to do one's job well; you must also contribute to the group. Lynn Williams advised:

> If you're incompetent at your job, nothing will save you. If you're not cooperative and at least doing the minimum in the other duties, that's a recipe for disaster. You can win an awful lot of points by being attentive to those communal tasks. There are extras you can do: organising things, doing the projection,[11] hairdressing, all those extra things that are useful to the group. Those sorts of activities add to your acceptance in the group.

This is harder now, because there were more communal jobs on the old stations and that helped bond the group. Lynn added: 'The insecure social person who always needs time and attention can be an irritant in a group like that when everyone's quite self-reliant.' Rather, as 'J' observed: 'You need to be ready to take over and relieve another person—in other words, to behave like a good family member.'

These comments underline the fact that those in Antarctica both live and work together. Being tolerant and flexible are considered very important. 'The greatest assets in Antarctica are humour and flexibility,' Fiona advised. 'You need a fair dose of both to go and you need them to get you through, especially the winter with the lack of social stimulators.' Lynn added that it is important to have 'a sense of perspective with other people. You can't be too rigid; you're going to have to sort of fit with whoever happens to be in your group and you're going to have to make some accommodation for success of the group in a sense.' Kerrie's advice was to 'make it easy on yourself by trying to get along with others, and recognising that they're good at their job, and not necessarily there to help you'. Ulla also stressed thoughtfulness: 'You just have to get on with other people, you cannot be selfish down there, it ruins too much. You have to be able to jump in and chip in where help is needed.' 'J' summarised: 'A good expeditioner is one who makes an effort to get on well with everyone as much as possible, you have to curb your tongue a bit—if you don't get on, you can't just go home!'

Such advice needs to be applied to women *and* men, or it may lead to the silencing of one group in the interests of another, as discussed in Chapter 5. There is also the individual aspect: 'I'm non-confrontationalist: if I found something irritating or infuriating, I sublimated,' Heather Adamson admitted, but continued: 'It's a good strategy—you don't have any fights; if you fight there it's very difficult.' She elaborated: 'You need a sense of your own worth there and the ability to gain respect of the opinion leaders.' Another senior scientist, Maret Vesk, added: 'You need to put in a certain amount of humour and cynicism. I guess I've always had a fair amount of self-confidence in some ways. I probably would have challenged them, but I'm not a very aggressive person. All the nonsense that went on about letting women go down is hopefully fading.' A young scientist, Jenny Selkirk, asserted: 'Some say that women are the root of all problems in Antarctica. That's bullshit. The sooner it's a more normal life, with normal interactions, the easier.'

Relationships

Groups and sub-groups do form, and what happens within and between them can be extremely intense. Finding a 'comfortable' smaller group provides an anchoring point both for closer association and for negotiating the larger one, even though clique formation is frowned on. If you have not been to field training in Tasmania, and especially if you have come from overseas just before the ship departs, anxious about getting your project operational, the social situation can be daunting. Elaborate social events, especially on Saturday nights, are valued, since work schedules and locations separate people during the week. 'Renate' observed:

> I think it's important to have friends down there that you can spend time with who don't demand too much—people you feel comfortable with and can relax with. Because you can't go home and leave them at night you have to develop groups with whom you can relax, people you can trust, etc. Often there might be many such people and you do different things with different people.

During her first year, Denise Allen went through a process of self-development which involved gaining confidence in the decisions she made.

> The first time I learnt my limits, what I would accept and what I wouldn't in relationships in general. The first month or so there's sussing out. When you give them a clear message of your stance, the pressure that comes on you the first month falls away, they realise you're going to be consistent, and stick to your point. But if you give signals that say 'I might change my mind next week' then the pressures are still on you. There's a lot of sexual energy there. In one instance a guy came to me at a party, just came at me: 'You ... bitch, etc., etc.' 'What's the problem? I think what you're experiencing at the moment is sexual frustration, I'm the only woman on the station and you're taking it out on me.' I treated it as a generic rather than a personal issue.'

147

Denise recently affirmed that she considered 'I was correct in this instance as the frustration developed towards me as I represented something they wanted but was unavailable. Similar attitudes and comments could also be detected during movie nights towards female stars.'

Many women feel it is easier for solo women to control and set their own standards, whereas it can be more difficult when there are several women winterers who have different standards. 'GD', another solo female winterer, explained that she:

> decided to set the tone, take the initiative in how they were to relate to me. I took a firm line—played 'the lady'. I never said anything but there were men who said 'don't swear in front of her'. They knew it would be easy for the station to degenerate to 'locker room behaviour' for the whole year, and most men are bored silly by that, and I let the moderate men in the group use my presence to prevent foul behaviour in the group. It obviously happened when I wasn't around. It was accepted and understood that it was their right to do that when I wasn't around. Basically that locker room behaviour is quite boring for more intelligent or decent men. They used me like that. Almost all of them at some stage said I reminded them of a woman in their life at some stage. I was clearly filling a symbolic role of the civilising influence, and didn't mind it. If only they knew how medical students carry on!

An important message to convey is that one's person, not one's gender, is the relevant factor, as Pia explained: 'I try to be just a person doing my job, but it can be different for females. You feel like you are on display.' Tracey P. said: 'People generally get that message and don't treat me differently.' And there are other strategies, especially on the ships, as Pia found, such as 'never being by yourself at the bar, checking out how many women are there, never close the door of your cabin with a guy there so the rumour mill doesn't go into overdrive . . . you get into a habit'.

Overcoming isolation: female companionship

'Charlotte' described the emotional needs that emerge:

> I remember one time towards the end of the first year feeling just
> a total emotional desolation ... suddenly there was this wave of
> total loneliness, you know that stuff, just 'whoomph!' I thought,
> 'Yes, I can sit on this rock and it will go away in a bit. I just might
> see if "Davina" is around', because 'Davina' was the only other
> woman on the station. While we were not very close, I did
> definitely know that if push came to shove and all else failed, we
> would be there for each other. So I went to where I thought she
> might be, and she was there, and I just walked in the door and
> said 'Eh, "Davina" ' and she took one look at me and said, 'Come
> here "Charlotte", you need a hug'.

Friendship can be critically important in Antarctica. Some
women enjoyed relaxed times together, including off-station
trips, though they sometimes felt they were 'on show' to prove
they could handle the vehicles and conditions without men. Over
winter, the number of women is relevant, as Lynne noted: 'There
were five women out of 30, above the percentage for a minority
to be victimised. The women never got together as a group—we
were friendly to each other, but our interests, friends were
different.'

'Janelle' said it was 'refreshing to have women socially, the new
station leader was a woman and was very good. It was good to
talk to one of the women from the previous winter, if there was
anything I wanted an opinion on in a tricky situation, or that was
personally important. It depended on feeling we shared a viewpoint.' Liza confirmed this: 'Women support each other by being
themselves, being women. They talk!' It was the relaxed female
conversation that was either missed or enjoyed by women, even
though there was sometimes competition, lack of support and
even conflict between them. 'Caitlin' described how, one season,
'all the summering women lived in the same unit. There were
eight of us, we could have a great gasbag session. You could let

go and relax, laugh, walk out of the shower in your towel.' Lynne 'missed having a really close woman friend over winter. In summer there were more than four of a similar age and views on science. This was very refreshing, really nice!' Melanie enjoyed a marine science voyage where 'there were lots of women on board, and I worked with a group of eight people [not all women] where we could sit around and really talk about things of shared interest'. Jane was 'looking forward to female company by the end of the year, and I was really glad that some of the women I'd met the previous summer were coming back'.

All the women got together when Denise Jones was at Mawson. 'It was nice to do that. Conversations with women were more intimate, not on such a shallow basis. A closeness is there in friendships with women that you don't get with the men. You need to keep some distance with the men, when it gets to that level.' Denise recorded the success of MUFF (the Mawson, later reappearing as the Macquarie, United Feminist Front), when the five women banded together to provide a humorous opposition to various forms of male sexism, eventually publishing the *MUFF Magazine* complete with male centrefolds.

Women described how friendship made a difference:

> We get on very well, we could talk to each other but also watch out and assist each other, so that released the pressure incredibly and she's very quick and clever at responding to me instead of going off feeling awful. I felt more confident, knowing someone else there was terrific, that really helped. We could assist each other emotionally and started to protect our needs more.

Two others realised the importance of getting on: 'The most important thing in the whole expedition was our relationship. All work, etc. hung off that.' It was a joint project and they shared a camp on Heard Island with two other women.

> The wind made us bad-tempered. I especially had a problem with that. So we stopped working. I had a level beyond which I felt ratty, etc. and not safe to go on: wind speed and my grumpiness

were correlated. We worked it out quite quickly. I saw a bit of social tension on Heard Island. This prompted us to raise it as an issue with each other. It would be such a disaster if we fell out, so we made sure how we felt, especially in the wind equals grump factor, and developing a strategy to cope.

Things don't always work out between close work partners, regardless of their gender, which throws each back on to others for support. This may be very stressful when based in the field. It may also be difficult to find support, or to realise one doesn't have to put up with friction. Helpful station leaders have organised regular relief and returns to station. The situation is complicated when rumours are spread about the relationships between people at a field site. This can affect how one feels about others on station, and one's willingness to ask for help. Amanda Nimon, who spent three summers on Cuverville Island off the Antarctic Peninsula with three others, found it a 'sharing situation', where each 'had responsibility and authority'. However, during one of those summers, Pam Davies recounted her anger that 'our supervisor was down, there were three women and people said disgusting things like: "He can have a different woman each night".'

Men are attracted to women socially too, to talk about personal issues, tacitly recognising the different interaction. This can lead to pressure on women to socialise with all, reducing their time with a more compatible and supportive small group. Jenny Mackenzie put this positively, seeing it as a desire for female company and conversation: 'The guys don't miss the sex so much—they say they can switch off—but they miss the hugs.' This suggests women are a communal resource. It provides special agonies for lesbian women. Homosexuality has been a very taboo topic in Antarctic circles, which must be extraordinarily difficult for gay men.

There is a tacit assumption that if there are even two women, they will be friends. Women find this assumption trying. 'Geraldine' commented: 'I think one other problem for women is that people assume that women should get on; people are always watching how women get on.' Denise Allen noted: 'The pressure on women wintering with other women to be friends is huge, from AAD and from the group. But you don't pick your friends by gender, rather by personality. It's not true at all that two women will get on—it's a ridiculous assumption when you look at society in general.' Peta agreed: 'The pressure for two women to be friends is not so good; you can't pick a friend.' Monica mentioned that 'sometimes women can be lumped together with other women and regarded as a source of entertainment. You're not seen as individuals.'

'Helena' has experienced women who are 'outrageously competitive and threatened by other women and it was most uncomfortable'.[12] This can be very destructive. Angela Rhodes agreed, but also pointed out that women 'are better at giving emotional support to each other'. This point was repeated by a number of women, Estelle adding: 'It's hard to confide in men, especially female experiences.' 'Helena' felt: 'It's a tragedy when women are against each other, the reverse is so wonderful. Women seem to deal with emotional issues differently to men, it's good to have someone who understands how your brain works.' As a result, as 'Pippa' found, victimisation by a woman 'was particularly hard. I'd never been victimised before, and the emotions it brought up, having problems with another woman, and having to deal with it, were very difficult'. 'Thelma' admitted, reluctantly, that: 'There've been women who've been utter bitches—there's no other word for it—to other women.'

However, Jenny Mackenzie was surprised that, with only two women: 'We never became confidantes or anything like that, which is not what you'd have expected.' But people differ in their friendship patterns and needs. Some women do not miss other female company, or find that phone calls and emails suffice. Erica wintered solo and found: 'I certainly benefited in some ways from being the only woman. There was no possibility of rivalry; I had a special role.' She was 'really nervous to start with' when a woman came in at the end of the season, though they did get on well 'and soon became friends'.

More problematic have been some groups with five female winterers of diverse occupations and amounts of prior Antarctic experience. It is unlikely that all would be friends, and their divisions resemble the majority/minority dynamics between men and women. Female disharmony is not expected by men, and has led to indignant reports by station leaders. There can be complex dynamics, involving women taking on male expectations of them and using this to exercise power over other women. More simply, women may just find it hard to explain why they have not been compatible!

Far more common are the stories of the great times women have had together, when they have developed easy enough friendships to publicly enjoy occasional all-female gatherings. Jenny Selkirk told of one long summer on Macquarie Island when 25 per cent of expeditioners were women. They could gather in the evenings in a public place with handicrafts such as knitting and embroidery, usually hidden in bedrooms. This happened because of their numbers, their self-confidence in their sexual identity, and the permissive social environment. 'Girls' night' in the sauna, and a dress-up women's picnic, were other celebrations of female companionship.

Personality, attitudes, reactions and outlets

Personality affects one's experiences in Antarctica, as elsewhere, as Maret pointed out:

> If you're terribly intense and take yourself seriously, you will have
> trouble, and it won't improve with age! You can see through
> statements, even body language, that some will cause problems,
> the male or female aspect will stand out, in a very limited number
> of people. There's an incredible mix of people, who are bound to
> have problems as it's hard to get away in the closed society.

The two contrasting views below illustrate Maret's perspective. 'Molly' advised:

How you feel as a woman depends on how flexible you are,
whether you are going to be terribly affronted by [what is]
essentially still a male-dominated environment . . . It's human
nature to always attack the weak. If you're upset by something
they'll play on it. If something did genuinely upset me, I'd not go
where it's likely to occur, or would say something. It's the way you
approach the issues. If you go in with all guns blazing and a piece
of legislation in each pocket you've got Buckley's. You have to go
in and play the situation according to the personalities, and
background of the issue.

Keen at first to argue rationally about issues that were important to her, 'Britta' got sick of trying to convince the men of
something 'that is already accepted and in the legislation. Why
should I be having to argue a case that is open and closed, that's
been done in the 1970s and 1980s and that's probably not something that I should have to do any more. So then I left it and
basically withdrew and kept away from the group that was the
most against me.' After her return, she found:

The further away you are from it, the more you can put it in
perspective . . . I can admit my own mistakes in the way I behaved.
At the time I felt I was not going to compromise, would stick to
my guns, under any circumstances. Now I can see that there's
more than one way of sticking to your guns and that I should have
a better repertoire in future of how I'd avoid conflict or deal with
the conflict that came up.

At the time she found she had to use denial.
Other forms of denial are also used, such as withdrawing into
oneself, putting up a protective shield or just creating a private
zone. Not allowing oneself to respond to jokes or taunts is
another form of denial. This is potentially stressful. Jane W. said
she tended towards a 'reasonably positive view of the world and
of people. I don't let a lot of negative stuff in, can turn the
tide of sexual stuff using humour, for example'. Jenny Mackenzie
also did this, adding: 'I'm basically shock-proof but I could shock
them. I advised another woman not to jump at these things. If

you jump routinely when people say something, then they'll do it just to watch the show, because they're bored.'

Catharsis is also used. Several women admitted that they found crying helpful as an outlet, whereas others lacked consolation and found it made things worse. Diaries were also used. Denise Jones recently reread and burnt her first winter's account, as it 'started out basically and got more emotional'. Three female station leaders mentioned using them. Sometimes it was even too emotional to write at the time, and Joan said she sat and poured her heart out for seventeen pages when she got on the ship to go home after her first winter. Diana said: 'I used my diary extensively, I've never shown it to anyone and probably won't. It was about personal feelings, and was an outlet for anger. I used it like girlfriends back home. Women use personal networks, long-term friends to "talk about things from the heart".' Fewer people keep a diary on subsequent expeditions. The monologue can relieve feelings, serving the dual function of hiding one's most vulnerable feelings and recording what is often so difficult to share with others outside the situation. 'Going away so often, you find out who your real friends are,' explained 'Derani'. 'The worst thing when I was feeling in the doldrums was to ring the family. I got off the phone feeling worse.' Elizabeth Bulling found it hard to keep all her friends in the picture, though a sister empathised: 'She works in a school for "problem" girls and she'd say, "It's like the Year Nines!" She helped me put it into perspective and realise it's basically the same dynamics as the silly stuff that kids do at school. That was really good.'

Diversion is often the best 'cure'. Skiing is popular, and it is sometimes possible to do it alone. 'Whenever the weather was good and time was available', Midj went outside. 'It was a general break from the humdrum, allowing fresh air, and fresh thoughts. In Australia, you have to go away from town for that. In Antarctica you only have to go outside, even for five minutes!' For Robyn C.: 'Getting outside worked wonders for low spirits, to rug up and battle around in the wind for even half an hour always helped.' Melanie skied far enough to dampen even the noise of the generator on the icy plateau at Law Dome. The gym is usually well used.

Few women indulge in solitary indoor hobbies, but many enjoy reading. Now there is the luxury of the occasional hot bath or spa. Photography is popular.[13] There is the chance to learn skills from others, and several women have learnt a new language, or undertaken correspondence study—Mandy, for instance, completed most of an external degree during her second winter. A tolerance for monotony coupled with an ability to be self-contained are considered personal characteristics that contribute to a successful winter.

Jenny Mudge added another dimension: 'You've got to know yourself, what you're capable of coping with, of handling. It's very difficult if you can't handle yourself properly. You don't know what others go through; you've got to respect and trust other people—don't judge them. A lot of the time, that's the problem—you view people with your own expectations.' There is also a need for confidence in oneself, both with work and relating to others.

Some issues remain unresolved on return. Ann pointed out: 'You have to be able to let go.' This was not so easy for those who found that the inner storm is the one you bring back with you. Jane Wilson said: 'Difficult experiences encourage learning and reflection. You develop skills when you're out on a limb and stressed.' Monica suggested that self-forgiveness is important but, as the examples show, this does not happen easily for some. Being heard 'confidentially is important to me', Ruth E. recognised. Being heard—and believed—and realising that your experience was not unique, can promote healing.

Creating space

The need for personal space is still acknowledged, though it may be difficult to attain. Two female biologists, for example, lived in an aircraft engine packing case: 'There's no personal space. It took incredible discipline to hold it together when we were exhausted, busy, frustrated, exhausting weather that takes it out of you. You have to do everything with the other, and I am really proud of how we made it work and got through the program.' They each set up a personal shelf and, like others, used a Walkman to create personal space. Reading can also signal 'stay away', and Kirsten realised that 'visual space is a form of privacy, being able to not see someone you don't get on with'. Curtains can be very useful, too. Estelle sketched 'as a form of meditation'.[14]

Space is also at a premium on the ship, and Ruth learnt to 'seek a group of people to relax with, confide in, to unwind, talk with, share confidences. You're vulnerable there. Sometimes you can't even go outside due to bad weather. You keep telling yourself it's your job. You learn quickly who you can/can't talk to. It is important for me to be heard confidentially.'

HOW CAN THINGS BE IMPROVED?

For most, experience is a critical factor in dealing with the whole social situation in Antarctica. 'Katrina' found: 'The social side was a real learning curve, which I value highly. I always got on with a range of people, but talking when I didn't want to was a challenge. I grew up a lot in Antarctica.' Most women over 30 felt their age was an advantage. Sharon admitted she would:

> much rather be there as a woman in my thirties than in my twenties. There's that impressionable thing, and you develop confidence. You're much less bothered about what others think of you than fifteen years ago, and have a more balanced idea of people's image of you. There are male and female students I wouldn't send as they lack the personal strength to deal with the isolation and intensity there. I think partly it is experience and it comes with age and the range of different life experiences, working in different places.

Jane W. spelt out an important aspect of this: 'I could draw the lines I wanted to draw, and they were respected. I felt confident that my needs were accepted—no approval or disapproval.' Estelle added: 'When you get to a certain age and have a certain amount of life experience, you can deal with propositions and they aren't a trauma', while Patricia found: 'It didn't faze me, my self-image is not tied up with being the life and soul of the party!' despite a mixed reception when she arrived at Casey in 1981.

Barbara S. suggested: 'It was no additional strain being a woman, but there's more for younger ones, with families, or in new relationships.' Experience of working with diverse men is an advantage. Midj suggested: 'If you work with men all the time, you can watch how they relate to each other, and can sift what's personal and what's just the way they are.' Having worked with the men for several years, Ursula added: 'Despite pressure at the end, there were no major conflicts because each knew the other well', though she thought at Davis, where young women are 'thrown in the deep end, it's harder being a woman'. Mandy pointed to a double edge with lengthy exposure to a male environment: 'As I've been brought up in an all-male household with brothers, except for my mother, I never felt my sex was an issue. In fact, on the rare occasions when discrimination reared its ugly head, I had difficulty in recognising it as such. I usually took it as some sort of deficiency or inadequacy I had.' Others felt that being 'isolated and protected from a normal cross-section' was a distinct disadvantage.

Emphasising the value of prior experience of group life, Tracey P. thought: 'It didn't feel claustrophobic. I had lived in group houses for over ten years so it didn't feel different; rather, it was better. There was someone to cook your dinner!' Others who had experienced boarding school or university college life seemed to step into station life more easily. And it was usually easier on subsequent expeditions, even if the group wasn't so compatible. A number wanted to 'have another go', to 'get it right this next time', for in a sense the first time is a trial. Those who fail to be reselected can have great difficulty in letting go, whether the first time was a good or a bad experience. Some explanations for their rejection raise messy issues of discrimination, the assessment of expeditioner performance, and selection criteria and panels.

Young women mature, and acknowledge their naiveté, some-times after intensely painful self-analysis and condemnation. Poor communication between expeditioners is now pinpointed as a major source of misunderstanding and distress. So can better ways be taught? First, a need must be admitted, both officially and by expeditioners. Women would like more pre-departure briefings and training, especially for communication and con-flict-resolution skills, and an ongoing network on specific issues and information-sharing. There is an informal network of women who have been to Antarctica, and Pene Greet, Mary Mulligan and Maria Turnbull have made themselves available for consultation by women. Most find out by rumour, and experience.

Is there hope for change? Janet Thomson, though speaking of BAS, believes the trend is positive: 'It's been a gradual process to get women accepted into Antarctic activities.' Change has been more rapid since the mid-1980s, with increased female numbers, anti-discrimination legislation and some change in public attitudes. 'It's made life a little hard for all,' Maria Turn-bull admitted. Erica noticed that 'in 1988, things have changed dramatically in the last few years, like perceptions of sexual dis-crimination or sexual harassment, what is acceptable and what isn't. It's changed very quickly', though even in the late 1990s, some women have not felt this about ANARE. 'Janelle' suggested that problems stemmed from 'immature management' and others added that structures needed to be challenged, especially those perpetrating sexual politics and power on stations.

Five issues are repeatedly raised when women discuss change. One is the amount of alcohol on stations, which is implicated in many of the unpleasant interpersonal incidents. The second is improvement in the appeals procedures. This includes more effective briefing of expeditioners about EEO issues and pro-cesses, and countering the belief that to complain jeopardises not only your position on station, but your future chances of selection. Men as well as women have been inhibited from lodging formal complaints. No investigation can take place without the formality. Improvement in dealing with issues on station is also urgently needed yet, as Elaine Prior found in her recent study,[15] there has been a particular 'silo' mentality at head office and amongst some experienced expeditioners that resists such change. Deliberate attempts at change, especially from the top, may be difficult, and can easily be subverted in the relative isolation of the stations if mechanisms to reduce this are not in place and observed, even though bureaucracy is resented by so many.

Resistance to change may also affect another major concern: selection and assessment procedures. 'Krista' said: 'I feel strongly that the selection processes to get down are not strong enough. I think a lot of women would say the same.' Of major concern to women is the fact that men who have harassed others are sometimes re-selected. Identifying potential harassers may be difficult, though lack of experience with women and anti-social attitudes should be detectable. Re-selecting known perpetrators also points to flaws in the assessment of performance on station, despite several revisions. The station leader still has a lot of power in this respect, which inhibits complaints and also places stress on leaders who have to discipline, mediate and assess, and still live with the people concerned.

The main issue, however, is the gender balance in expeditions. The more female numbers approach males ones, the closer it will become to 'normal' society, though this may be abnormal for some who go South, and it is still hard to find qualified women for some positions. Apart from the change in the social and emotional environment that should follow, it will release another pressure on women: to 'look after' the men. And while some of the problems stem from the fact that stations are small communities, with the pressures and limitations that implies, women's minority status remains the major issue.

SEVEN

'It just blew my mind away!'

While tales of exploration and hardship are one inspiration for going to Antarctica, it is the place itself—the sense of untouched nature, of unharnessed forces—that draws people South. There is a longing today for wilderness, for places where the imprint of urban lifestyles is absent. We may create an imaginary landscape to meet our needs, or simply respond to what is there. The Antarctic is a place that invites us with its solitude. It is empty of people, though seething with wildlife in summer. Colours take on a particular intensity there, and the vistas of white and black and ice and rock contrast with the incredible depthlessness in the blue caverns and green surfaces of huge icebergs, wind scours and crevasses. Then there is the sky, the dramatic rising and setting of the sun over limitless horizons, the haloes and pillars created round the sun by ice crystals hanging in the clear air, and the mysterious swirling aurorae, like wind-tossed theatre curtains. It is elemental, and from the time when people first envisaged the polar ice, Antarctica has challenged visitors to make sense of the experience and to find ways to convey it to others.

A litany of words is used to describe the place: 'pristine', 'fragile', 'amazing', 'magical'. We feel 'privileged' to have lived there. Melanie described the sensations:

It was peaceful, it made me smile, just being there! Going down on the boat was like going into fairyland, going through icebergs, the change from pinks to purples to mauves—there's just no white in Antarctica, it's all shades of white. What impressed me most was the silence: inland it was just flat and white all around and you could ski away from the base and the generator noise and just be in a silent environment. I have never experienced anything like it.

Colours, textures, silence—these make the memories of Antarctica that endure, together with the smells, sounds and sights of the breeding wildlife on tussock and cliff and stony island beach.

As Astrida said: 'You don't forget the feelings you have there, for example of our arrival at Davis, at the edge of the fast ice.' Her images give deeper meaning to the sense of Antarctica as a frontier:

The ship has to pound itself in quite a long way to the base to make a ship–base connection to transport fuel. It hit the fast ice and went pounding through it for about twelve hours. We could see the base, and it felt like we were penetrating a membrane. This was the break between winterers and summerers, the contact with the animals—it really hit you, touched you inside. We were really going into this other place.

It was hard to sleep:

There was almost a full moon, my whole orientation in terms of space was disrupted—the sun and moon positions—and I questioned whether we were still getting the glow of a sunset or even moonrise or sunrise; it was an extraordinary sensation. I had a continuous feeling that I didn't want to sleep, I wanted to be out in it. I slept out on many occasions in my bivvy bag. I wanted to be a short way away, to witness the moon, the snow petrels flying and breeding, the storm petrels. Seals were calling not too far away, and there was continual activity. I wanted to be part of it all of the time. It's like nothing else!

Our senses struggle to deal with this huge new world. In the Southern Ocean, Tonia vividly remembered: 'There's the exhilaration of going out on deck on a crisp clear day and seeing the scenery—it's mind-blowing, each bit is different. You take a deep breath and feel wonderful. You feel like a little speck, very insignificant, it's so vast and goes on forever. It puts things right in proportion!' Elizabeth Hynes found that: 'Macquarie Island got hold of me in a big way. The colours are very, very vivid—greens, the clouds, the rocks—it's just stunning. You can walk into cloud. There are reflections in lakes, and it's just perfection on mirror still days.' Macquarie 'could be a lot less monotonous, it's just white on the continent. Looking at the blues of the continent, that could get hold of me in a bigger way and it would blow up. It's so huge, and ancient. It stores the ancient part of the world, it's spooky, you don't want to confront what it is . . .'

WORKING OUTDOORS

Tracey Rogers' doctoral research was on leopard seal behavioural acoustics:

> I'm interested in the vocalisation repertoire, the behavioural significance of sounds. Being solitary animals, I'm interested in how they find mates—they call for periods up to eighteen hours in a 24-hour period. I tracked them with helicopters, left a paint mark on them, then drove out with quads and recorded their vocalisations from the fast ice. They're pack ice animals who come into the continent to feed on penguins. As the ice retreats, the seals follow them in. The sounds travel—they can be recorded from 5–10 kilometres—but I like to get close: you can pick them up in the 40 mHz to 8 kHz range. The female in oestrus calls too—that's unusual, it's supposed to be only the males that call. It's very active work. I got up early, went out and marked, did tissue biopsies, came back and rested, then went out to start to record early in the afternoon, in a six-week cycle.

She 'always had to be aware of the ice', she recalled, and recounted an incident that brings out the danger, the transience and the sensuality of the environment. Alone one night, she:

heard it go—it just went 'boom'—and noticed that it was a different sound. My blood curdled, I felt cold down my back, and went 'oooooh . . .' and thought: 'OK, there's a crack opened up behind me.' I thought I'd get my equipment and move back—the crack had just opened, and I thought I'd keep walking just to make sure there weren't any more cracks. I kept walking and walking and the tide was going out. So I went back and packed up all my equipment, put it on my back and ran—by the end I was jumping floes! I remembered Rod Ledingham's words at field training about not to panic, just to keep calm, don't lose your head, run in. I arrived back by 3.00 a.m. The next morning I went out in the helicopter about 10.00 a.m. There was no pack there, it had all gone. If the wind comes up, they're like big sails then, they just float away.

Nevertheless:

The fast ice edge is to me the most beautiful place—it's where it's all happening—and you've got the sounds of it all, the creaking and the seals singing. I always record at night so it's all pink, and the birds—the penguins—think that you're a flock of penguins and they're all around you and giant petrels swoop on something dead on the ice, and the leopard seals come to check you out to see if there's something to eat. It's a really lovely, lovely place, it's really special. Being stuck on the station the whole time would drive you potty.

Over and over, women expressed this preference for being outdoors, for working from a simple field camp. Trudy covered over 90 kilometres of Macquarie Island's coastline for her albatross study.

I still get flashbacks to certain scenes—out away from people. Initially you are amazed, then you lose that, and start to get right inside it all—the total wildness, isolation, no other people. Sometimes when you've been out there for a while, you start to take it for granted and then you come to a point where you feel a part of it, somehow. It's hard to describe—you've lost the amazement, but you've started to become part of it. It's the total wildness, it's unspoilt, it carries on as it always has done and hopefully always will. For me the high point was that . . . it was the time away from station really.

Susan Ingham recorded:

Mary, Stefan and I went for a morning stroll to Handspike
Point ... A short way farther on, there was something white. It was
the Handspike Point wandering albatross on its nest. That was a
wonderful bird. It was first seen I think in '48, and it was still
going on 20 years later, breeding, as far as my records went. The
most beautiful white male bird.

Barbara Wienecke took up the story:

I never had a boring moment! The entire winter experience was a
constant 'wow!'—it was fantastic. The second I was away from
station and back into the field was just marvellous—I wouldn't
have lasted in the field without that attitude. I love being out in
the field away from people.

It took time to get used to the station again, 'but the showers
were nice, and not sleeping with things in your sleeping bag to
keep them liquid!'

In the cold, windy darkness of midwinter, Barbara marvelled
at the birds:

Especially the males carrying the eggs. They shuffle on their heels
though they can go up to 30 centimetre steps without eggs, only
5 centimetres with eggs, and they walk for kilometres like that.
They can't extend their flippers as that may dislodge the eggs.
When the females return, all these dirty skinny little males roll
around stretching! They are such good parents: they sing to the
eggs, and show them to each other. The ice looks like a huge Pro
Hart painting where they defecate! They rely on fresh snow to
maintain their fluid balance—they will go off even alone to get to
fresh snow on ice, and will even go across tide cracks on their
belly with their egg.

Then in July the females came back.

They were ever such a sight to behold! The forecast was for not
particularly good weather, with a bit of wind and snow, but we got

out to look at the colony and do another egg collection before they were buried in snow. Out of the blowing snow we saw six females coming out of the shadow—they were huge, big, clean, really showing off the little dirty males. The females were birds with a mission! They were tobogganing at first, then they got up, marched, bullied their way in between the males, and started to sing to locate their mates. They disappeared into the first huddle and became part of it, and nothing much happened for the next days, then a solid string of females came in, the noise level vastly increased, then they continued a cycling of birds in and out.

The Weddell seals started to return and pup in early summer.

This was quite exciting. There was nothing but cloud and stars above for months, then there were flying birds which was great—skuas, giant petrels, Wilson's storm petrels—they were just marvellous. Then there was a moving boiling big black band and a whole group of Adélies scooted on past the colony to the islands—they stood up to the big Emperors! As the tide cracks opened, the Emperors began to use them as bathtubs and swimming holes, including the seal holes. There was a marvellous interaction between the seals and penguins. The serenity of winter was well over! It's just so beautiful I wouldn't care if I died out there. What a place to leave this planet!

Anitra added:

As a place it is awesome, beautiful, it really is at the end of world, so far away. You have a sense of immense privilege to be there and see it. Ice diving, I had some of the most spectacular Antarctic experiences of anyone—I may go the rest of my life and never have experiences as utterly wonderful again. It's hard to imagine anything that good. The first dive was off the planet, though I nearly killed myself on it. At the end of that first day, we were photographed. I look at it and it brings back a sense of a turning point day in my life. I did something beyond belief, and it was incredibly important for each person.

Anitra is an experienced diver, but:

This was the best visibility I'd ever seen. I got in, saw 2 metres of ice, and stretching ahead under the ice with the sun shining above, it was incredibly beautiful. There was an abundance of huge sponges, seaweeds, and I felt completely 'lost'—there was sensory overload. A huge flock of Adélie penguins dived in and around us and you think you'll burst!

Gina described the depths from above:

The ink-blue darkness of the cold water—it was almost like looking into death. That was a bit scary—a facade of ice over water. I thought I'd be too scared to go on to the sea ice, but you see others there and do it. There were calved 'bergs from previous years. I went to bed one night while two fellows were skiing on those 'bergs. The next day the 'bergs were a mile out to sea!

A film crew arrived to make the first IMAX large-frame film and Anitra spent several weeks diving for them.

We went by helicopter to look for an inland crevasse with water . . . I jumped with Malcolm into a pool that led to a vast system of caverns, pools, chambers, all of ice. It was glacial meltwater and completely clear as there were no bacterial sediments. It was a 400 foot [140 metre] chamber, which was light in places, a phenomenally beautiful natural formation. I nearly drowned on my first dive from screaming at the beauty. We filmed for two weeks in it, but never again—it was incredibly dangerous. One day I was sitting in 1 metre deep water, waiting. The sun was sparkling, and I was aware of something, and a VW-sized piece of ice had broken off and was floating. I was hauled in suddenly by the others. Malcolm carried us with his passion to ignore dangers and persuaded us to do one more day. We found there were no caves any more, it had all collapsed and where we'd parked had fallen in—it could have happened while we were in! Good sense would tell us never do it again!

The variety and numbers of wild creatures bring the continent to life in summer, but cannot rival the effects of the sheer numbers of creatures on Macquarie Island. 'There's nothing to compare with standing at Lusitania Bay with 100 000 penguins around, seeing a whale. It makes up for being saturated, and cold—it's the most extreme biological life I'll get to see! It's the most fantastic experience!' Jennie exclaimed. She felt incredibly lucky to have seen such things: 'It is extremely beautiful.' The extremes of climate are matched by the extremes of landscape and biology.

Pauline echoed the impact of the quantity of wildlife:

To look down on a colony of thousands of penguins is unbelievable! Some Royals nested up on the plateau—you were hit by the smell and the babble of their noise—they were a pecking distance apart. The nests were awash with mud, guano, pebbles they kept pinching from each other! I sat in a large group that was pecking distance apart, and became a penguin then . . .

Lynn Williams did not hesitate to say that a high point was

seeing the glowing, snowy cone of the active volcano Big Ben exposed, and seeing the pastels and the soft lights on dog trips in the afternoon, the really remote physical splendour, just icebergs, big icebergs, icebergs around Auster rookery, a lot of the physical splendour, maybe seeing whales from the ship—it's hard to get a balance really . . . the really pronounced, prolonged sunrises, sunsets, four hours of bright lights in the sky, the aurora, it would definitely be all those physical things. Watching some of the animals, certainly at Macquarie, watching the nesting patterns, and the full cycle, that sense of being part of it continuing, being that close to nature, would definitely be the highlight. Sometimes at Macquarie it would be like a jewel in the Southern Ocean and there'd be just a thousand kilometres of open water and you'd just have this glorious coloured water along the beaches, you'd have these beachscapes and this vivid turquoise water, and blue, just some of the colours you'd see. And watching some of the albatrosses, when they're flapping their wings at chicks, or watching the mating of some of the blackbrows . . . all the highs are nature-related. That sort of feeling you're just so privileged to see all of that.

And there's 'the sheer pleasure of walking up and down the island—the physical feel of walking':

I have always enjoyed that with bushwalking, so I remember some of those trips. There was more of that sort of pleasure at Macquarie than at Mawson because you're just that much closer to it. At Heard Island you're close to the animals again, and the birds, all those visual sightings, the rare sightings, or your first experience of a particular animal or bird, watching the moulting of the penguins, they're really tame. Lying in a hut at night listening to them going on with their noises—Macquarie has some wonderful, wonderful scenery and walking opportunities. Careering down huge scree slopes or some of the coastal rim, it has such a rugged coastline and it's just fantastic. It doesn't rain heavily very often, it's really a drizzle and a sea spray, what they call precipitation, really not rain so you see dots on puddles often. You get wind, and when it's strong you get blasting sand, there are grey sandy beaches, but I really see that as an inclemency of the climate and more of a hassle. It really stings your face as it whips along, but I don't remember rain as a negative. Basically you rug yourself up and you've got a pair of woollen long johns and a parka and you're going to be wet, you've got wet feet, you're not going to get from one end of the island dry anyway, so once you accept you've got wet feet it's all right.

Ulla has been another multiple visitor to Antarctica. Nature is also the highlight for her. She talked about 'nature, the stillness. It's very difficult to put all that into words. It's unreal.' Attempting to tease out the specific attractions, she continued: 'I can't put it in words—I love cold areas . . . I remember one night alone on Macquarie Island with a breeze through the tussocks—it's being at one with nature, the walks alone at Davis wandering around the rocks and looking at shapes even in winter.' Here, she and another woman went for a five-day walk in temperatures down to −30°C. They skated on one of the lakes.

For the first time, I got vertigo. I went on to the lake and looked down and could see the bottom through the ice. Everything was spinning and it was my head! When I got my balance back, we both skated on the lake in the twilight in the falling snow. It was nearly dark, huge snowflakes came down and we just skated from one end of the lake to the other, over and over. Just the two of us, and the silence, it was as if we were the only ones in the world.

The same feelings were there for Lucinda:

Some of my best memories were being on top of little mountains, having collected all the lichens, put them away in my bag, and sitting down out of the wind and just looking out over the glacier, with this huge expanse of white, I couldn't see my field partner, only the glacier. That was good. It was everything that I hoped it would be, I enjoyed every single aspect—the voyage down there, station life at Mawson, living out in the field, and I had a great time collecting.

Working with the huskies was the peak experience for some fortunate to be in Antarctica at the right time, and prepared to put the time and effort into it.[1] With a dog team, there is the thrill of moving through the quiet environment. This is also appreciated on skidoo trips over the sea ice, and at special places like Scullin Monolith. Louise elaborated:

There is nothing more wonderful than when the dogs are running well, the ice is firm, you're gliding along past icebergs and the sun's shining—you have a far greater sense of connection to the environment, of being part of it, than you do in a vehicle, where you're insulated and cocooned. And it's the right speed—the dogs run at about 6–7 kilometres per hour, a good steady jog for a person, and everything slides by, and you've got a companion, and the dogs are companionable, and when it's like that, it's bliss, it's absolutely unimaginable!

Experiencing the self as physical is part of the exhilaration. High points for Pene at Mawson were working with the dogs, combined with 'the big open space, the expanse of sky with aurorae splashed across it, the pinks, purples and blues of the long polar twilights that really inspire me. In summer the wildlife is fascinating. I enjoy the absence of people.'

PERCEIVING AND REPRESENTING ANTARCTICA

Words to describe the experience of Antarctica are hard to find. According to Ros: 'Even with the visual knowledge given by present-day media presentations, the Antarctic will be an imagined landscape for the majority of this generation.' Those who do visit see and perceive it differently, through the lenses of their profession, their personal expectations, their reason for and manner of being there, their culture and so on. Some of those professionals speak here about their impressions and understandings.

Ros's doctoral thesis examines the notion of the wilderness and aesthetic values of the Antarctic.[2]

> It started from simple problem-solving. What is the meaning and the implications of 'wilderness and aesthetic values in the Antarctic'? It spans disciplines, especially philosophy and landscape architecture. The Antarctic poses particular dilemmas: the joy and beauty of coffee table books on Antarctica is [that of] a moving, disintegrating landscape. Can you assess it? How do you assess a landscape in winter when you can't see it? And it is often assumed that there is one set of aesthetic values, although there are different cultural understandings of landscape—for example, between the British and Americans. And 'landscape' has only been used recently with respect to the Antarctic—we use 'environment' but have not specified what that means. So what is the Treaty language, and why have they used it?

Her thesis is a complex unfolding of some answers to these questions. Her personal response is one of 'wonder, awe, majesty—without question that feeling, thrill, excitement'. She added: 'I speak from a background of personal conviction as a straightforward Christian, biblically based. Therefore— inevitably?—a sense of wonder and joy that says "Thank you, Lord, for the majesty and pleasure to be there and see it".'

As official photographer, the first obligation for Jutta during her five trips South was to capture the human operations in Antarctica. But she was captivated by the environment, and

published her photographs.³ Her description of arrival at Casey
evokes strong sensory impressions, and the phenomenon of
'knowing' intellectually, followed by the physical encounter:

> When we neared the coast, I got a chance to go by helicopter to
> film the ship's arrival. Casey station was the replacement station
> for Wilkes—they had planned and built it in my time, so I'd seen
> all stages of it from planning, testing the aerodynamic designs in a
> wind tunnel. I 'knew' what it looked like. We flew in with the
> helicopter, sitting in that tiny little bubble, and I saw the station
> down there. It was real at last and I really broke up: it suddenly
> became real. I didn't think anyone noticed with the big goggles on
> against the glare, but I was really overwhelmed to see the rocks,
> and you see the ice down behind, the ice edge, and the blue sky,
> and it was absolutely overwhelming to see in reality what I'd seen
> in all the photos and plans.

Of Macquarie Island, Jutta noted:

> It's a contrast, there's no ice or snow but rainfall almost every day,
> very little sunshine, and a rough climate as such. Antarctica was
> different. It was such a tremendous experience. On Macquarie
> Island, I particularly enjoyed the walking. The first trip was brief
> because we had a storm, but I had the chance for some walks
> along the coast. The second trip I had the chance for a longer
> walk and to stay in one of the huts away from camp overnight.
> That was a superb experience. I used to do a lot of bushwalking—
> I still do—and felt in my element there! It was such a tremendous
> experience.

Those sentiments about Macquarie Island were echoed by every
woman I spoke to.

Jutta continued:

> It's different, the air is so extremely clear, the views in the
> distance, especially from the helicopter. That gave a perspective, a
> feeling for place. At the station in summer, you don't get the right
> impression, because the snow has melted—there's still some ice by
> the sea but it's quite different to the winter. At one stage I got

inland. That was a superb experience. It was quite cold, even though it was sunny, beautiful weather. On the first trip to Casey in 1976, we experienced one of the summer blizzards. The wind came from the land, the ship was dragging anchor and in the short distance between coast and ship the steep and heavy short waves built up, the ship was permanently leaning. We couldn't have a shower as the water couldn't get away because of the lean. I was able to photograph big waves breaking over the landing barge tied to the side of the ship.[4]

Those experiences were shared with Elizabeth Chipman:

It was not dangerous, I didn't feel threatened by the landscape though it was overwhelming and I felt just a small dot of humanity—it's like that in the Australian desert too. I felt awe, not that it was threatening. It's a big magnificent stage to be strutting or crawling on! So many clichés come to mind—that it was breathtaking was literally true at one stage. I was so stunned I was gasping. One day I was out in a helicopter catching a seal with two others, and Jutta was filming. I went off a bit behind a slight hill—alone—and dropped to my knees and as an atheist didn't know what to do! It seemed like a religious experience and I didn't know who to pray to! And being there at last too.[5] Part of the effect the place has on you is that emotions overcome you! The silence, the distance you can see, the clarity of the air. We had a blizzard at sea—it was magnificent! The ship was listing 45 per cent but I was not frightened! I'd never thought of it snowing at sea—it was a wonderful experience. Penguins are a symbol of the struggle of survival, especially the Emperors!

Clare Robertson explained the role of perception in what we 'see' in an environment. Using photographs, sketches and a diary to record her impressions, then reflecting on all the diverse sources of information, the painting finally began. Clare talked about the task of the artist in attempting to convey—both to an audience who is familiar with the place, but also with a much larger, unfamiliarised one—the feelings and meanings that Antarctica held for her. She reflected on the techniques that she employs as an artist to create the paintings:[6]

To me the essential feeling I wanted to transmit was one of fear and beauty inextricably combined. It has to be one of the most beautiful places on Earth, but everything is dangerous. The beauty is mesmerising and pulls you forward while the sense of peril restrains you. It is a very powerful combination. Another constant emotional theme of the paintings was the conflict between fear and beauty, fear of the unknown, the sheer perilous beauty of the ice. Fear repels and beauty attracts, but fear can also attract us despite ourselves.

According to Clare, the untrained viewer can:

take these images at face value, as simply providing information about a site they probably do not know much about. For example, with [her painting] 'Ice Spur', it depicts typical sea ice, and this site is 300 kilometres out to sea, and all the so-called landforms are in fact various types of ice. There is no solid land at all in this image, although it has all the characteristics of a landscape. But then you start playing other games, and this quite attractive place turns out to be something else entirely. The foreground is slick and insubstantial, the whole place is obviously unstable. So despite its superficial appeal, it is a threatening image.

One of the commmon themes of the paintings is:

a sense of loss. This sense of loss is both personal and for humanity as a whole. Another essential element is a lack of sense of scale. If I were a proper landscape artist, every picture would have to have a penguin or a seal or something else that is familiar, to anchor the image and allow the viewer to work out the relative positions of forms and hence the scale. But the lack of a sense of scale is one of the most striking characteristics of Antarctica, and it was fundamental to the construction of the paintings. Because the atmosphere in Antarctica is almost completely free of moisture, there is no atmospheric haze. Because there are no trees or other foliage, you have nothing against which to compare. In other words, you cannot tell whether an object is a small rock 10 metres away on the crest of a small rise, or whether it is the tip of a distant mountain. The helicopter pilots said they would sometimes have to open the door when coming in to land, so they could see when the skids touched the ground [because there was nothing else to guide them].

It is a fractal-dominated landscape. On the surface of the ice, the formations are exactly the same in a smaller scale as the same landscape seen from the air. So you have that marvellous image within an image within an image that is extraordinarily difficult to relate to a sense of scale. This was one of the characteristics that the paintings had to have, and again it is very unnerving.

The place she became so enmeshed with was:

a fabrication of my own mind, like a dream, and it doesn't exist, least of all there in the real place. It is not enough to paint a picture of Antarctica that is merely pretty. Anyone can do that because the place is so rich in images. You have to go beyond the content and give the viewer some real insight. When you make the effort, you are amply repaid because people can become quite passionate about the images.

Both Ros and Clare wanted their work to have a practical outcome and, while Clare has gained immense satisfaction from the 'recognition' of place when expeditioners view her work, she also wanted to invite others to discover, and then to become carers for, the place: 'The central theme of the whole project is related to the larger view of global civilisation and the point that it has now reached. The work is not overtly political, but it does intend to make people aware and get them to think.'

She noted:

On the voyage, we were intensely aware of being at the very end of an immensely attenuated supply line tracking back for thousands of kilometres over the stormiest seas in the world, the product of the high technology of the late twentieth century. This was our umbilical cord, the only thing which kept us alive in that environment which is essentially unsuitable for human life. The slightest malfunction would have spelled disaster. I was always aware of the sense of intense vulnerability.

Caroline Caddy also wrestled with ways to depict Antarctica:

That blue—that's the one thing that you're going to find amazing,[7] and Clare found amazing. I keep reading over and over about artists and writers and even the explorers themselves trying to describe it—that no matter what you say or try to tell people, you cannot capture that colour and unearthly glow that it has. It's like some technology from another planet: it's there and it's all around you, it's obviously so natural but there's no way you can explain this without bringing in terms that don't exist.

We talked about the role of imagination and our interaction with the information from our senses. She unfolded this through uncovering the layers of her poem, 'The Music Makers'.

> Over ice that's humped
>   like buried harps and pianos
> through wind scoops
>   melt pots of ancient
>   Chinese music
> all day we peer into the distances
>   of a bushman's song
> about a tree mistaken
> for a man.
> The sun slides on we stop
>   in the huge ocarina
>   of Antarctica.
> La da da da da I explain
>   ni naw ni naw ni he says.
> We stamp our feet and blow into
>   our cupped hands
> the colours of Neptune Jupiter and Mars
>   leaning in
>   to hear.

I felt it was like recording the songs of humans ... I've got people out on the ice and what they're saying comes out as 'la-de-dahs'. That 'ni-naw-ni' the Spanish use in place of 'la-de-dah' absolutely fascinated me when I first heard it, and that fed right into this idea that there is no language in Antarctica. So I have these people right on the ice and when they talk to each other it comes out as 'la-de-dahs' and 'ni-naw-nis' to anything listening to the universe, which at the end of the poem is the colours of that endless sunset that you get in the sky there at the end of the summer. It's the colours of the close-ups when you see Neptune and Jupiter and Mars, those soft bands of colour.

When I think of the poem now, I feel like someone who's been out on the ice recording the songs of the seals and yet that is a poetic coalescence of images and things because it never really happened. The feel of the colour of the sky brought in the planets, and that brings in the music because of the old classic thing about the music of the spheres. You don't even have to know these things in a good poem because you'll get something else out of the imagery.

The shapes of the snow and the ice are always in your mind when you're thinking about Antarctica and trying to write about it, the shapes and the sound of the wind which is always strong, it's *the* sound in Antarctica. And the wind makes its own noise over the snow when it blows the snow—that 'chi-tacky-chi' of the snow over the ice, and through wind scoops. At the time I'd been listening to some of the old Chinese music played on pottery instruments, what we used to know as an ocarina. And that idea of wind scoops, wind scours, listening to the Chinese music, ocarina and musical instruments, the word 'ocarina' suddenly came out— and in the poem we stop—we're going along somewhere, we stop, the sun keeps going, because it's always sliding down the horizon. We stop and there's this huge ocarina of Antarctica . . .

THE IMPACT OF ANTARCTICA ON HUMANS

Clare articulated those indefinable feelings evoked by Antarctica, and found:

Going to Antarctica creates a bond, because only another person with the same experience will understand how you feel, and you know you will not need to explain yourself. Those who know will understand and all the rest will not. To try to explain is like describing colour to someone who is colour blind; you can manage the cold facts, but the emotional aspects are meaningless.

You have to ask yourself: 'Just what is it about Antarctica which has such a powerful effect on so many people?' For some, it takes them out of their normal context to an extent that they have never before experienced. It is as if they have up to this point been shielded from ever having to think, and suddenly they find themselves in circumstances where they have time to reflect on the larger issues of life. It can be a confronting experience for the average person who is unaccustomed to it. Artists think like this all the time as a fundamental part of their work, but still Antarctica is a shock for them too. People discover things about themselves, or others, that they never knew, or confront aspects that they were hiding, or come to deeper realisations about our culture and civilisation as a whole. For others, it is simply an enormous privilege to be somewhere that is so exquisitely beautiful.

There is some sort of experience of coming to terms with themselves as a human being. It requires the absolute peak of human endurance to survive unaided. You cannot take your existence there for granted. Nothing can be taken for granted. You must respect and acknowledge everything that goes to keep you alive, and you have to respect the planet in the larger sense and realise our place in it.

For Elizabeth Chipman: 'It's difficult to describe what it's like and it looms very large in my personal life, still colours every day, because I deliberately set out to work on it, am immersed in it.' Now a writer, she commented that: 'You write for the pleasure and it leads you on, you feel you must stay with it. I feel I must stay with the Antarctic too. After [my current book], I'd like to write a novel with an Antarctic setting.'

The sense of loss that Clare mentioned earlier is also felt by others. 'I really, really miss Antarctica at times,' 'Jade' exclaimed. 'The place was it! There were times when you'd just get out and look and see for miles and feel so isolated and struck by the beauty.' And the place inspires:

I have a healthy respect for it. I felt very small and vulnerable at times. The first really cold day I headed out skiing, it was –29°C, it was scary cold. We were out for five hours and I had the feeling my fingers were going. We got caught by the weather going back and had to bivvy. I was very aware of my hands that night. I went out in winter a lot. I loved winter, it was fantastic; I enjoyed it more than summer, it's the 'real Antarctica'! Or just to be on Davis Island, just to think we are only the second people there— it was amazing—we'll never be so isolated again. It puts you back in your place.

Isolation, wildness, cold: these beckon human beings.

The Antarctic as frontier is a human construct, just as the concept of 'wilderness' is. As Clare pointed out:

> Antarctica is more than just a physical place. To many people it represents a state of mind, a precious place unlike any other. As an artist, I use my intense feelings for it as a yardstick against which all other sites and emotions can be measured. In short it is extreme, one end of the spectrum, and must be understood. It allows me to ask the question 'What then is the other end of that spectrum?' Is it the overcrowded and fashion-obsessed city, remote from first-hand knowledge of the natural world, where everything is pressed into service of humanity? It was a privilege to be able to experience a site of this importance.

Ultimately, it is the internal changes that remain. Pauline said:

> It was a testing time for myself, and showed me that I had enough strength to be able to cope with the conditions, so I was strengthened by the experience. Also I wanted the experience, and having had it, it went way beyond expectations. All of us have dreams—most don't come true. This did and it wasn't a nightmare! It was so beautiful—the stark black of the rocks outlined against a paling sky was like a sculpture, the pounding of the sea, the light, I had no feeling of fear or that things could go wrong, there was no tension.

How could one? In Clare's words: 'It is simply an enormous privilege to be somewhere that is so exquisitely beautiful!'

EIGHT

'There's no room for heroes there!'

Experiencing Antarctica begins as the physical frontier is reached: 'The extraordinary jewellery box of Antarctica has opened and there are greater treasures in store as we enter the pack,' wrote Phillipa Foster.[1] This chapter highlights the ways in which women have gained deep satisfaction from their Antarctic sojourns, and looks at their hopes for the future.

HEROES, HEROINES AND THE LIKES OF YOU AND ME

In the public imagination, Antarctica was discovered by men who risked all in the stormy, frozen South, battling unthinkable extremes of climate and suffering horrendous physical and even mental torment—heroes, in a word, though this has at least two meanings: an individual who triumphs over adversity, one of the 'great men of history'; and one whose deeds are located in the moral context of the welfare of others.[2] In Western culture, there are few such female models, and one of them, Joan of Arc, is almost an ungendered person. Traditionally, women's role has been to deliver and succour the hero, giving him up to the greater good.

Tracey Pitman has suggested that there is an inevitable linking of Antarctica and heroism: 'The heroic element is alive and well.

It will take a long time to go, and may always be there as it is a bit special—not many get to go. Some will always express that specialness in heroic-type acts.' She noted that 'having women there normalises it, it's part of the levelling'. One woman asked why else one would go to Antarctica if not to approach the heroic, which renders attempts to implement public service norms 'at their very worst, emasculating one of the last bastions of true masculinity, profaning this hall of heroes'. This is, however, a reason why other women feel uneasy about the 'culture' and its traditions: invoking the heroic era makes women feel that 'we don't belong here'.

Perhaps it is time we had some Antarctic *heroines*. So is it helpful to know about previous women in Antarctica, and should women's achievements—both in earlier times and today—be acknowledged specifically? Wendy suggested heroines 'would be outgoing, confident, competent—and they wouldn't have a beard!' She also pointed out that 'it's not exceptional to have gone' to Antarctica, though 'not many women spend a year in isolation'.

Most women felt: 'If an ordinary person such as me could go there, it's nothing spectacular!' The message they want to broadcast is that Antarctica is a place for men *and* women, and that women *are* there, participating in every aspect of the station work and life, and revelling in it. This view stands beside a sense of privilege to have been there, a feeling that it has been a life-changing experience, and frustration that it can be difficult to share the experience with others.

Women tend to emphasise the experience, not the individual. Lucinda spoke for many women:

> I don't have a sense of having achieved something for womankind by going there—maybe if I'd been a station leader; there's something unusual about a female being a station leader, though I can't see that there should be something unusual about it . . . To me, there's nothing extraordinary in that I, a female, have gone down there to be a field assistant . . . I don't make a big thing about being a woman caver, a woman blackbelt, a woman who's been to Antarctica or whatever, there's just things I've done as a *person*.

Erica elucidated the meaning of the experience: 'I don't think of heroines or think of it in that way. I was part of a team, part of the group and felt really privileged that it worked out well and I was a good part of the group. I don't see that as at all heroic.' Multiple-winterer 'Davina' added: 'There's no scope for heroism on bases now; you can't do it unless you break rules! [But] I'd include the first woman who chose to winter by herself. That was quite heroic.'

Lyn Goldsworthy suggested there were two sides to the heroism issue. On the one hand, Antarctica is 'about the last place where *man* can test his testosterone or whatever it is he's testing when he goes out and walks 400 kilometres in the cold', a place that 'also gives people some sort of strength, it's nice that you can still test your own endurance and strength of mind'. Women are doing that too, with each summer bringing some new 'first'. And, as Liv's account makes clear, testing the self—rather than competing with others—is a compelling motive. Lyn continued:

> Women shouldn't 'rise up' to the masculine concept of the heroic age. The whole issue of men going out and walking for X days and getting their feet frozen off—what can I say? Some men seem to need to do this. A few women seem to need to do it too [but] the whole concept of heroism from that perspective of frostbite and climbing the highest mountain, this is very old-world male, and not something that women should set out to emulate.

Even more explicit in her dismissal of such images was Vivian Schenker:

> I have trouble with the concept of hero—it's such a boy's concept! What's so virtuous about suffering? I can't understand why we make heroes out of those who suffer, not based on what they *achieve*. This is a problem to women—if the emphasis was on achievement, it would encourage people to look at it differently. But it's part of boys' culture and their resentment and that's why it's hard for women.

Liza elaborated: 'Men need to conquer things. They need to throw themselves off cliffs, throw themselves down holes, and go beyond the edge of safety on the ice! Women know the limits. Very few women I have met need to be like the fellows.' And Estelle pointed out the different ways of telling stories: 'Heroes are a stupid idea, the true heroes are unfussy: they just do it. Females don't need it. It's male myths and that macho image to make it more terrifying and scary than it really was. That's the way they tell the stories, to make them seem more brave.'

Fiona spoke for many when she said: 'Setting anyone up as a hero is pretty silly. It's as bad to see women doing this as perpetuating the male myth.' Ruth Eriksen added: 'What we do today is advanced technology; heroism is mostly perceived by other people [who haven't been]. [But] it *is* something special to work there.' Angela McGowan voiced a point that was echoed by other women, 'Those who want to be heroes don't like to see those who are not particularly heroic coping!' She cited as evidence the concern the men had to check out her all-female camp and offer advice, even though 'The women just laughed—we'd been fixing the generator, etc.'. Women clearly look at present realities, not past myths, in narrating their Antarctic presence.

Heroines

Women responded to the idea of Antarctic heroines in ways that reflected their view of heroes. As Helen Pearce pointed out: 'There weren't a lot of female heroines. As a kid you took on male heroes. I never thought that what they did was just male. I just thought you could do whatever they did. Perhaps this belief more than anything else is what distinguishes women who go to Antarctica, and those who do not consider the possibility.' Then, too, as Jenny Mackenzie said: 'if you're looking at the old-style heroes, they survived some incredible adventures and great hardship and personal sacrifice ... someone would have had an awfully horrible time if they became an Antarctic heroine and I wouldn't wish it on anyone!'

Melanie reflected:

I wonder if we're then setting up for ourselves something akin to
the hero and that's not something that I want to do for women.
I don't think women need any definition of what an Antarctic
heroine is. But we do need a range of role models who've been to
Antarctica, women who are going there. I just wonder what it is
we're doing by picking out women—are we necessarily going to
show people who have achieved something in Antarctica, or are we
just going to choose them because of their gender and highlight
what they've done? I guess the only reason I'm hesitating is
because I know there's going to be a backlash for doing that sort
of thing. Generally among people there's certainly no feeling of
who are some famous women who've been to Antarctica, whereas
everybody's heard of Phillip Law and all the old cronies, and
people don't have a real sense of what the modern Antarctic
expeditioner who's a woman does. Like in so many areas, women
remain anonymous—they're only there. It's part of our story now.

Of those who concede that 'female Antarctic heroines
wouldn't do any harm', women who quietly cope are repeatedly
cited. As Alison explained, 'They would demonstrate resiliency,
tenacity, a sense of humour, not taking themselves too seriously
(which is the worst possible thing!), self-confidence and the
ability to portray that.' Women like Liv Arnesen and Brigitte Muir
are extraordinary people whose exploits have inspired men and
women. Elizabeth Chipman said they 'led the way' for women in
Antarctica, but went on to explore the notion of 'extraordinary':

There are not that many women heroes (that we hear about)
throughout history except the suffragettes. They've not been in
the exploring game, involved in the adventuring except the
Victorian women. But women have led extraordinary lives. I have
looked personally for female role models. There are strengths in
very ordinary women—one starts with one's mother—and I looked
for these strengths, in tram drivers, connies, anyone who showed
some wit. One looks for them, hopes to recognise them, but one's
total life cannot be lived as a hero: there's always the times when
heroes do not live up to one's expectations. Scott was hardly a

hero! I remember as a child looking for heroes; they were always men. What we women need is a woman hero recognised by both men and women; we need to see women doing things and achieving in fields that are recognised as 'good' by both men and women.

'Those first four women were closeted on board ship, like boarding school. I see those as Antarctic heroines,' said one woman. Sue Baker also looked up to them. She was teased by a man for reading *Women on the Ice* in Antarctica; he thought such a book was silly because 'women can't be compared to the men that have been written about, such as Mawson'. But Sue, like many other women, felt she wanted 'to be able to identify with other women who've done similar things'.

Others nominated female scientists, if not for heroic status, then for inspiration. Mary Gillham dedicated her book about Macquarie Island to 'Professor Lily Newton who set my feet on the naturalist's trail'. For others, both male and female mentors have played a role. On Macquarie Island, people like Jenny Scott, who has conducted field research there since 1979, stand out: 'She's outside for hours and hours doing her transects. People would often tell stories about women in a kind of parallel sort of way . . . and maybe on Macquarie there's not such a tradition of male heroes . . .'

Patricia Selkirk, whose first visit coincided with Jenny Scott's, is also spoken of with admiration for her work, for 'flying the flag for science' in a quiet, competent way, and for her tactful support of younger people, especially first-time women. Jennie Whinam elaborated: 'I feel that Patricia Selkirk is a wonderful role model. Patricia is very generous with her support and assistance and I have enjoyed my contacts with her.'

Like others, Jennie also enjoys having younger women come through, full of inspiration and keenness. Not many senior, experienced scientists spend time in Antarctica now; those who do, and who go out of their way to be helpful to others, are mentioned enthusiastically. They include Margaret Clayton, who has worked on the joint Argentinian–German stations, and on a

Chilean station. In nominating her, Anitra also said that it was more physically difficult for the early women in science who worked in the bush than for women on Antarctic stations in recent decades: 'Some women inhabited large boots and trod where no woman has trod before.' Combining pathbreaking with personal qualities, female station leaders were also considered as possible Antarctic heroines. 'I'm glad I wintered with Louise [Crossley],' said 'Davina', 'she's another model of how to do things, and a good role model as leader.' Diana Patterson has also been named for her outstanding skills in managing people in a small community. She feels that she has been a role model for women in middle management, has support from women and men in Antarctica, and takes her responsibility 'very seriously'. Considerable distress has been caused to a number of women by perceived lack of support from male station leaders. Joan Russell, too—controversial for her actions against harassment and pornography—stands out to others for her support and example. As station leader at Macquarie Island, her change strategies were much appreciated by other women, and her caring approach was welcomed. 'Helena' added: 'If a fat, middle-aged woman [Joan] could walk the length of Macca in the middle of winter in rubber boots, anyone can! This was breaking myths. There are Antarctic heroines and they are not acknowledged. Joan did so much for Macca, and Di Patterson is achieving many things.'

Role models and mentors

There was a strong suggestion in the discussion of heroines that the high achiever is not relevant to ordinary women's lives: 'Has the fact that women have flown around the planet, cruised all the oceans and gone into space made a single difference to any other woman? I don't think that Antarctic heroines are going to make a difference to women in Antarctica in general. That's possibly because I've always believed that if you want something, you go and get it yourself,' says Barbara W. Some women gain such confidence and the ability to act, but others seem barely able to dream. Women who go to Antarctica have those qualities of daring and confidence, coupled in many instances with incredible persistence in the face of initial rejections, and they exhibit patience and determination. Sadly, experiences there can severely shake their self-confidence and sense of self.

There have to be pioneers to venture into new fields—both women and men—who show that it is possible and how it might be achieved, and these have inspired women. Many of the women who have returned from Antarctica enjoy going into schools, especially all-female ones, 'very much aware of actually going there to show these girls that well, if you really want to you can do anything, study science, go to Antarctica', as Corinna pointed out.

Role models can suggest that it is possible to be there and to succeed in new circumstances. Making a strong case for role models, Sue Baker said: 'In very male-dominated fields, having female "role models" who have "succeeded" helps you to feel that maybe there's a chance for you to succeed also.' However, success can be intimidating: 'If you want role models rather than heroes, you have to look at successful people. I don't mean successful in that they publish wonderful papers, but just the ones who got along . . . I value common sense more than anything.' Phillipa probably speaks for many women, saying: 'I feel I'm a classic female and am surprised when I do a new thing well.'

How women present themselves to others, and the relationship between acceptance and conformity with others' expectations can be complex, and in the uncertainties of Antarctica, these things can become very confusing. The ability to be oneself was stressed by Elizabeth Bulling, who suggested that a role for mentors is to demonstrate that it is normal to be there, without needing to be labelled 'successful'. There's a need to have someone who knows what it's like, who can listen, and who can pass on her experience, validating both the way newcomers feel and their right to be there.

Confidence in the person and her ability to inspire it in others has earned the high regard of women. An aspiring expeditioner said of one field training officer: 'Heather [Kirkpatrick] is confident, skilled, good with people—she'll be a guiding light for women five years hence.' Skills with handling people were also mentioned by Suzanne, an experienced voyage leader: 'I would rather like to have female role models, doing a good job, getting on with people.' Kerrie found yet another important aspect in her role model: 'She brought a very humanitarian approach to lecturing which I hadn't experienced before.' This woman applied to go to Antarctica in 1973, 'and they just laughed at her!'

Respect is another quality that is admired—for example, Diana Patterson was 'very professional—people respected that even if they didn't like her'. With so few women in senior positions in the Antarctic Division, experienced female expeditioners inspire others. Yet, over and over again, they stress their ordinariness. Estelle exemplified this: 'I went in as a small girl, who still can do it. It was very challenging [but] really in my heart of hearts I don't think I've done anything special.' Ulla added:

> When I graduated in 1979, it wasn't all that unusual [to have] female radio operators, but unusual enough that my whole family was quite shocked that I went to sea as a female, and on most of the ships I was the only female. But once you started working, you don't regard yourself as unusual, it's just part of your life . . . As far as I'm concerned, I haven't done anything special. We all have choice and I've done what I did.

Like others, she is proud and perhaps a little surprised that she was chosen, but then plays down her achievement.

In a remote place visited by few people, and fewer women, pride and denial walk hand in hand. I suspect that one reason for this duality in women's accounts of their Antarctic experiences is the struggle for esteem—the battle between reliance on external sources of validation and self-acceptance, and perhaps a fear that, having dared to reach high, they do not want to place burdensome expectations on themselves or others.

Women's sense of themselves is central to issues about encouragement and support. Annie Rushton pointed out:

Part of the problem of women's sense of self is the lack of continuity from one generation to the next. Women have always done unusual things but we don't know about them. One of the greatest tools of suppression/oppression can be seen in the writings of Henry Lawson's mother—they're extremely interesting and to the point— so we keep reinventing feminism as the 'corporate memory' is lost from one generation to the next. One of the functions of a mentor in the public realm is to ensure that the experiences, knowledge and learnings of that period become public knowledge (*not* public property). So, too, do the experiences and learnings of those affected by the 'mentor'. When one woman achieves some level of public recognition, others are inspired to speak out more confidently. Put bluntly, in 2000, role models seem not necessary in an Antarctic context. Women are doing it and the reasons women don't go aren't because they're afraid, think it's inappropriate or are not encouraged, but they're stuck in ways that are inimical to women's lives back here—not because it's Antarctica.

This point was raised by a number of women, especially with respect to the way the whole operation—AAD, the research grant system and ANARE—overlooks responsibilities for children.

A PLACE FOR PEACE AND SCIENCE?

The fact that Antarctica is a special place, where even a misplaced step can damage a fragile plant that takes years to repair, is the reason most women want to work there. Antarctica as 'a place for peace and science' is enshrined in the Antarctic Treaty which, together with the 1991 Madrid Protocol, commits signatory nations to cooperative, non-exploitative strategies.

Barbara W. wanted to 'develop the sense of responsibility. I was in love with those birds and both scientifically and personally wanted to know what was happening in summer'. Astrida elaborated:

There's an underlying potential conflict depending on how religious or puritan you want to be. We talk about the importance of Antarctica and the contribution of data to understanding

189

climate change and the greenhouse effect, but we need to ask ourselves some strategically chosen questions regarding research to be done in future, to justify being down there. We have to be responsible. The infrastructures that have been developed even at Davis look safe for humans, but there are potential pollution problems to look at. Do we need to have winterers down there?

Patricia Selkirk put the scientific argument for a human presence on Macquarie Island:

There's huge scope for fascinating research on Macquarie. The sub-Antarctic is very important to know a lot about, as the edge of anything is likely to be the place where change first occurs, and the edge can give important indications of change. The sub-Antarctic is the key to the polar zone. There's a lot of detectable change in the sub-Antarctic. It is, however, the poor relation when it comes to political interest in Antarctica. It's seen as 'not the real Antarctic', rather than being of intrinsic interest on its own. This is a significant mistake in regard to the world environment: the sub-Antarctic environment is significant but support for research there is diminishing, leading to big holes in our understanding. Antarctica is an ice-covered continent; the sub-Antarctic region in itself is of intrinsic interest and is also important for the whole global picture.

The majority of expeditioners to whom I spoke, both male and female, were cynical about the reality of the official commitment to science, though there have been changes in the last year or so. But expeditioners point to the new continental stations, which are half empty in winter when little scientific activity can take place, and wonder about priorities. According to 'Gemma', many think bureaucrats and politicians view science as the most 'flexible' part of the Australian program, with the Australian presence more important than 'contributing to understanding of the place. Too much goes into infrastructure, compared to the science programs.'

'Where's it going?' worried Isobel Bennett, who in her late eighties is still an ardent environmental advocate. 'We hear stories of what the French have done and are doing,[3] and the mess of McMurdo. I don't know what it's like at the Pole, and I wonder what they are achieving . . . One wonders how much communication there is between the different nations, how much they are working together and not duplicating things—from hearsay, the state of stations is so sub-standard, it worries me.' She is also worried about 'the krill on which everything in Antarctica ultimately depends'. She concluded: 'It's all very well having a treaty against the taking of whales, but will some nations, or the next generation, care? Antarctica is more or less sacrosanct now from the point of view of industrial mining and that sort of thing, but with increasing technology, more tourist vessels, unless severely monitored, you wonder what will happen.'

There is a spectrum of opinion on whether or not humans should be there at all. While some of the women wanted to preserve Antarctica in a pristine state for future generations, most accepted that we are there, and have left a mark. In addition to the arguments about the importance of the Antarctic biosphere for understanding global phenomena like climate change, life can be studied there in a relatively undisturbed state, even as a testing ground for the possibility of extra-terrestrial life. Anyone familiar with the ideas of quantum mechanics will respond that even our presence changes that which we seek to observe. And it is almost impossible to study without some interference. So should we do it? Opinions are divided, with good arguments on all sides. Sensitivity to the way we are present, and its potential harm, is the baseline.

Two senior Greenpeace campaigners, Lyn Goldsworthy and Janet Dalziell, have been involved in national and international monitoring and policy development for Antarctica. Lyn elaborated: 'The formal vision is for Antarctica as a World Park. We've got on to the last pinnacle of the mountain, got on to the last ascent having thrown out the minerals convention, but I know it's going to come up again. There are three things that provide the points of my vision for Antarctica in the future. We haven't quite got there yet: we're at the bottom of the last steep ascent.'

The first thing mentioned by Lyn was Antarctica as a place of peace: 'This is very important in a world with so many conflicts, a place where people can cooperate, that needs strengthening, in terms of sharing facilities and sharing scientific programs.' It is also 'a place of inspiration. We've got to have one place we've not wiped out, even if you don't go there, it's important. It became more important to me after I'd been there, it provided and still provides massive inspiration to know there's one place we haven't totally destroyed.' And thirdly, Antarctica is seen as a place of 'baseline conservation studies. It's very important in this world where we put more and more pollutants into the air and into the water that we have one place where we can get some concept of what it is that we're actually doing'.

Janet has a five-fold vision for Antarctica's future. This involves cooperative research done with international standards of environmental impact assessment; management more jointly done with the Treaty secretariat and an inspectorate; rationalised stations where we can take the high moral ground because there's no native population and establish some world models; combining the bringing out of all waste with recycling and re-use there; and controlled tourism with no wildcat operators and no land facilities. She added: 'Keep the wild/adventure side!'

In Antarctica, Janet found:

On station, people wax lyrical about how wonderful the place is and how they love it. The difference comes with what people consider to be important or significant environmental issues— some would tell me how disgusting they thought quite minor issues were, while others said they were taking the station and its impact as a given, and talking about bigger issues like tourism without seeing that the station itself had an impact on the environment or that their practices needed to change: considering how they handled fuel, sewage output, the dogs, the vehicle use. That really shocked me, especially with spread-out new stations; there's a huge amount of vehicle use on station, utes and quikes in addition to the heavy equipment for unloading. What is the threshold for using vehicles? How far one should walk before one should get on a vehicle is set by custom! The more available vehicles are, the less likely we'll walk, and vice versa. Fuel is the problem. People are quite prepared to be told what the acceptable standards are, but until then, they assume you do what you do at home in Australia—for example, in field huts what do you do toilet-wise? The answer was usually 'common sense', but that's not an acceptable answer—people don't know about bacteria and faeces and their effect on the environment. They need quite specific instructions about what's acceptable—always do it in buckets.

Many expeditioners see tourism as a threat, despite findings suggesting that, when it is ship-based, it can be quite sensitive.[4] Lyn would 'really love lots of people to go as an adventure, ship based so they can experience the thrill of being totally unimportant and vulnerable. It gives you a profound understanding of how violent and all-powerful nature is. It's a very important thing for people to experience, because it helps them to get things back into perspective and create a respect for nature, which we need.' Another strong argument is that people are more likely to want to preserve Antarctica if they have experienced it. They need a good sense of the vulnerability of the frail ecosystem, as well as the might of natural forces. And there is also a sense of fairness: I can't stop others if I've been.

CAREERS, ANTARCTIC CAREERS AND JOBS

Work is what enables most women to go to Antarctica, so how has the experience impacted on subsequent employment? Most of the women were under 30 when they first went to Antarctica, and were therefore in the early stages of a career, though this is not necessarily how they saw themselves. They are well qualified and professionally active, even when they have small children.[5] The majority thought that their Antarctic work had made little difference to their careers, and they hadn't done it for that reason anyway. A number had not thought beyond the experience and what it might entail, so strenuous were their efforts to get South. Unpaid volunteers for others' projects accounted for

28 per cent of the trips made by women in the study, and 34 per cent were gathering material for a degree, often in addition to working for someone else.

Antarctic service is least useful for medical careers, a side-step almost, and most doctors who do additional research gain little formal career benefit. However, the community, tired of the world of specialist medicine, may benefit as doctors for Antarctica must be generalists and need some experience in surgery and anaesthetics, basic dentistry and physiotherapy. The female doctors felt they gained valuable experience in Antarctica.

Field training officers, too, seek extra qualifications and experience before applying to go to Antarctica. The service would not be considered negative on a *curriculum vitae*, though they may have to choose, in Ann's words, between 'secure permanent work and really adventurous, rewarding work'. Others also gained confidence. Of the three female station leaders in public-sector middle or senior management at the time of going South, one lost ground for a while as a result, and one certainly went for considerably less pay. The fourth, a squadron leader in the Air Force, and the first female air traffic control instructor, neither gained nor lost from the experience, and a fifth changed direction on return. However, the station leader position is on no specific career path.

Chefs, who are required to have considerable experience to be selected, find few exciting career outlets based on their Antarctic service. It is more complex for radio operators and technicians, a number of whom go to Antarctica on leave from positions in the Armed Forces. Antarctica is one of the remote stations for Meteorological Bureau staff, and for a small number of AGSO and TasPAWS staff. Like AAD staff, it is a possible posting at the lower levels with few direct career path benefits. Division staff with no recent Antarctic experience lose credibility with expeditioners, though some are tired of the repeated disruption to family life and work. A number of the Division's science positions are two and a half- to three-year expeditioner contracts, which require at least one winter South. Career issues arise from the short contracts and the lack of new permanent positions.

In science, some of the women interviewed had been doing Antarctic-based research for ten or more years.[6] Others, especially academic scientists, have been deterred by factors like the long voyages and shipping schedules which clash with the academic year. Others again are not career oriented, and some are happy to be able to continue to work in Antarctica in a variety of positions. Some say it hasn't done their careers any harm: they learnt additional skills and demonstrated their adaptability. The archaeologists and conservators had problems with obtaining leave. The lack of new permanent jobs in science generally means that specialisation in Antarctica, a field with a small international research community, can be problematic.

Women expressed uncertainty about following a single-track career, as Judy suggested: 'I have no great career goals, I'm happy to do something interesting.' Some perceive that successful careers involve closing off other interests.[7] Melanie said: 'There's an element of how female scientists construct work and a sense of themselves as professionals in it.' This included questioning, as Pene pointed out, 'work towards a hierarchical position'. Several have abandoned nearly complete PhDs, disillusioned by the perception that success entails an undesirable single-mindedness and tunnel vision. This is not limited to women in Antarctic science. More attractive are applied fields and 'hands-on' work with more human contact. And women from all fields have dismissed the idea of a career, seeing work as a means to earn money while the significant parts of their lives are in other spheres. For some, the Antarctic experience has been part of a search for new ways to gain meaning and enhance life options.

FAMILIES AND ANTARCTIC SERVICE

Life is more than a career. It is also affected by Antarctic work. One in five of the summerers interviewed had children when they went South, including nine children under five years. Beth Gott wrote to her family: 'I slept very well last night, but I missed everyone this morning. It was so quiet—no Miranda saying "Mum, Mum",[8] no Margaret and Jim getting ready for school, no Dad snoring in bed.' Others spoke of 'deals' done with partners to 'repay' the child-minding time at a later date, and all have said they would not have contemplated wintering without their children. As 'Hilary' found: 'The premise that ANARE is based on is that we don't admit to family life. We deny families, in head office and at the stations. We don't talk about it, we don't talk about the issues. It's a very anti-family organisation. You assume that people will drop tools and off they go to Antarctica, and you have to be like that if you want to be in an important job.'

The situation is particularly difficult where both partners are involved in Antarctic work, but cannot be there together because of children. Private expeditions get around this. The whole Poncet family have shared their yacht-based Antarctic experiences, and Susan Barr has been both pregnant and breastfeeding during fieldwork in the Arctic on Svalbard. There seems to have been an outbreak of babies since the interviews began, underlining the different phases of women's life course: education, work, travel, children, with or without ongoing employment but limiting its location in most cases.

An account of Antarctic service would be incomplete without mentioning the partners left behind. Ros Bowden interviewed women from the Antarctic Wives (now Family and Friends) Association in 1987. They valued supportive families, full-time jobs, the Association and a sense that it would have been bad for their relationship to stand in the way of their partner's wintering. It is much harder for partners left behind with children, and imagine how it has been when children, including twins, have been born after their fathers went South. Separation is an important aspect of remote service.[9] As 'Martha' explained, 'Antarctica changes people, sometimes significantly. Expeditioners experience difficulty in settling back into life at home—some are "monsters"

196

after they return—unhappy, disinterested, unsettled—they feel
as though they don't fit into our society any longer ... Readjusting is difficult.' This affects both parties, especially where women
left behind discover new competences and independence, things
that are not easily relinquished.

Friendships formed in Antarctica are a lasting memento, as
expressed by Jennie: 'Some of my fellow expeditioners, both
male and female—have made my visits South enjoyable and my
work easier. I have enjoyed those few occasions when I have been
out working with other women. It meant an awful lot personally.'
Elanor simply said that one of the high points was 'the special
friends, those who I know I will be in contact with for the rest
of my life'. Robin Thomson elaborated: 'I achieved a greater
social success than I've ever had before. I made some fantastic
friends down there and we all share a kinship because of what
we experienced together.'

'IT'S A LIFE-CHANGING EXPERIENCE'

Antarctica changes people. In the exquisite yet stark, unyielding
world of Antarctica, where physical and mental survival depends
on what we bring with us, wonder and beauty and small miracles
abound. Estelle conveyed the actual and metaphorical impact:

> It's changed my whole vision of everything. Nothing is usual
> visually or the same again—I saw with new eyes, everything was so
> different and exotic, and it made the ordinary things here very
> special as if I'd never seen them before. It was such a powerful,
> overwhelming, good, mind-expanding experience, it gave me a
> sense of calm. I can't describe being on the icecap—it's not just
> seeing it, it's being in it.

It widens horizons on life. Janet Hughes acknowledged: 'It
changed the focus of my life ... I found it a very profound realisation that something so unknown can have a profound
influence on the whole climate of the earth.' Margaret Werner

expressed the effect of Antarctica on the human spirit: 'It is wonderful to go to areas without pollution, water as clear as glass, mountains unclimbed, undisturbed. You find an essence of yourself; you learn about yourself there. Being in Antarctica heightens your instincts and feelings of well-being; you get in tune with the environment and yourself down there.'

Practical knowledge and experience gained are rewarding. Polar historian Ann Savours said it 'added something very special, helped me to know what Macquarie Island was like. It was practical knowledge as opposed to book knowledge—for example, the effects of a gale, the great albatrosses. It enhanced my work.' Jennie found: 'It's given me a different biological context to put things in—for example, the rabbit impact: you can alter a whole flora with one introduced animal and see the effects in a lifetime.' Debra now has 'a wealth of experience to draw on later, a wonderful band of memories ... What's so attractive about Antarctica is being able to challenge yourself on more than one plane.' This sentiment was repeated over and over.

When sensory stimulation is minimal, and social stimulation is low, one can open the door to inner life. For Susan, 'the almost total lack of daily life stress, with time schedules, telephones, shopping, etc., is a wonderful, rejuvenating, experience, as is also the quietness and untouchedness of the polar regions'. Debra discovered that: 'Trying to assess what's important in your life, the bottom line of everything, is hard, [but] in an environment that removes a lot of distractions and humdrum, you can focus on other things that matter. You're able to get down to the nitty gritty.' Above all, whether or not things are smooth, there is the chance to learn about oneself and others, to test oneself physically, mentally, emotionally, to reflect and learn from others far from the crowded busyness of the everyday world. It is not stress-free, though sometimes the physical or mental draining allows renewal. Jane Wilson found: 'I tuned into the learning experience and determined to gain more autonomy. Difficult experiences encourage learning and reflection.' Mandy added:

'I guess I am more self-reliant, more tolerant of most things, more self-directed.'

'IT WASN'T EASY, BUT I WOULD DO IT ALL AGAIN!'

This description of Antarctic service must resonate with most who have encountered this remote continent, from the explorers onwards. I asked women to reflect on what they felt proud about for having been, what they would like others to know. Two who found the experience particularly difficult quickly replied: 'Just tell them I survived!' That is not such a simple thing; however, women downplay their achievements in Antarctica.

A significant element for most, apart from the personal challenges, was the opportunities Antarctica presented, especially to encounter new people and situations. Mandy recounted:

> One of the good things is to get involved in extra station positions like theatre, SAR and photographer, and other people's work, especially some like Ruth's which is with live beings,[10] or going to places you wouldn't get otherwise. Also learning new things on station from people who have other skills such as computers, carpentry. One of the plant operators helped me and the female storeperson to get our 950 licence (the *big* earth mover).

For 'Davina', working with the huskies was 'on a personal level, the major part of my year', as it was for several others. She described the teamwork, the planning for trips, the chance to be alone and 'talk' to the dogs, sharing affection, and the marvellous feeling of 'running behind them in weather so cold one's breath freezes. The Kloa round trip tests your physical and mental limits. To work with dogs not only involves caring for them daily, disciplining large, tough working beasts, but learning how to maintain and mend the harnesses and sledging equipment.' She also learnt to weld there, and did 'some carpentry and a little metal lathe work', as well as conducting her scientific work program 'quite competently and I think they'd be eager to have me do it again'. She is proud of these things, but she did not want to draw attention to herself.

Most downplayed being the first in their field, but the warmth of Phillipa's pleasure as the first female deputy voyage leader deserves sharing:

> I'm always really proud of the fact that I led the way. I was the first—and I have to say I've liked a lot of what I've seen of the women that have come through after me. What they love about it, and they are refreshed by this whole new world that opens up, is this industrial world, it's opened the window and they've just marched straight through into this whole new world of wharfies and stevedores, of forklift trucks and cranes, of 'lifts' as in a load of weights and measures and nuts and bolts, and they're thrilled by it, because it's something that most women don't ever get a chance of being familiar with. You talk about hatches and holds and 'tween decks—it opens up another language for you, another world, another culture, the seafaring culture. And it's the learning stuff . . . they occasionally get to sneak in and experience it really at close quarters and they love it!

There is also the day-to-day satisfaction, and pride, in doing one's job in those circumstances, as Robyn Carter experienced after a good day's work weighing penguin chicks: 'If we managed to keep chaos to a minimum, and managed to account for all or the majority of the chicks we'd tagged, we'd feel a sense of achievement! At the end of the season when all the work was finished there was a sense of achievement that we'd done it all to the best of our ability—we felt we'd done a pretty good job.' Antarctic work opens up wider horizons on one's strengths and possibilities. In contrast to those who turned to other aspects of life, some scientists confirmed their aptitude and enthusiasm for research, as Adele acknowledged: 'Professionally, the research work went very well: it's world-leading research, far ahead of BAS, applying advanced techniques to the field situation. At that time [on the way down] I was having my PhD examined, coming out from being a PhD student to a fully fledged scientist, and getting a post-doctoral fellowship was good: I felt a fully fledged professional.'

On the eve of her return for a second winter, Jane Goddard admitted that doing her job well was the greatest challenge, and that she had an 'overall a sense of having done the job reasonably well—that wasn't a super high, that was just a sort of a nice gentle swell as opposed to a peak!' Amanda Nimon may have 'gob-smacked' people on board the luxury cruise ship that dropped her and her three companions on to a small island to live in cramped conditions. But she does not flaunt their achievements. Satisfaction with managing is what so many women display. Tracey and Lynne were in a lab, 'doing all the work including all the maintenance. It was a very good experience—it's not usually done as part of the job'.

For station leaders, aspects of group interaction were critical. Angela wanted to be remembered for 'people enjoying their year under my leadership, that I was seen as a good leader. Ex-peditioners' opinions were more important than the Division's.' A key aspect of this for Alison was to be remembered because 'they all got home safely—this was my overriding aim—they were scared, but they did what they had to and came home safely. The constant fear was there. It was put at the top of everything. I hated the view from my window of the memorial to Steve Bunning who died in 1987.' And while Diana did not say she wanted to be remembered for it, she found a great deal of chal-lenge, and personal satisfaction, in dealing with others who were going through personal trauma, including one accidental death on station during her second stint as leader. Similarly, Louise mentioned that 'everyone knew you cared about them and that was good. I don't care in a sort of slushy kind of way—but I guess what that meant was that I demonstrated that I did have their well-being at heart, and was considerate of what they needed and wanted and tried to work that into the whole thing.'

Joan's concerns for people and her experience in equal employment opportunity and management were expressed in action for cultural change to create a safer and more productive workplace. She encountered tremendous challenges to that, but was able to conclude: 'Well, I think that the ground I broke at Casey in 1990, and paid for with blood, sweat and tears, has had a very positive result. The young women scientists with whom I worked last year on Macquarie Island take it as an absolute that they have a right to work free of harassment, both sexual harassment and gender discrimination.' Louise recently confirmed the changing ethos, and said she had a sense that strong, competent women had set the tone on Macquarie for the winter of 2000.

Meredy gained greatest satisfaction from her value to the group. Like many other women, she acknowledged others:

> My parents were so proud, so happy I'd done something worthwhile, and I felt good that the fellows had appreciated my work—it made you feel good someone took notice of what you're doing when the governor talked to me about it. Expeditioners feel it's blowing your own trumpet—I felt it too—when he mentioned the things I'd done they were things I took for granted. Barbara [Wienecke] rang to congratulate me, backed up that I'd saved their lives providing food when they came in from traverse. I didn't go to Antarctica to get a medal but to experience it, have a lot of fun and work hard and make people feel happy.[11]

The chefs also get more direct feedback from others about their performance. Carol Pye, for example, was pleased to readily discover and cater for people's likes, dislikes and special needs and generally get on with people in such a closed community: 'I discovered the hidden dimension to the chef's job, too—ordering, managing a fixed supply with no new supplies for months, providing variety from that supply, and fewer recreational opportunities, all rarely externally acknowledged.'

Gaining respect within their group was more important to nearly everyone than any outside acclaim. But slowly, thoughtfully, pride was also expressed, and a willingness to share this with others.

Women who have been to Antarctica try to downsize the image that others might have of them. Peta, the first wintering female geophysicist, explained:

Going to a place like that is not life-threatening—at the turn of
the century you might have been proud of that, but now you only
put yourself under as much physical duress as you choose, so—
as you don't have to—you're not so proud of it when you do it.
[However] the two years have had a big impact on my life: people
feel there's something different about women having gone
South—I feel, for example, that I should do careers talks as I may
have something to contribute. I don't think there's anything
special about women being there, but you have to get girls to do
the physical sciences.

Her work outcomes were most important: 'I know I did a good
job for the BMR [Bureau of Mineral Resources] from feedback
from them—I know they're happy and that feels good. It's a good
feeling to have had a good time in the institution and be welcomed back.'

Some are satisfied at having been to Antarctica, and while they
miss aspects of it at times, have new priorities. Others long to
return. There is a sense of trying to 'get it right' or 'do it better'
a second time. More importantly, there is a nostalgia, expressed
by Fiona in the words: 'I would never say "never again"!' Surprise and gratitude underscore the opportunities. Helen Keenan
expressed another common view—'I don't really know'—when
asked what she'd like others to know about her work: 'I guess I
just feel really lucky to have got somewhere like Macquarie.'
Robyn C., like other women, acknowledged 'pride in having
been—I can't quite believe it'. She still asks 'Why me?' Denise
Jones said she had a sense of pride, but also 'of being fortunate
I've been paid to go. I work in a male dominated field, so I don't
go round bragging, it is just a job I've done.' Perhaps the most
important thing is to embrace the experience wholeheartedly, in
Denise Allen's words, because 'You've only got one life and you
need to live it to the full!'

Just to go to Antarctica brings deep satisfaction. The journey
itself is the purpose. Liv undertook her solo expedition 'for
myself, to fulfil an old dream, but if it's inspired others, then I'm
glad'. The most important aspect was 'to ski, to be a part of

nature. It's hard, cold, dangerous (crevasses), and I put a lot of effort in the planning and training. I knew I could do the physical thing and knew I was mentally strong, but you can never be sure of crevasses, despite my experiences of glaciers and climbing. Beforehand I visualised problems, falling into glaciers, problems with pitching the tent but I always came through in the exercise, so I knew I'd be all right.' For Liv, the achievement was deeply personal: 'It was the expedition/tour of my life, my batteries are loaded for the rest of my life, and I rely more on my intuition now ... I learnt to listen to this feeling, and it's persisted since I came home.'

Kirsten added: 'I feel I am a happier, and a better person for having gone through it all. I looked forward to contributing to the station, and I've learnt a lot.' More than anything: 'I've been there, fulfilled my lifelong dream and was not disappointed, it just blew me away. It's the best thing I've ever done!'

The meaning of the experience becomes part of one's way of being in the world. Gina suggested: 'There's a sense of adventure, answering those needs and desires rather than feeling "I've done it!" I like to push myself, not to get to the top. I loved running with the dogs in Alaska. I was out to enjoy being in it, running in the valleys rather than going to the top of the mountains. I loved the experience, I milked the experiences, did not go for achievement. Also the exploration—satisfying curiosity is reverence for life.' 'Tamara' said she gained perspective there: 'My biggest experience was one of inner peace—almost serenity— which I only finally came to at the very end of my winter whilst in the field. Plus the knowledge of what I was capable of and of my strength and powers of self-discipline. I feel I have done my best professional work at Macquarie Island or in association with the place.'

'Davina' felt:

So many women don't do things because they're not encouraged to believe they can do it, it doesn't enter their mind. It doesn't enter my head that I couldn't do it because I'm a woman, or others' heads about me. I don't think 'X is a man so he can do it, but not me'. But I feel women don't see enough women doing things. It needs to be made acceptable that women do 'that' too. I may be not as physically strong—for example, in a dog run—but you can get round it—for instance, by having three rather than two to a sled, and better equipment and I have other strengths.

———

This story began with the expectations that women brought to their Antarctic sojourn, and has drawn out the different threads of experiences there—good and bad. But it is appropriate to close with a celebration of the unique environment of Antarctica. In Clare's words:

> All the distinctive rocks are still there at Davis, the ground is littered with frost-shattered garnets and other crystals and the ice has just retreated, exposing a typical ice-age landscape. This made me realise what a blunted environment we have become accustomed to, and consider normal. Antarctica is not for humans, yet in time we will 'conquer' it, perhaps never fully realising that because an environment is harsh to humans it may not be strong. Antarctica is one of the most fragile ecosystems on earth. We have to remind ourselves that these places are not put here for our use, that we are irrelevant to them in the longer view.

Women participating in this study and their Antarctic service

Listed by year*, type of stay, station/s, job, subsequent visits**.
* For winterers, the year of wintering, not when they left Australia; for others, the year of departure is listed which does not indicate the length of the 'summer' or voyage.
** Information on this is incomplete and indicated by just 'yes' before or a '+' after the number of known visits (up to the 1999–2000 season) to indicate there may have been more.

ANARE EXPEDITIONS, INCLUDING THOSE WHO HAVE GONE ON OTHER NATIONAL OR PRIVATE EXPEDITIONS

Erica Adamson (1988, winter, Casey, expeditioner-scientist, yes 2 summers)
Heather Adamson (1987, summer, Casey, scientist, yes 1 summer)
Denise Allen (1985, winter, Macquarie Island, Met. observer, yes 3 more winters, deputy station leader on last one)
Morag Anderson (1990, winter, Davis, volunteer microbiologist)
Sue Baker (1995, summer, Casey, field assistant, yes)
Evlyn Barrett (1984, round trip, AAD librarian, yes 1 round trip)
Helen Beggs (1987, winter, Macquarie Island, expeditioner-physicist, yes one winter, 5+ marine science voyages)
Elanor Bell (1996, winter, Davis, biologist)
Isobel Bennett (1959, round trip, Macquarie Island, biologist [Isobel describes her position as 'supernumerary'], yes 3 round trips)
Hope Black, née MacPherson (1959, round trip, Macquarie Island, biologist, yes 1)

Nerida Bleakley (1994, summer, Scott Base, higher degree student;
1997, 1 summer at Davis)
Pru Bonham (1993, marine science, biological oceanographer, yes)
Elizabeth Bulling (1995, winter, Casey, medical officer)
Caroline Caddy (1992, round trip, Mawson and Davis, poet and
writer)
Robyn Carter (1990, summer, Davis, volunteer field assistant, yes
1 summer)
Elizabeth Chipman (1967, round trip, Macquarie Island, AAD clerk/
field assistant, yes 2 round trips)
Judy Clarke (1990, summer, Mawson, volunteer biologist, yes
5+ summers, 1 at Terra Nova)
Alison Clifton (1989, winter, Macquarie Island, station leader, yes
1 winter)
Lucinda Coates (1991, summer, Prince Charles Mountains, field
assistant)
Tonia Cochran (1986, summer, Macquarie Island, PhD student,
biologist, yes 7 marine science voyages)
Peta Colebatch (1993, round trip, Casey and Macquarie Island,
political observer)
Laurence Cordonnery (1994, round trip, Dumont D'Urville, PhD
student, yes 1 summer at Casey)
Louise Crossley (1991, winter Mawson plus summer field leader,
PCMs, yes winter 2000 and visits as lecturer on tourist ships)
Janet Dalziell (1991, round trip, Antarctic Peninsula with
Greenpeace, voyage co-leader, yes round trip with ANARE as NGO
observer, Greenpeace round trip)
Gillian Deakin (1986, winter, Davis, medical officer, yes 1 round trip)
Maria De Deuge (1987, winter, Mawson, expeditioner-physicist, yes
2 winters)
Trudy Disney (1993, winter, Macquarie Island, biologist)
Robyn Downey (1985, winter, Mawson, radio operator, yes 1 winter)
Ruth Eriksen (1993, marine science, hydrographer, yes 2 marine
science voyages)
Liza Fallon (1991, marine science, biological technical officer, yes
2 marine science voyages and 1 summer)
Melanie Fitzpatrick (1992, summer, Law Dome, glaciology
professional officer, yes 1 summer and 1 sea ice voyage)
Phillipa Foster (1981, round trip, voyage management, yes
7+ including 4 summers)
Lorraine Frances (1987, round trip, yes 1 as voyage leader to Heard
Island)

Jane Goddard (1993, winter, Davis, medical officer, yes 1 winter)

Lyn Goldsworthy, AM (1984, round trip, Casey, environmental impact assessor, yes 1)

Beth Gott (1963, round trip, Macquarie Island, botanist)

Robyn Graham (1988, round trip, Casey and Macquarie Island, staff familiarisation, yes 1 as deputy voyage leader)

Pene Greet (1982, summer, Mawson, PhD student, yes 3 summers, and 2 winters as expeditioner-physicist)

Annette Hackett (1996, winter, Casey, medical officer)

Kathrine Handasyde (1988, summer, Macquarie Island, volunteer field assistant)

Elizabeth Haywood (1989, round trip, Casey, familiarisation, yes 1 round trip)

Louise Holliday (1981, winter, Davis, medical officer)

Mandy Holmes (1993, winter, Casey, chef, yes 1 winter)

Jutta Hösel (1967, round trip, Macquarie Island, AAD photographer, yes 3 round trips)

Janet Hughes (1985, summer, Cape Denison, conservator, yes 2+ private expeditions and 1 ANARE)

Cindy Hull (1993, summer, Davis, biologist, yes 3 summers for PhD research)

Elizabeth Hynes (1980, winter, Macquarie Island, radio operator)

Susan Ingham (1959, round trip, Macquarie Island, AAD biological secretary, yes 2 round trips)

Anne Jackson (1993, winter, Casey, expeditioner-biologist)

Jeannette Johanson (1993, summer, Mawson, volunteer field assistant)

Denise Jones (1985, winter, Casey, communications officer, yes 3 winters)

Midj Jones (1993, summer, Davis, Met. forecaster, yes 1 summer)

Helen Keenan (1990, summer, Macquarie Island, PhD student, yes 1 summer)

Peta Kelsey (1983, winter, Macquarie Island, BMR geophysicist, yes 1 winter)

Anne Kerle (1978, summer, Macquarie Island, volunteer field assistant)

Elizabeth Kerry (1975, Macquarie Island, scientist, yes 8+ summers)

Heather Kirkpatrick (1992, summer, Davis, field training officer, yes 1 summer)

Ulla Knox-Little, née Sommers (1980, radio officer on *Nella Dan*, yes 3 winters and 4 seasons on ships)

Ruth Lawless (1993, summer, Mawson, volunteer field assistant, yes 3+ summers and 1 marine science voyage)

Estelle Lazer (1984, summer, Cape Denison, archaeologist with
Project Blizzard, yes 2 summers with ANARE at Heard Island and
Cape Denison)

Jean Ledingham, née Syme (1977, Macquarie Island, medical officer,
yes 1 winter, 1 summer and 4 round trips)

Michelle Leishman (1992, summer, Davis, scientist, yes 1 summer)

Kirsten Le Mar (1994, summer, Davis, volunteer field assistant, yes 1
summer)

Angela McGowan (1985, summer, Cape Denison, archaeologist with
Project Blizzard, yes 1 with ANARE at Heard Island)

Jenny Mackenzie (1992, winter, Macquarie Island, medical officer, yes
1 winter)

Cheryl McRae (1995, winter, Casey, expeditioner-biologist)

Doreen Marcheson (1992, Macquarie Island, volunteer field assistant,
yes 1 summer)

Astrida Mednis (1993, summer, Macquarie Island, volunteer field
assistant, yes 1 summer)

Jenny Mudge (1995, winter, Macquarie Island, TasPAWS ranger)

Mary Mulligan (1988, round trip, AAD EFLO, yes 1 round trip)

Pia Orr, née Geijsel (1990, marine science, Heard Island, professional
officer, yes 4 marine science voyages)

Diana Patterson (1987, summer, Casey, station leader, yes 2 winters)

Bridget Payne (1989, round trip, Mawson and Davis, familiarisation,
yes 4 round trips)

Helen Pearce (1985, summer, Davis, Met. forecaster)

Tracey Pitman (1992, winter, Davis, biologist, yes 1 round trip for an
NGO)

Adele Post (1987, summer, Casey, scientist, yes 1 winter and
1 summer)

Gina Price (1985, winter, Mawson, expeditioner-physicist)

Carol Pye (1989, winter, Davis, chef)

Lynne Rankin (1992, winter, Davis, expeditioner-scientist, yes
1 summer)

Pauline Reilly, OA (1977, round trip, Macquarie Island, ornithologist,
yes 1 summer)

Angela Rhodes (1994, winter, Casey, station leader)

Ricarda Riley, née Ortner (1987, winter, Mawson, Met. observer)

Christian Clare Robertson (1988, round trip, Mawson and Davis,
artist)

Sharon Robinson (1996, summer, Casey, biologist, yes 2+ summers)

Tracey Rogers (1992, summer, Davis, PhD student, yes 2+ summers,
1 private voyage)

Annie Rushton (1998, summer, Casey, researcher)

Joan Russell (1990, winter, Casey, station leader, yes 1 winter and 1 summer)

Ursula Ryan (1992, summer, Law Dome, glaciology professional officer, yes 2+ as deputy voyage leader)

Vivian Schenker (1986, round trip, journalist, yes 1 round trip)

Fiona Scott (1992, winter, Davis, biology professional officer, yes 1 winter and 1 marine science voyage)

Jenny Selkirk (1989, summer, Macquarie Island, volunteer field assistant, yes 2 summers)

Patricia Selkirk (1979, summer, Macquarie Island, botanist, yes 8+ summers, 2 with NZAP)

Gwen Shaughnessy (1985, summer, Heard Island, volunteer biologist, yes 1 summer)

Natalie Shilo (1997, summer, Casey, MSc student)

Ann Shirley (Ann Savours, pseud.) (1960, round trip, Macquarie Island, historian)

Liz Sikes (1993, marine science voyages, oceanographer)

Barbara Smith (1999, summer, Davis, glaciology professional officer)

Suzanne Stallman (1979, summer, Casey, geographer, yes 1 summer, 5+ round trips as deputy or voyage leader)

Leslie Stephenson/Frost (1989, round trip, Macquarie Island, heritage assessor, yes 1+ round trip)

Corinna Sullivan (1994, summer, Davis, volunteer research assistant)

Kerrie Swadling (1987, summer, Davis, volunteer field assistant, yes 1 winter and 2 summers as a PhD student)

Robin Thomson (1995, summer plus marine science voyage, Casey, volunteer field assistant)

Karen Townrow (1986, summer, Macquarie Island, archaeologist, yes 1 winter and 1 summer)

Maria Turnbull (1988?, round trip, Casey, AAD public relations officer)

Maret Vesk (1987, summer, Casey, scientist)

Wendy Welsh, née Prohasky (1984, winter, Macquarie Island, BMR geophysicist, yes 1 summer)

Anitra Wendin (1989, summer, Davis, ice diver and field assistant, yes 1 summer)

Ann Wessing (1987, summer, Casey, field training officer, yes 2 summers)

Jennie Whinam (1987, summer, Heard Island, botanist, yes 3 summers)

Barbara Wienecke (1994, winter, Mawson, expeditioner-biologist, yes 1 summer at Dumont D'Urville)

Lynn Williams (1981, winter, Macquarie Island, medical officer, yes
 1 winter and 1 summer as field leader, Heard Island)
Jane Wilson (1993, summer, Macquarie Island, volunteer biologist,
 yes at least 2 summers)
Suenor Woon (1995, summer, Law Dome, glaciology professional
 officer, yes 1)
Meredy Zwar (1994, winter, Mawson, chef, yes 1 winter)

OTHER NATIONAL OPERATIONS

Margaret Clayton (1986, summer, King George Island and South
 Shetlands, biologist, yes 1 summer at Juveny)
Debra Enzenbacher (1986, summer, McMurdo, shuttle driver, yes
 1 winter at South Pole, 2 summers independent expeditions)
Julie Hall (1994, summer, BAS, ice chemist, yes)
Judi Hansen (1988, summer, McMurdo, scientist)
Janet Thomson (1977, marine science, South Orkneys and Antarctic
 Peninsula, geologist, yes 1 summer and 2 marine science voyages
 with BAS)

EXPEDITION ARRANGED BY AN INSTITUTION INCLUDING THE SCOTT POLAR RESEARCH INSTITUTE STUDENT FIELDWORK EXPEDITIONS

Susan Barr (1989, historian: member of film crew from the
 Norwegian Polar Institute, to Dronning Maud Land)
Rosamunde Codling (1980, round trip, fieldwork, yes 1 summer visit
 to 2 BAS bases)
Pam Davis (1991, summer, Cuverville Island, PhD student, yes 1)
Monica Kristensen-Solås (1980, summer, Weddell Sea, glaciologist, yes
 6 including 1 private expedition)
Amanda Nimon (1992, summer, Antarctic Peninsula, PhD student,
 yes 2 summers)

PRIVATE EXPEDITIONS

Liv Arnesen (1994–95, skied solo to the Pole)
Ros Bowden (1995, tourist visit)
Margaret Werner (1987, bicentennial expedition to Mt Minto, cook,
 yes 6+ with tourist voyages)

Demographic portrait of the women, compiled in August 1999

AGE

1   Age when first went to Antarctica
mean = 32.17 years, median = 30 years, range = 21–59 years
Of the women 45.3 per cent were under 30 years of age, 18.7 per cent between 30 and 34 years old.

2   Age in relation to type of first visit
Winter: 57.6 per cent were under 30, range = 21–49 years (up to 1998)
Summer: 45.2 per cent were under 30, range = 22–54 years
Round/marine science: 33.3 per cent were under 30, range = 23–59 years

QUALIFICATIONS

Number of qualifications, not number of women with the qualification; the estimate following the first visit is conservative as not all qualifications have been notified to me. The plural is used because some women have more than one qualification—for example, one woman has two PhDs.

1   At time of first visit
Certificate(s):   8
Diploma(s):   5 (includes both pre- and postgraduate)
Bachelors degree(s):   71 (MBBS = 1 degree here; includes degree with Honours)

Masters degree(s):	19
Doctoral degree(s):	15
Other qualifications:	2

2 Up to mid-1998

Certificate(s):	16
Diploma(s):	31
Bachelors degree(s):	105
Masters degree(s):	32
Doctoral degree(s):	44
Other qualifications:	13

ANTARCTIC EXPERIENCE AND SELECTED PROFESSIONAL OUTCOMES

1 Average number of visits
   Winter = 1.5, range = 1–4
   Summer = 2.4, range = 1–9
   Round trip = 2.2, range = 1–6

2 Average number of job changes since last visit: 2.5 (this includes from student to paid employment and vice versa, job to unemployment and vice versa, job to full-time parenting)

3 Number who have published on their Antarctic research/ experience = 75

4 Total publications = 373, mean = 4.97, range = 1–35

5 Years between last visit and interview: average = 4.4 years; range 0 (= conducted on station) to 35 years

SIBLINGS, PARTNERS AND CHILDREN

1 Siblings (one only child)
   Number of children in family of origin: average = 3.3, range = 1–9
   Birth order: oldest child = 42 per cent; youngest child = 29 per cent
   Number with older brother(s) = 40; younger brother(s) = 47; older sister(s) = 30; younger sister = 38

2   **Partners with Antarctic experience**
Current partner has been to Antarctica: 65 per cent
Have been in Antarctica at the same time as current partner: 46 per cent
Met current partner while in Antarctica: 20 per cent

3   **Children**
Had children at the time of first visit = 28
Number of children: mean = 1.9, range = 1–3
Ages of children at time of visit: range = 1–16 years (9 were under 5 years)

Appendix 3

Women's writings about Antarctica

New books still appear on the early Antarctic explorers, and their exploits are configured into many Anglo-Nordic consciousnesses. But we do not have many images of contemporary Antarcticans, and that alone was reason for some women to embrace my project. For others, there was a desire to show that ordinary women can go to places still considered extraordinary, to record their experiences, share their joy and disclose the costs. Through the scope of this project, the particularity of individual stories and the generalities of going there as a woman are held in sometimes-uneasy balance. The intent is to place women in the picture we have of the world's driest continent and its sub-Antarctic jewels, a picture detailed by neither the increasing tourist nor wildlife spectaculars.

There are four categories of women's writing about Antarctica. The first includes historical accounts and contemporary interpretations. There are five books about women in Antarctica, and three more general accounts. Women have also written on historical aspects, including some who have themselves been to Antarctica. Then there are the scientific research writings, some of which are books.

Creative writing is a third form. Several women referred to the Ursula Le Guin short story about a Latin American women's expedition to the South Pole a year before Amundsen. They leave no record of their achievement, their participation sufficing for reward, but want their views conveyed to their children. Some of the women I interviewed articulated similar perspectives on recording their experiences. Finally, there are memoirs, from early women who accompanied their partners and private expeditioners to tourists. There are also short pieces, newspaper articles and interviews in various magazines and the daily press. There is an experiential gap of 30 years between the brief sections in Mary Gillham's and Isobel Bennett's books of everyday life as a working expeditioner on an Australian station, and the record of wintering women by Pene Greet and Gina Price. There is also an account of women's presence in Tim Bowden's official jubilee history of ANARE.

WOMEN IN ANTARCTICA

Barbara Land, *The New Explorers*, Dodds, Mead and Co., New York, 1981; Elizabeth Chipman, *Women on the Ice*, Melbourne University Press, Melbourne, 1986; Kerry Edwards and Robyn Graham, *Gender on Ice: Proceedings of a Conference on women in Antarctica held in Hobart, Tasmania, under Auspices of the Australian Antarctic Foundation*, AGPS, Canberra, 1994; Pene Greet and Gina Price, *Frost Bytes*, Doubleday, Sydney, 1995; and Esther D. Rothblum, Jacqueline S. Weinstock and Jessica F. Morris, eds, *Women in the Antarctic*, The Haworth Press, Bringhampton NY, 1998.

GENERAL ACCOUNTS

Elizabeth Chipman, *Australians in the Frozen South. Living and Working in Antarctica*, Thomas Nelson, West Melbourne, 1978; Linda Clark and Elspeth Wishart, *66° South*, Queen Victoria Museum and Art Gallery, Launceston, 1993; and Tracey Diggins, comp. *Travelling South: Journeys into Antarctica: A Multimedia Education Kit by the Wilderness Society Education Unit*, The Australian Wilderness Society, Melbourne, 1994. Other accounts by women are listed in Chipman's extensive bibliography in *Women on the Ice*.

HISTORICAL ACCOUNTS

Ann Savours, *The Voyages of the 'Discovery': The Illustrated History of Scott's Ship*, Virgin Publishing, London, 1992; Rosamunde J. Codling, 'The Antarctic paintings of Edward Seago (1910–1974)', *Polar Record*, vol. 33, no. 186, 1997, pp. 213–22; Rosamunde Codling, 'HMS *Challenger* in the

Antarctic: Pictures and photographs from 1874', *Landscape Research,* vol. 22, no. 2, 1997, pp. 191–208, and Louise Crossley, ed. *Trial by Ice: The Antarctic Journals of John King Davis,* Bluntisham Press/Erskine Press, Huntingdon, 1997.

SCIENTIFIC RESEARCH WRITINGS

For example, two by the first women to go to an Australian station: Mary Gillham, *Sub-Antarctic Sanctuary: Summertime on Macquarie Island,* Victor Gollancz, London, 1967; and Isobel Bennett, *Shores of Macquarie Island,* Rigby, Adelaide, 1971. See also Meg Thornton, ed., *Heard Island Expedition 1983,* Spirit of Adventure, Sydney, 1983; Karen Townrow, *Sealers, Scientists and Shipwrecks: Archaeological Survey of Macquarie Island, Summer 1986/87,* Department of Parks, Wildlife and Heritage, Hobart, 1987; Estelle Lazer and Angela McGowan, *Heard Island Archaeological Survey 1986–1987. Report to the Australian Heritage Commission* (mimeo); P.M. Selkirk, R.D. Seppelt and D.R. Selkirk, *Subantarctic Macquarie Island: Environment and Biology,* Cambridge University Press, Cambridge, 1990; and Pauline Reilly, *Penguins of the World,* Oxford University Press, Melbourne, 1994. Louise Crossley has written a useful, concise introduction to the continent and scientific understanding of it: Louise Crossley, *Explore Antarctica,* Cambridge University Press, Cambridge, 1995.

CREATIVE WRITING

Nikki Gemmell, *Shiver: A Novel,* Vintage Books, Sydney, 1997; Sara Wheeler, *Terra Incognita. Travels in Antarctica,* Vintage Books, London, 1997 (faction); Caroline Caddy, *Antarctica,* Fremantle Arts Centre Press, South Fremantle, 1996 (poems); and Ursula K. Le Guin, 'Sur. A Summary report of the Yelcho Expedition to the Antarctic, 1909–1910', *New Yorker,* 1 February 1982.

MEMOIRS

Jennie Darlington, *My Antarctic Honeymoon: A Year at the Bottom of the World,* as told to Jane McIlvaine, Doubleday, New York, 1956; and Nan Brown, *Antarctic Housewife,* Hutchinson, Richmond, 1971; Liv Arnesen,

Snille piker går ikke til Sydpolen ['Nice girls don't go to the South Pole'], N.W. Damm & Søn a.s., Oslo, 1995; and Monica Kristensen, *Mot 90° Syd* ['Towards 90° South'], Grøndahl & Søn, Oslo, 1987; Dorothy Braxton, *The Abominable Snow-women*, A.H. and A.W. Reed, Wellington/Auckland/Sydney/Melbourne, 1969; and Jean Bailey, *Antarctica: A Traveller's Tale*, Angus & Robertson, Sydney, 1980.

NEWSPAPER AND MAGAZINE ARTICLES

Jutta Hösel, 'One woman's Antarctic diary', *Habitat Australia*, no. 5, Jan. 1978, pp. 3–5; Christian Clare Robertson, 'Ice edge. Excerpts from an Antarctic journal, 1989', *Northern Perspective*, vol. 12, no. 2, 1989, pp. 1–22; Sally Poncet, 'Raising a family in the Southern Ocean', *Australian Geographic*, vol. 32, October–December 1993, pp. 94–111; and Phillipa Foster, 'Phillipa's feeling for ice', *40° South*, no. 2, 1996, pp. 6–8.

Notes

INTRODUCTION   'I WANT TO GO TOO!'

1 The artist Nel Law, who went as a guest of the Danish shipping company Lauritzen, with the Antarctic Division Director and expedition leader, Dr Philip Law, her husband: Elizabeth Chipman, *Women on the Ice: A History of Women in the Far South*, Melbourne University Press, Melbourne, 1986, pp. 84–85.
2 The majority of the interviews took place between June 1994 and October 1995, though they continued after that, with the last in February 2000.
3 There are 39 acceding states to the Treaty, representing 'the overwhelming majority of humanity': A. Herr, H.R. Hall and M.G. Hayward, 'Antarctica's future: Symbols and reality' in *Antarctica's Future: Continuity or Change?* eds R.A. Herr, H.R. Hall and M.G. Hayward, Tasmanian Government Printing Office, Hobart, 1990, p. 12.
     International collaboration for scientific purposes, and for the protection and conservation of the Antarctic environment, is prescribed under international treaties: *Antarctic Treaty Act* 1960; *Antarctic Treaty (Environment Protection) Act* 1980.
4 Chipman, *Women on the Ice*; Tim Bowden, *The Silence Calling: Australians in Antarctica 1947–97*, Allen & Unwin, Sydney, 1997.
5 This was enabled by two research grants and a period of study leave.
6 The path was not easy and Robyn's efforts have been largely unacknowledged. Dr Peta Colebatch and Dr Louise Crossley, members of the Australian Antarctic Foundation Board, were also involved in making the conference happen. They all deserve warm thanks.

1   'FINALLY WE WERE ON OUR WAY'

1 Kay Shaffer, *Women and the Bush: Forces of Desire in the Australian Cultural Tradition*, Cambridge University Press, Cambridge, 1988.

2 Elizabeth Chipman attempted 'to draw together the names of the women about whom anything is known, and to set them against the background of the exploration, exploitation and scientific research of the Far South'. Elizabeth Chipman, *Women on the Ice: A History of Women in the Far South*, Melbourne University Press, Melbourne, 1986, p. 12.

3 Marnie Bassett, *Realms and Islands: The World Voyage of Rose de Freycinet in the Corvette Uranie 1817–1820*, Oxford University Press, London, 1962.

4 Chipman, *Women on the Ice*, pp. 71–76. Diana Patterson coordinated the location of the memorial cairn and in 1996 went to Norway to interview Caroline, now Mrs Mandel: Diana Patterson, 'The Vestfold Hills: the Norwegian connection' *ANARE News*, no. 76, 1995–96, pp. 43–44.

5 Barbara Land, *The New Explorers: Women in Antarctica*, Dodds, Mead and Co., New York, 1981; Esther D. Rothblum, Jacqueline S. Weinstock and Jessica F. Morris, eds, *Women in the Antarctic*, The Haworth Press, Binghampton NY, 1998.

6 All Australian stations are serviced by ship, though air transport is under review now (2000).

7 The ANARE Club defines a winterer as 'having spent six continuous months including Midwinter Day, at the station or on field trips originating from it': M.J.C. [Max Corry], 'ANARE wintering expeditioners at "new" Casey', *Aurora*, vol. 16, no. 2, 1996, pp. 15–16.

8 Stephen Pyne, *The Ice: A Journey to Antarctica*, Arlington Books, London, 1987, pp. 66, 68.

9 Large tracked vehicle used for transport on ice.

10 This applies to the three Australian continental stations.

11 Conversations about the relative merits of particular years are especially heard between men who have multiple winters behind them.

12 JoAnna Wood, Sylvia J. Hysong, Desmond J. Lugg and Deborah L. Harm, 'Is it really so bad? A comparison of positive and negative experiences in Antarctic winter stations', *Environment & Behavior*, vol. 32, no. 1, 2000, pp. 84–110.

13 See Chipman, *Women on the Ice*, pp. 77, 81. Subsequent details are also based on her account. This book is recommended for readers interested in the early days, and in greater detail about women from all Antarctic nations. The movie *Hell Below Zero* was based on the novel *The Winter South* by Hammond Innes.

14 C. Swithinbank, *Forty Years on Ice*, Book Guild, Lewes, 1998, p. 190.

15 Reported in the *Koori Mail*, 16 November 1994.

16 This Belgian-born Australian is the first woman to scale the highest mountain on each continent.
17 *The Mercury*, 22 November 1930.
18 Melbourne *Sun*, 12 December 1963.
19 *The Examiner* (Launceston), 15 September 1992.
20 *The Australian*, 18 October 1985.
21 *The Age*, 10 July 1999.
22 This was widely reported in the Australian daily press on 6 and 7 December 1963.
23 *The Age*, 9 October 1957.
24 *Telegraph*, 5 March 1959.
25 Elizabeth Chipman, 'Casey in the summer of 1975–6', *Aurora*, vol. 13, no. 1, 1993, pp. 10–11.
26 Martin Stevenson, 'Even the huskies were upset', *The Examiner*, 9 December 1993.
27 Alan Trengove, 'There goes another haven', Melbourne *Sun*, 7 March 1975.
28 Louise Bower, 'Antarctic adventure breaks the ice', *The Mercury*, 26 January 1985.
29 Barry Martin, *Annual Report*, Officer-in-Charge Casey Station, 1986 (mimeo).
30 J. Smart, Macquarie Island 1983. OIC station leader report, 1983 (mimeo).
31 Trengove, 'There goes another haven'.
32 Tim Dalmau, 'Cultural change by remote control. Reflections on changing the dynamics of Antarctic communities', background paper prepared for the fifth SCALOP Symposium, San Carlos de Bariloche, Argentina, June 1992 (mimeo), p. 9.
33 Elaine Prior, The Australian Antarctic Program: Conflict, culture and vision, thesis in partial fulfilment of the requirements of the Bachelor of Antarctic Studies with Honours, Institute of Antarctic and Southern Ocean Studies (IASOS), University of Tasmania, Hobart, 1999 (mimeo).
34 Wood et al., 'Is it really so bad?'

2   'I HAD THIS DREAM . . .'

1 Eric Wood, *Famous Voyages of the Great Discoverers*, George G. Harrap & Sons, London, 1949: 1910.
2 Paul Simpson-Housley, *Antarctica: Exploration, Perception and Metaphor*, Routledge, London and New York, 1992, p. xvii.

3 Stephen Pyne, *The Ice: A Journey to Antarctica*, Arlington Books, London, 1987, p. 68.
4 For example, Mary Morris, ed., with Larry O'Connor, *The Virago Book of Women Travellers*, Virago, London, 1996.
5 The Norwegian leader of the first expedition to reach the geographic South Pole, 1911–12.
6 Perhaps the negativity is reflected in the title of her book about the experience, *Nice Girls Don't Go to the South Pole* [Liv Arnesen, *Snille piker går ikke til Sydpolen*, N.W. Damm & Søn a.s., Oslo, 1995].
7 Two more women have since won these medals, Judy Clarke and Meredy Zwar.
8 Heard Island, 1985 summer.
9 Pauline Reilly, *Penguins of the World*, Oxford University Press, Melbourne, 1994.
10 Her infant daughter.
11 Carol Gilligan, *In a Different Voice: Psychological Theory and Women's Development*, Harvard University Press, Cambridge, MA, 1982.
12 Brigitte Muir, *The Wind in my Hair*, Viking, Ringwood, 1998, p. 9.
13 ibid., p. 23.
14 Dea Birkett, *Spinsters Abroad. Victorian Lady Explorers*, Basil Blackwell, Oxford, 1989, p. 16.
15 ibid., p. 22.
16 ibid., p. 27.
17 Morris, *The Virago Book*, p. xvi.
18 ibid., p. xviii.

3   'I JUST WANTED TO DO MY JOB WELL!'

1 These positions are common to all stations. The station leader is still frequently referred to as the OiC, from the former title, Officer in Charge.
2 Macquarie Island is part of Tasmania and administered by the Tasmanian government. It, Heard and MacDonald Islands were inscribed on the World Heritage list on 4 December 1997: Alec Marr, 'Islands in the wind: A celebration of success', *Wilderness News*, no. 150, summer 1998, p. 2.
3 The obvious reason is that there is no wildlife except for Emperor penguins on the continent during winter, and rocks and flora are covered with a deep layer of snow. The situation is different on Macquarie Island, though there can be a deep snow cover in some places.

4 Recorded message from the AAD voyage information line.

5 'Just another fucking observer'.

6 The birds become victims of long-line tuna fishing where they get caught on baited hooks. Numbers are low and they only begin breeding at twelve years, and then only every two years, so the population is vulnerable.

7 This, like a number of other regular monitoring programs, is part of the work of the Convention on the Conservation of Antarctic Marine Living Resources (CCAMLR).

8 Feral cats, rabbits and rats were all introduced by humans to Macquarie Island and are a threat to the indigenous wildlife. One of the jobs for the rangers is their eradication.

9 The women I interviewed who had worked on Heard Island were there between 1985 and 1987. Heard Island expeditions do not occur every year, and when they do occur expeditioners live in what is still usable of the cramped early and now deteriorating buildings. These are also supplemented with fibreglass huts and tents.

10 TDRs (time-depth recorders) record how long the birds stay away and how deep they dive. The radio transmitters, weighing 60 grams, are used to locate the position of a bird, so distance travelled can be calculated. Because they can affect the efficiency of a bird's foraging, they are usually removed after one trip from colony to sea and back, and any trace of glue disappears with that season's moult.

11 The nearby Chinese station.

12 Station routine is a do-it-yourself breakfast with substantial hot snacks at smoko, which is at 10.00 a.m.

13 Elizabeth Chipman, 'Casey in the summer of 1975–6' *Aurora*, vol. 13, no. 1, 1993, pp. 10–11.

14 Not a universally appreciated designation of the role of female chefs!

15 Part of the chef's job is keeping the pantry in the mess stocked from the various forms of storage (both warm and cold) outside the main building, which requires using a forklift.

16 That was 1977; better communications now mean that conferencing about a case can take place, and the Internet is bringing telemedicine to the Antarctic. However, the bottom line is that there is still only one doctor on the spot except briefly in summer when a ship comes in.

17 Some training is undertaken at the Melbourne Dental Hospital before departure.

18 Susan Yola Headley, Women in Management on Australian Antarctic Stations, a thesis submitted in partial fulfilment of the

requirements for the degree of Bachelor of Arts with Honours in the Department of Sociology, University of Tasmania, Hobart, 1992, p. 34 (mimeo).

19 See reviews in Peter Suedfeld, 'Polar psychology: An overview', *Environment & Behavior*, vol. 23, no. 6, 1991, pp. 653–55; Lawrence A. Palinkas, 'Going to the extremes: The cultural context of stress, illness and coping in Antarctica', *Social Science and Medicine*, vol. 35, no. 5, 1992, pp. 651–64; and Robin Burns and Peter Sullivan, 'Perceptions of danger, risk taking, and outcomes in a remote community', *Environment & Behavior*, vol. 32, no. 1, 2000, pp. 32–71.

20 Peter Murphy, Australian Army Psychology Corps: personal communication.

21 Wind-corrugated ice, which may be many centimetres deep.

22 For example, Anne Spencer and David Podmore, eds, *In a Man's World*, Tavistock, London, 1987; and Rosemary Pringle, 'Ladies to women: Women and the professions' in *Australian Women: Contemporary Feminist Thought*, eds Norma Grieve and Ailsa Burns, Oxford University Press, Melbourne, 1994, pp. 202–14.

23 Lenora M. Yuen and Devora S. Depper, 'Fear of failure in women', *Women & Therapy*, vol. 6, no. 3, 1987, pp. 21–39.

24 Heard Island is not on the ANARESAT system, so communications are very basic and weather dependent, and the occasional expeditions there have been small.

4   'EVERYTHING YOU DO IS NOTICED THERE!'

1 A 'virtual' experience of a station can be found at the Australian Antarctic Division website: http://www.antdiv.gov.au

2 Seven of the seventeen deaths of Australians in the Antarctic, or as a result of accidents in the Antarctic, have occurred on Macquarie and Heard Islands, five of them on Macquarie.

3 An example of the critical role of shipping schedules is that 27 people wintered on Macquarie in 2000 because a special expedition to Heard Island in spring meant no early ship into Macquarie, so those following particular biological cycles had to be there over winter to arrive in time. There were, however, 21 there the previous winter.

4 'Operations' ('Ops') houses administration, communications and the meteorology office. Buildings are often referred to by the bright colours in which they are painted—for example, the 'Red Shed' for living quarters.

5 These are converted metal sea-containers housing four people in bunks during summer.

6 Dongas, the term still used for the sleeping quarters, is a hang-over from the days when each man had a cubicle containing a bed, desk, chair and table simply divided from his neighbour by heavy canvas curtains.

7 The new stations consume large quantities of fuel for heating, electricity, etc. and cannot be shut down for a season, enforcing continuous occupation. Over winter, the living quarters are more than half empty, though overflowing in summer when even a few centimetres of desk space in a laboratory can be hard to find.

8 The high salinity prevents them from freezing.

9 At Law Dome, 120 kilometres inland from Casey station, where the icecap is over 1200 metres deep.

10 Joan Russell, station leader.

11 Variation is partly due to the vagaries of the sea ice and shipping schedules, and partly to the nature of tasks to be undertaken. Senior staff, especially from universities, have difficulty with the lengthy absences from Australia that the shipping schedules require.

12 See psychological studies in A.J.W. Taylor, *Antarctic Psychology* (DSIR Bulletin No. 244), Science Information Publishing Centre, Wellington, New Zealand, 1987; and A.A. Harrison, Y.A. Clearwater and C.P. McKay, eds, *From Antarctica to Outer Space*, Springer-Verlag, New York, 1991.

13 Gloria R. Leon, 'Individual and group process characteristics of polar expedition teams', *Environment & Behavior*, vol. 23, no. 6, 1991, pp. 723–48; Pauline Maki Kahn and Gloria R. Leon, 'Group climate and individual functioning in an all-women Antarctic expedition team', *Environment & Behavior*, vol. 26, no. 5, 1994, pp. 669–97; and Esther D. Rothblum, Jessica F. Morris and Jacqueline S. Weinstock, 'Women in the Antarctic: Risk-taking and social consequences', *World Psychology*, vol. 1, no. 1, 1995, pp. 83–112.

14 The term 'recidivist' is used for those who repeatedly go to Antarctica; there is a sense that some find life easier there than in more complex society, and need fewer social skills. The ANARE Club has branches in most states and encourages all expeditioners to join. They publish a journal, *Aurora*, and organise events like annual midwinter dinners. It is dedicated to preserving the history of ANARE, especially its wintering parties, and its committees tend to be dominated by men from the era before women wintered.

15 Syd Kirkby, 'The spirit of ANARE', *Aurora*, vol. 17, no. 1, 1997, pp. 2–5.

16 Rod Mackenzie, 'Report of ANARE Club representative Voyage 4, 1996–1997', *Aurora*, vol. 16, no. 3, 1997, pp. 11–13.

17 An alcohol allowance has been part of ANARE, as has home brewing on station. The amount of alcohol available on the ships was reduced several years ago, and the alcohol allowance on station has been abolished, but group duty free alcohol purchase is organised amongst expeditioners. Home brewing continues as a sacred ANARE tradition.

18 The BAS stations are closer to tourist routes and receive more summer visitors than the Australian ones. Macquarie Island has averaged two tourist ship visits annually.

19 The club centres on the bar, and such 'decorations' as scanty women's underclothing may still be displayed there almost as a gauntlet. It is the space on station where many women feel least comfortable, because of the association between excessive drinking and harassment. It is also where male fights are likely to erupt.

20 Tim Bowden, *The Silence Calling. Australians in Antarctica 1947–97*, Allen & Unwin, Sydney, 1997, p. 220.

21 A 1995 review of the psychological assessment procedures for ANARE suggested that the following were reasons for excluding applicants, which gives some idea of current expeditioner requirements in addition to relevant skills and experience:
   1 not performing their job effectively due to behavioural characteristics (rather than technical or professional ability);
   2 not coping with their period of service in the Antarctic such that they cannot effectively undertake their work, or cause others to be less effective;
   3 conducting themselves in a manner which will disrupt the harmonious working or social operation of the station community (harassment of others is included here);
   4 not meeting other particular requirements as indicated by the Antarctic Division (which applies especially to supervisors, station leaders, and people on traverse or isolated scientific teams).

22 25 April, remembering the slaughter of Australian and New Zealand troops at Gallipoli in 1915. Lampooned for some decades as merely an occasion for old mates to get together and drink, and a perpetration of militarism, in the past few years there has been a resurgence of interest in marking the occasion and passing on the legend to the new generation. See K.S. Inglis, *Sacred Places. War Memorials in the Australian Landscape*, Miegunyah Press, Melbourne, 1998.

23 Office of the Status of Women (OSW), *Women in Australia 1999*, OSW, Canberra, 1999.

24 Carrying a firearm in the field in the Arctic is necessary because of the presence of polar bears. I have a photo of Susan from 1982 in the field in Svalbard. She has her baby on her back, and a gun over her shoulder: Bjørg Evjen, 'Women in polar research—exotic elements, intruders or equals?', *Ottar*, vol. 3, no. 226, 1999, pp. 31–41.

5   'IF YOU PAT ONE, PAT THEM ALL'

1 It took a long time for the AAD to obtain supplies of the issue clothing that were small enough for a number of women. Gloves, waterproof pants and 'freezer' suits have been in particularly short supply. The occupational safety issues raised by ill-fitting clothing have helped provide a better range of clothing in the Division's store.

2 Anne Summers, *Damned Whores and God's Police*, Penguin, Melbourne, 1975.

3 Susan Yola Headley, Women in Management on Australian Antarctic Stations, a thesis submitted in partial fulfilment of the requirements for the degree of Bachelor of Arts with Honours in the Department of Sociology, University of Tasmania, Hobart, 1992 (mimeo).

4 Isobel Bennett, *Shores of Macquarie Island*, Rigby, Adelaide, 1970, p. 31.

5 Elizabeth Chipman, 'Casey in the summer of 1975–76', *Aurora*, vol. 13, no. 1, 1993, pp. 10–11.

6 Paulo Freire, *Cultural Action for Freedom*, Penguin, Harmondsworth, 1972.

7 Clare Brant and Yun Lee Too, eds, *Rethinking Sexual Harassment*, Pluto Press, London, 1994.

8 Freire, *Cultural Action*.

9 This figure is derived from the interviews and from a review of expeditioner records by John Kelley, Army Psychology Corps (personal communication).

10 Joan added: 'You get a sexual harassment complaint, you withdraw the source of the complaint. You fix it. But people didn't see that. What I had failed to assess was the iconic value of page 3 in the newspaper and the difference between my comprehension of issues like sexual harassment and the average level of comprehension on the station.' She was later deliberately exposed to much more explicit pornography which she said affected her physiologically as it would 'a 17-year-old who accidentally stumbles into the men's dunny'.

11 I have been reminded on more than one occasion, listening to accounts of Antarctic incidents, of the depiction of raw male power in William Golding's *Lord of the Flies* (Penguin, Harmondsworth, 1960).

6 'TELL THEM I SURVIVED!'

1 An excellent case study of this phenomenon is found in Inger Agger, *The Blue Room: Trauma and Testimony Among Refugee Women. A Psychosocial Exploration*, Zed Books, London, 1994 [transl. Mary Bille].

2 Interestingly, there is some evidence that winterers are using the open-ended questions in a study of mood and the immune system as a form of catharsis, if not counselling. They enter answers regularly on a computer, and meet the American researcher in Australia at pre-departure briefings, thus personalising the process (personal communication, Dr Des Lugg).

3 Monika Puskeppeleit, 'The Untold Story: The German All-Female Overwintering Party' in *Gender on Ice: Proceedings of a Conference on Women in Antarctica Held in Hobart, Tasmania, under auspices of the Australian Antarctic Foundation*, eds Kerry Edwards and Robyn Graham, AGPS, Canberra, 1994, pp. 49–52.

4 W. Walter Menninger, 'Adaptation and Morale. Predictable Responses to Life Change', *Bulletin of the Menninger Clinic*, vol. 52, no. 3, 1988, pp. 198–210. See also A.J.W. Taylor, *Antarctic Psychology*, DSIR Bulletin No. 244, Science Information Publishing Centre, Wellington, New Zealand, 1987; J. Rivolier, R. Goldsmith, D.J. Lugg and A.J.W. Taylor, eds, *Man in the Antarctic: The Scientific Work of the International Biomedical Expedition to the Antarctic (IBEA)*, Taylor & Francis, London, 1988; A.A. Harrison, Y.A. Clearwater and C.P. McKay, eds, *From Antarctica to Outer Space*, Springer-Verlag, New York, 1991; Lawrence A. Palinkas and Deidre Browner, 'Stress, coping, and depression in U.S. Antarctic Program personnel', *Antarctic Journal of the United States*, vol. 26, no. 3, 1991, pp. 240–41; and JoAnna Wood, Sylvia J. Hysong, Desmond J. Lugg and Deborah L. Harm, 'Is it really so bad? A comparison of positive and negative experiences in Antarctic winter stations', *Environment & Behavior*, vol. 32, no. 1, 2000, pp. 84–110.

5 'RTA' is shorthand for 'return to Australia' and there are printed 'RTA' stickers for cargo. It is often used also as a verb in Antarctica, as in this quotation.

6 He recorded this in the station log too, which I don't think 'Alicia' realised.

7 Taking time off without pay has been mentioned. Until now, volunteers have also had to provide their own expensive insurance coverage and, earlier, their own special clothes. Some are covered by the research grants of their supervisors, but not all look after their volunteers in that way. They also miss out on field training, or pay the fares themselves, because of inability to leave jobs, or reluctance to use grant money for that purpose.

8 See Taylor, *Antarctic Psychology*; Rivolier et al., *Man in the Antarctic*; Gloria R. Leon, 'Individual and group process characteristics of polar expedition teams', *Environment & Behavior*, vol. 23, no. 6, 1991, pp. 723–48; J.R. Godwin, 'A preliminary investigation into stress in Australian Antarctic expeditioners', *SPRI Polar Symposia*, no. 1, 1991, pp. 9–22; Lucy Johnson, Women's Role in Antarctica: Past, Present and Future, dissertation submitted in partial fulfilment of the requirements for the Graduate Diploma in Antarctic and Southern Ocean Studies with Honours from the Institute of Antarctic and Southern Ocean Studies, University of Tasmania, Hobart, 1992 (mimeo); Tim Dalmau, 'International Approaches: Reflections on Managing Women and Men in Antarctic expeditions' in *Gender on Ice: Proceedings of a Conference on Women in Antarctica Held in Hobart, Tasmania, under auspices of the Australian Antarctic Foundation*, eds Kerry Edwards and Robyn Graham; Pauline Maki Kahn and Gloria R. Leon, 'Group climate and individual functioning in an all-women Antarctic expedition team', *Environment & Behavior*, vol. 26, no. 5, 1994, pp. 669–97 and Wood et al., 'Was it really so bad?'

9 I initially included questions to try to replicate an American study of women's sense of risk in going to Antarctica (Esther D. Rothblum, Jessica F. Morris and Jacqueline S. Weinstock, 'Women in the Antarctic: Risk-taking and social consequences', *World Psychology*, vol. 1, no. 1, 1995, pp. 83–112), but soon dropped the questions because they did not resonate with ANARE women. In a survey of risk perceptions amongst expeditioners, people displayed great acumen in relating hazards, level of preparation for going out, and behaviour (Robin Burns and Peter Sullivan, 'Perceptions of danger, risk taking, and outcomes in a remote community', *Environment & Behavior*, vol. 32, no. 1, 2000, pp. 32–71).

10 The three major approaches are found in Aaron Antonovsky, *Health, Stress and Coping*, Jossey-Bass, San Francisco, 1979; Suzanne C. Kobasa, 'Stressful life events, personality, and health: An inquiry

into hardiness', *Journal of Personality and Social Psychology*, vol. 37, no. 1, 1979, pp. 1–11; Richard S. Lazarus and Susan Folkman, eds, *Stress, Appraisal, and Coping*, Springer Publishing Company, New York, 1984; and Richard S. Lazarus, 'Coping theory and research: Past, present, and future', *Psychosomatic Medicine*, vol. 55, 1993, pp. 234–47.

11 Film nights have been an important feature of winter life. Large-screen videos are more popular now, but the films are still sometimes shown. In the early days, some expeditioners said that by the end of their time they were running the films backwards, they had seen them so often!

12 The ways in which men disrupt female solidarity and friendships is discussed in Susie Orbach and Luise Eichenbaum, *Bitter Sweet: Love, Envy and Competition in Women's Friendships*, Arrow Books, London, 1988.

13 Each station has a darkroom which is regularly used.

14 Estelle showed me some of her exquisite, finely detailed sketches. She had a problem holding the pen in the cold!

15 Elaine Prior, The Australian Antarctic Program: Conflict, Culture and Vision, thesis in partial fulfilment of the requirements of the Bachelor of Antarctic Studies with Honours, Institute of Antarctic and Southern Ocean Studies (IASOS), University of Tasmania, Hobart, 1999 (mimeo).

7   'IT JUST BLEW MY MIND AWAY!'

1 Mawson was the last station to have huskies, those at Davis and Wilkes (later located across the bay and named Casey) having been withdrawn in the late 1960s. The young dogs at Mawson were sent to Alaska in 1992, and the remaining five elderly ones were repatriated to Australia in late 1993, where several were still alive in 2000. They were withdrawn under the terms of the Madrid Protocol, as an 'introduced species'. Their loss has been felt strongly by old hands. They are an effective means of polar travel, and they provided an irreplaceable emotional and recreational outlet on station. Nearly every woman interviewed who spent time at Mawson was involved with the dogs.

2 These are enshrined in the Antarctic Treaty as a rationale for the Treaty's approach to international management of the continent.

3 Jutta Hösel, *Antarctic Australia*, John Currey, O'Neil, Melbourne, 1981.

4 Jutta added: 'I photographed it and the film was used by the press and on TV. There was a double-spread picture over all Australian newspapers, with an absolutely terrible picture of me in the corner, and journalistic lies like "the women who are huddling in the cold" and so on. We were probably sitting in the saloon drinking beer!'

5 Elizabeth had—still has—a passion for the Antarctic and a dedication to getting there. Her commitment helped her to move from the typing pool to become scientific secretary and publications officer for the Antarctic Division. Most of her working life was spent at the Division but it was some years before she was allowed to visit Antarctica.

6 Clare kindly invited me to stay with her in Darwin, and I was able to view not only her paintings on public display, but the slides she took in preparation.

7 I interviewed Caroline at her retreat near Albany, staying overnight at her generous insistence, while waiting for the *Aurora Australis* to be repaired in Fremantle, on my way to Casey.

8 Caroline Caddy, *Antarctica*, Fremantle Arts Centre Press, South Fremantle, 1996, p. 69.

8   'THERE'S NO ROOM FOR HEROES THERE!'

1 Phillipa Foster, 'Phillipa's feeling for ice', *40° South*, no. 2, 1996, pp. 6–8 (p. 8).

2 Both versions were propounded in the nineteenth century: see Thomas Carlyle, *On Heroes and Hero-worship*, Oxford University Press, Oxford, 1965: 1841; and Charles Kingsley, *The Heroes*, Thomas Nelson & Son, London, 1856 and the ideas linger today, though the term has been downsized through over-use, for example, in the context of sport.

3 She was referring to the building of a crushed rock runway for air transport which not only affected a penguin rookery, but was found to be unusable.

4 For example, Rosamunde J. Codling, 'Sea-borne tourism in the Antarctic: An evaluation,' *Polar Record*, vol. 21, no. 130, 1982, pp. 3–9; and Leslie Stephenson, 'Managing visitors to Macquarie Island—a model for Antarctica?', *ANARE News*, Autumn 1993, pp. 8–9.

5 More details of the demographic profile of women in this study and their work histories are found in Appendix 2.

6 In Australia, Patricia Selkirk is the outstanding example. Younger women are *de facto* career Antarctic scientists, after ten years or more

on Antarctic work, though a number would not see themselves that way. One relevant factor is the way research is 'located'. One issue is the theoretical questions it addresses, which may lead to a general problem where Antarctic data provides interesting insights, or can only/best be answered *in* Antarctica, rather than a more descriptive question *about* Antarctica. The second factor is the choice of publication outlet: small readership, less discipline-specific Antarctic journals, or general disciplinary ones? For academic researchers, the answer is often, clearly, 'go for the general', not least because of the need to keep up with a broader field for teaching purposes. The situation is different for glaciologists because most of their work *has* to be done in polar regions.

7 This seems to be a trend with younger people anyway, who know that they will probably have to change track several times in the course of a working life. For more detail on female scientists' views, see for example Sandra Harding, *The Science Question in Feminism*, Cornell University Press, Ithaca and London, 1986; Margaret Wertheim, *Pythagoras' Trousers: God, Physics and the Gender Wars*, Random House, New York, 1995; Robin Burns, 'Access, Employment Opportunities and the Pursuit of Scientific Interests: Issues from a study of women scientists with Antarctic experience', *GATES*, vol. 3, no. 1, 1996, pp. 1–10; and Sue V. Rosser, ed., *Women' Studies Quarterly* special edn, nos 3/4, 1999.

8 Miranda was one year old.

9 The AAD employs an 'Expeditioner Family Liaison Officer' (EFLO) to provide support and assistance while people are in Antarctica and during readjustment afterwards.

10 Ruth Lawless, penguin biologist. When the ship bringing Ruth to Antarctica was delayed, Mandy and others did the preliminary work as the penguins had arrived and claimed their nests. Nature doesn't wait for ships! Such situations also emphasise the importance of email and telephone for contact with stations.

11 Meredy is referring to the award of the Antarctic Medal for outstanding service.